BETWEEN HEAVEN & EARTH

Spiritual Gifts & Heavenly Manifestations of Latter-dau Prophets

BETWEEN HEAVEN & EARTH

Spiritual Gifts & Heavenly Manifestations of Latter-day Prophets

GLENN T. H. KIMBALL

CFI
An imprint of Cedar Fort, Inc.
Springville, Utah

Paperback ISBN 13: 978-1-4621-4960-5
eBook ISBN 13: 978-1-4621-4961-2

Published by CFI, an imprint of Cedar Fort, Inc.
2373 W. 700 S., Suite 100, Springville, UT 84663
Distributed by Cedar Fort, Inc., www.cedarfort.com

Library of Congress Cataloging Number: 2025932757

Cover design by Shawnda Craig

Edited and Typeset by Liz Kazandzhy

Printed in the United States of America

10 9 8 7 6 5 4 3 2 1

Printed on acid-free paper

Contents

Preface

Two topics that perhaps receive more discussion among Latter-day Saints than any other are gifts of the Spirit and prophets. This book deals with both—the gifts of the Spirit as displayed in the lives of prophets of The Church of Jesus Christ of Latter-day Saints. While researching another project, I stumbled across many accounts in the Latter-day Saint history of prophets describing personal experiences with a gift of the Spirit—visions, dreams, answered prayers, tongues, and healings, for example. Some accounts are well known and some are lesser known, but all are fascinating and illustrate the unique nature of the Latter-day Saint religion. My purpose here is to present the reader with a book that discusses gifts of the Spirit as understood by Latter-day Saints as well as to show how these gifts have influenced the Church and the lives of its leaders, who are revered by millions of people worldwide.

While preparing the manuscript, I wrestled with the options of either presenting the accounts in my own words or presenting them as told by those who were at the scene when the event occurred. I chose the latter mainly because experiences of this kind are more powerful when related firsthand and not devotionalized, sensationalized, or otherwise distorted by an author living generations after the fact.

Some of the accounts, however, are not related firsthand, as firsthand accounts do not exist; therefore, they are retold in my words, in the words of other authors and biographers, or in the publications of family and friends of the individual.

I have organized the accounts not by chronological order or by prophet but by topic, which allows the reader to focus on one gift of the Spirit while comparing the accounts relating to that gift to one another. In addition, I have included a short introduction to each chapter that expounds on the nature of the spiritual gift, as well as a short section of commentary and insight at the end of each chapter, wherein I highlight certain aspects of the accounts or present additional teachings from the prophets.

I must also mention that not every account in existence of a prophet relating an experience with a gift of the Spirit is included in this book, as there are far too many to mention. I did not include, for example, many of Joseph Smith's early visions and angelic manifestations, as those are presented elsewhere. I have also omitted many of the most well-known accounts, such as Joseph Smith's prophecy of the Civil War, as well as those that are mentioned only briefly in passing—in journal entries and autobiographies, for example—or are otherwise unclear or without substance. Ultimately, my goal was to present those accounts that are (1) highly relevant to the spiritual gift in discussion, (2) refreshing and interesting to read, and (3) not widely known to the average Latter-day Saint.

I want to acknowledge the Cedar Fort staff for their hard work and dedication in bringing the manuscript to fruition. They are amazing, hard-working people.

Chapter One

An Introduction to Spiritual Gifts and Prophets

A "spiritual gift" (1 Corinthians 12:1), like the temple, is a link between heaven and earth. Individuals who have received their temple blessings are fully equipped and prepared to call down the blessings of heaven on their behalf and on behalf of others. Most people are familiar with the gifts that are listed in 1 Corinthians 12, Doctrine and Covenants 46, and Moroni 10. Among the many gifts mentioned in those three chapters are faith, testimony, knowledge and wisdom, revelation, teaching, healing, prophesying, interpreting and speaking in tongues, visions and dreams, beholding angels and ministering spirits, casting out evil spirits, and miracles.

While these gifts are the most discussed in the scriptures, they are not the only gifts available to the Saints. Hundreds more can be found throughout the standard works. Referring to spiritual gifts, Elder Bruce R. McConkie wrote, "In the fullest sense, they are infinite in number and endless in their manifestations."[1] Essentially, a spiritual gift is any gift that one receives through the Spirit to serve the Saints, "[edify] the Church," or "[fill] a particular need"[2] (see 1 Corinthians 14:12; Moroni 10:8; Doctrine and Covenants 46:16, 26). A gift of the Spirit may include anything that fits one of these categories; for example, an ability to make friends, a love and motivation for doing family history work, or even a unique ability to teach and motivate youth.

Gifts of the Spirit are available to "every man" (1 Corinthians 12:7) who "loves [the Lord] and keeps all [His] commandments" (Doctrine and Covenants 46:9) and who has received the gift of the Holy Ghost. The Prophet Joseph Smith taught that spiritual gifts "cannot be enjoyed without the gift of the Holy Ghost."[3] The Lord has revealed that "to every man is given a gift by the Spirit of God. To some is given one, and to some is given another" (Doctrine and Covenants 46:11–12). Joseph Smith also indicated that "a man who has none of the gifts has no faith."[4]

Women are also entitled to receive gifts of the Spirit, as Elder McConkie explained: "Where spiritual things are concerned, as pertaining to all of the gifts of the Spirit . . . [and] in all matters that pertain to godliness and holiness and which are brought to pass as a result of personal righteousness, in all these things men and women stand in a position of absolute equality before the Lord. He is no respecter of persons nor of sexes, and he blesses those men and those women who seek him and serve him and keep his commandments."[5]

Although every faithful and unselfish Latter-day Saint receives at least one gift, is it possible to seek to obtain more than one gift? Paul answered this question when he told the Saints to "covet earnestly" (1 Corinthians 12:31) and be "zealous of spiritual gifts . . . that ye may excel to the edifying of the church" (1 Corinthians 14:12). Elder George Q. Cannon explained that the purposes of spiritual gifts are not only to serve others but also to help God's children become like

---

1. Bruce R. McConkie, *Mormon Doctrine* (Bookcraft, 1966), 315.
2. *Encyclopedia of Mormonism* (1992), 2:544.
3. *History of the Church,* 5:27.
4. *History of the Church,* 5:218.
5. Bruce R. McConkie, "Our Sisters from the Beginning," *Ensign,* Jan. 1979, 61.

Him; therefore, "it is our *duty to pray for the gift* that will make us perfect." "Have I imperfections?" asked Elder Cannon, "I am full of them. What is my duty? To pray to God to give me the gifts that will correct these imperfections. If I am an angry man, it is my duty to pray for charity. . . . Am I an envious man? It is my duty to seek for charity, which envieth not. So with all the gifts of the Gospel. . . . For this purpose He gives these gifts and bestows them upon those who seek after them, in order that they may be a perfect people upon the face of the earth, notwithstanding their many weaknesses, because God has promised to give the gifts that are necessary for their perfection."[6] Elder Cannon taught elsewhere, "We cannot be the people that God designs we should be, unless we seek after and obtain these spiritual gifts."[7]

The Lord expects the Saints to use their gifts and talents to bless others. If one becomes prideful or complacent regarding their gifts and talents, the Lord will take them away. President Joseph F. Smith warned:

> We have found occasionally that men blessed with some peculiar gift of the spirit have exercised it in an unwise, improper manner. For instance, brethren strongly gifted with the power of healing have visited far and near amongst the Saints (to the neglect sometimes of other duties), until it has almost become a business with them, and their visits to the homes of the Saints have assumed somewhat the character of those of a physician . . . and he himself has sometimes grown to so feel, and not that he was simply an instrument in the hands of God of bringing blessings to their house. This view is exceedingly unfortunate . . . and is apt to result in the displeasure of the Lord. It has sometimes ended in the brother . . . losing his power to bless and heal.[8]

Elder Bruce R. McConkie boldly taught that not only will prideful, selfish people lose their gifts and talents, but they will also receive strict judgment: "Each is called to serve Him with all his heart, might, mind, and strength. Nothing less will do. The gifts came from God

---

6. *Millennial Star* 56 (Apr. 23, 1894): 260–61; emphasis added.

7. *Millennial Star* 62, no. 23 (June 7, 1900): 354.

8. *Juvenile Instructor* 37, no. 2 (Jan. 15, 1902): 51.

and are to be used in his service. When the Lord returns . . . each servant who had many talents and who doubled them receives the blessed benediction: 'Well done, thou good and faithful servant. . .' But the servant with little ability, who feared the Lord and hid his talent, is adjudged as wicked and slothful. . . . *Those who do not use their talents to save souls are damned.*"[9]

Ministering Angels, Visions, and Dreams

This book deals with at least eight spiritual gifts concerning the prophets: inspired prayers (Doctrine and Covenants 46:28, 30), beholding angels and ministering spirits (Moroni 10:14), seeing visions and dreams (Articles of Faith 1:7; Joel 2:28), casting out evil spirits (Matthew 10:1; Mark 16:17), prophesying (1 Corinthians 12:10; Moroni 10:13), interpreting and speaking in tongues (Moroni 10:15–16; Doctrine and Covenants 46:24–25), healing the sick (1 Corinthians 12:9; Doctrine and Covenants 46:20), and raising the dead (3 Nephi 19:4; 4 Nephi 1:5). I would like to expound here, however, on two of these gifts because numerous accounts in this book deal with them. They are beholding angels and seeing visions and dreams. (Additional details about these two gifts are found throughout the book, especially in chapter five.)

Regarding angels, the prophet Moroni asked, "Have [angels] ceased . . . to minister unto the children of men?" "Behold I say unto you, Nay," he answered, "For behold, they are subject unto him, to minister according to the word of his command, showing themselves unto them of strong faith and a firm mind in every form of godliness. And the office of their ministry is to call men unto repentance, and to fulfil and to do the work of the covenants of the Father, which he hath made unto the children of men, to prepare the way among the children of men, by declaring the word of Christ unto the chosen vessels of the Lord, that they may bear testimony of him" (Moroni 7:28–31). Moroni could have said the same regarding inspired visions and dreams.

---

9. Bruce R. McConkie, *The Millennial Messiah: The Second Coming of the Son of Man* (Deseret Book, 1982), 350; emphasis added.

The purpose of angels ministering to individuals and of people seeing inspired visions and dreams is to "bring to pass the immortality and eternal life of man" (Moses 1:39). Elder Wilford Woodruff taught, "The Lord never did nor ever will send an angel to anybody merely to gratify the desire of the individual to see an angel. The Lord sends an angel to perform a work that cannot be performed only by the administration of an angel."[10] Again, one could say the same thing regarding inspired visions and dreams. Elder McConkie explained that an inspired dream "is a vision given to a person while he sleeps. All inspired dreams are visions, but all visions are not dreams. Visions are received in hours of wakefulness or of sleep and in some cases when the recipient has passed into a trance; it is only when the vision occurs during sleep that it is termed a dream."[11] Using these terms interchangeably, Nephi wrote, "Behold, I have dreamed a dream; *or, in other words*, I have seen a vision" (1 Nephi 8:2).

Nevertheless, who does the Lord permit to see angels and visions? Elder McConkie indicated that every member of the Church is entitled to "get revelation from the Holy Ghost," "entertain angels," and "view the visions of eternity."[12] Elder McConkie taught elsewhere that signs follow faith: "If there are no signs, there is no faith. Where there is faith, there will be the gifts of the Spirit; there will be the ministering of angels and the working of miracles."[13] The Lord revealed that those who strip themselves of "jealousies and fears" and who are "sufficiently humble" might have the opportunity to see beyond the veil (Doctrine and Covenants 67:10). Elder Parley P. Pratt explained that to see an angel or discern things in the spirit world, "spiritual element must quicken a person in the flesh, the veil must be withdrawn, or the organs of sight, or of hearing, must be transformed, so as to be adapted to the spiritual sphere."[14]

---

10. Brian H. Stuy, ed., *Collected Discourses Delivered By President Wilford Woodruff, His Two Counselors, the Twelve Apostles, and Others* (B.H.S. Publishing, 1999), 5:233.

11. Bruce R. McConkie, *Mormon Doctrine*, 208.

12. Bruce R. McConkie, *Sermons and Writings of Bruce R. McConkie*, edited and arranged by Mark L. McConkie (Bookcraft, 1989), 154.

13. Bruce R. McConkie, in Conference Report, Oct. 1953, 125.

14. Parley P. Pratt, *Key to the Science of Theology* (Deseret Book, 1965), 127.

Many people have seen angels, visions, and dreams, but how can one know if these manifestations are from God, Satan, or even the product of imagination? Elder George A. Smith explained that a manifestation is of God when the mind is "illuminated," receives "vivid and pleasant impressions," and is "happy and comfortable."[15] Elder Smith also related an experience when he saw a dream but knew that it was not from God: "I remember once (when in Zion's camp) I was very thirsty, hungry, and tired, that I dreamed when I was walking on the road I could see a loaf of bread, a bottle of milk, and a spring of water. It was one of the pleasantest dreams in the world, and I dreamed it while walking along the road. At the same time a great many dreams, as men consider, are no more or less than open vision, and a great many dreams are the result, perhaps, of fatigue—of over-exercise—of overeating before retiring to rest, or some other cause."[16]

President Spencer W. Kimball mentioned that revelations might come from dreams; however, "most of our dreams are flighty and have no meaning."[17] President Wilford Woodruff counseled the Saints to disregard false manifestations unless their minds are enlightened and they feel that the manifestation has come from the Lord. Then, they must "pay attention to it."[18] In 1913, the First Presidency issued a statement to the Saints concerning manifestations and revelations as follows:

> When visions, dreams, tongues, prophecy, impressions or any extraordinary gift or inspiration, convey something out of harmony with the accepted revelations of the Church or contrary to the decisions of its constituted authorities, Latter-day Saints may know that it is not of God, no matter how plausible it may appear. Also, they should understand that directions for the guidance of the Church will come, by revelation, through the head.
>
> All faithful members are entitled to the inspiration of the Holy Spirit for themselves, their families, and for those over whom they are appointed and ordained to preside. But anything at discord

---

15. *Journal of Discourses*, 8:255.
16. *Journal of Discourses*, 8:255.
17. *The Teachings of Spencer W. Kimball*, ed. Edward L. Kimball (1982), 455.
18. *Journal of Discourses*, 22:333–34.

> with that which comes from God through the head of the Church is not to be received as authoritative or reliable. In secular as well as spiritual affairs, Saints may receive Divine guidance and revelation affecting themselves, but this does not convey authority to direct others, and is not to be accepted when contrary to Church covenants, doctrine or discipline, or to known facts, demonstrated truths, or good common sense. . . .
>
> Be not led by any spirit or influence that discredits established authority, contradicts true scientific principles and discoveries, or leads away from the direct revelations of God for the government of the Church. The Holy Ghost does not contradict its own revealings. Truth is always harmonious with itself. Piety is often the cloak of error. The counsels of the Lord through the channel he has appointed will be followed with safety, therefore, O! ye Latter-day Saints, profit by these words of warning.[19]

Latter-day Saints generally do not maintain that receiving spiritual gifts is an exclusive right but that anyone can receive them. While it is true that those who have received the gift of the Holy Ghost may possess any or all the gifts, it is also true that the Lord inspires many good men and women to perform His work, whether they have been properly baptized or not. For example, Nephi saw in a vision that the Spirit of the Lord "came down and wrought upon" Christopher Columbus and many other explorers (1 Nephi 13:12–13). Columbus recorded occasions when angels appeared and conversed with him concerning his mission. Latter-day prophets have taught that the Lord inspired many of the founders of the United States.[20] Trevan Hatch cited hundreds of people—who lived shortly before and during Joseph Smith's lifetime—who claimed to have seen visions, dreams, and angels. Many of these people—mostly from the Baptist, Methodist, Presbyterian, and other Protestant movements—believed

---

19. James R. Clark, comp., *Messages of the First Presidency of The Church of Jesus Christ of Latter-day Saints* (Bookcraft, 1965–75), 6:244–45.
20. See Donald Q. Cannon, *Latter-day Prophets and the United States Constitution* (Religious Studies Center, Brigham Young University, 1991).

that Christ's Church, as well as revelation and spiritual gifts, would soon be restored.[21]

It is worth noting that while most Christians reject the idea of revelation in the last days, John Wesley (1703–1791), the founder of Methodism, believed that men continue to receive revelation through visions, dreams, and angels. In 1739, Wesley penned in his journal the following: "What I have to say touching visions or dreams, is this: I know several persons in whom this great change was wrought in a dream, or during a strong representation to the eye of their mind, of Christ either on the cross or in the glory. This is the fact; let any judge of it as they please. And that such a change was wrought appears . . . from the whole tenor of their life, till then many ways wicked; from that time holy, just, and good." Wesley also wrote that "God does now, as aforetime" speak to men "often in dreams or in visions . . . [and] if it be not so, I am found a false witness before God."[22]

The Lord not only inspired Christopher Columbus and the Founding Fathers, but He also inspired and revealed certain things to inventors, Nobel Prize winners, US presidents, and many religious figures. For example, Captain Henry Bell recorded a manifestation he received in the 1630s. Apparently, Joseph Smith was not the only person commanded by an angelic messenger to translate a religious text. While in Germany, Henry Bell—a translator who worked for King James—discovered a work of Martin Luther called *Divine Discourses*, currently known as *The Table Talk of Martin Luther*. Bell learned that the emperor burned 80,000 copies of *Divine Discourses* several years prior to his arrival in Germany. The book contained theological discussions with German contemporaries who spoke out against the Catholic Church. Bell eventually found a copy of the book and desired to translate it into English but was unable to accomplish the task for several reasons.

Bell recorded a remarkable manifestation he received shortly after obtaining a copy of the book: "I being in bed with my wife one

---

21. Trevan Hatch, *When the Lights Came On: Joseph Smith and the Return of Heavenly Manifestations* (Cedar Fort, 2016).

22. Percy Livingstone Parker, ed., *The Heart of John Wesley's Journal* (Keats Publishing Inc., 1979), 51–52.

night, between twelve and one of the clock, she being asleep, but myself yet awake, there appeared unto me an ancient man, standing at my bedside, arrayed all in white . . . who taking me by my right ear, spake these words following unto me: 'Sirrah! Will not you take time to translate that book which is sent unto you out of Germany? I will shortly provide for you both place and time to do it' and then he vanished away out of my sight."[23] Bell eventually translated the book into English, which is widely read today.

Upon reading *The Table Talk of Martin Luther*, one learns that—like the Latter-day Saints—Luther believed in the premortal life, Satan, and angels who assist men and perform God's work:

> An Angel is a spiritual creature created by God . . . for the service of Christendom and of the church. The acknowledgment of angels is needful in the church. . . . They are good spirits and not evil; and here evil spirits also be spoken of, *not created evil by God, but made so by their rebellion against God*, and their consequent fall; this hatred *began in Paradise*, and will continue and remain against Christ and his church to the world's end. . . .
>
> The angels do minister unto us . . . in household and temporal policy, and in religion. . . . The angels are near to us . . . therefore *when the devil intends to hurt us, then the loving angels resist and drive him away*. . . . The devil is also near and about us, incessantly tracking our steps in order to deprive us of our lives, our saving health, and salvation. But the holy angels defend us from him, insomuch that he is not able to work us such mischief as willingly he would. *I believe that the angels are all up in arms, are putting on their harness, and girding their swords about them.* For the last judgment is nigh, and the angels prepare themselves for the combat, and to strike down [evil] into the bottomless pit.[24]

In 1865, President Abraham Lincoln recorded a fascinating and little-known experience that proved to be prophetic two weeks later when he was assassinated. Lincoln related that in his dream, "there seemed to be a death-like stillness about me. Then I heard subdued

---

23. Martin Luther, *The Table Talk of Martin Luther*, ed. William Hazlitt (Covent Garden, 1883), vii.

24. Luther, *Table Talk of Martin Luther*, 245–47.

sobs, as if a number of people were weeping. I thought I left my bed and wandered downstairs. . . . It was light in all the rooms; every object was familiar to me. . . . I kept on until I arrived at the East Room, which I entered. There I met with a sickening surprise. Before me was a catafalque, on which rested a corpse wrapped in funeral vestments. . . . 'Who is dead in the White House?' I demanded of one of the soldiers. 'The president,' was his answer. 'He was killed by an assassin!' Then came a loud burst of grief from the crowd." Just then, Lincoln awoke and could not fall back to sleep.

Several months prior to his death, President Lincoln survived an assassination attempt while stationed at a soldier's home. The assassin fired a gun at the president, but the bullet just missed his head and passed through his hat. Ward Hill Lamon, a bodyguard of the president, became worried about the president's safety and even chastised him several times for going to the theater alone. On one occasion, Hill said to President Lincoln, "You are in danger. Tonight, as you have done on several previous occasions, you went unattended to the theatre. . . . You ought to know, that your life is sought after, and will be taken unless you and your friends are cautious."

"Hill," retorted Lincoln, "your apprehension of harm to me from some hidden enemy is downright foolishness. For a long time you have been trying to keep somebody—the Lord knows who—from killing me. Don't you see how it will turn out? In this dream it was not me, but some other fellow, that was killed. It seems that this ghostly assassin tried his hand on someone else."

Lamon's constant badgering may have paid off. When President Lincoln went to Ford's Theater to see the comedy "Our American Cousin" on the night of April 14, 1865, he took his wife and an officer named Major Henry R. Rathbone. Despite this protection, however, John Wilkes Booth rushed into the president's box and shot Lincoln, who died nine hours later.[25]

Another example of an inspired manifestation was recorded by Otto Loewi, a German pharmacologist who won a Nobel Prize (in medicine) in 1936 for a discovery based on a dream. Loewi explained:

---

25. Philip B. Kundhardt, Philip B. Kundhardt III, and Peter W. Kundhardt, *Lincoln* (Alfred A. Knopf, 1992), 334.

> As far back as 1903, I discussed with Walter M. Fletcher from Cambridge, England, then an associate in Marburg, the fact that certain drugs mimic the augmentary as well as the inhibitory effects of the stimulation of sympathetic and/or parasympathetic nerves on their elfector organs. During this discussion, the idea occurred to me that the terminals of those nerves might contain chemicals, that stimulation might liberate them from the nerve terminals, and that these chemicals might in turn transmit the nervous impulse to their respective effector organs. At that time I did not see a way to prove the correctness of this hunch, and it entirely slipped my conscious memory until it emerged again in 1920.
>
> The night before Easter Sunday of that year I awoke, turned on the light, and jotted down a few notes on a tiny slip of thin paper. Then I fell asleep again. It occurred to me at six o'clock in the morning that during the night I had written down something most important, but I was unable to decipher the scrawl. The next night at three o'clock, the idea returned. It was the design of an experiment to determine whether or not the hypothesis of chemical transmission that I had uttered seventeen years ago was correct. I got up immediately, went to the laboratory, and performed a simple experiment on a frog heart according to the nocturnal design. I have to describe briefly this experiment since its results became the foundation of the theory of chemical transmission of the nervous impulse.[26]

Niels Bohr, a Swedish physicist, also won a Nobel Prize in 1922 for a discovery he made concerning the composition of an atom. He made this discovery from a dream, in which he saw "a huge sun with fiery flames radiating in rays away from the center. Then he saw little suns radiating similar flames, arranged in an elliptical orbit intersecting with the large sun. Then he saw another elliptical orbit with little suns and flares intersecting the first two orbits, and finally, a third elliptical orbit with little flares also intersecting with all other orbits. After he awoke, he wrote it down."[27]

---

26. Josef Donnerer and Fred Lembeck, *The Chemical Languages of the Nervous System: History of Scientists and Substances* (Karger S. Inc., 2006), 22–23.

27. Judith Aron Rubin, *Approaches to Art Therapy: Theory and Technique* (Taylor & Francis, Inc., 2001), 154.

Elias Howe invented the sewing machine based on a dream he had in 1845. In his dream, a "tribe of savages" captured him. They took Howe to their king, who said, "Elias Howe, I command you on pain of death to finish this machine at once." "In the vision," wrote one historian, "he saw himself surrounded by dark-skinned and painted warriors, who formed a hollow square about him and led him to the place of execution. Suddenly he noticed that near the heads of the spears which his guards carried, there were eye-shaped holes! He had solved the secret! What he needed was a needle with an eye near the point! He awoke from his dream, sprang out of bed, and at once made a whittled model of the eye-pointed needle, with which he brought his experiment to a successful close."[28]

The Lord inspires many individuals through dreams, visions, and angelic appearances to advance His work and build up His kingdom, which includes medical, technological, and moral advancements and ideas. The Lord also communicates to righteous individuals, like Abraham Lincoln, through dreams to warn them of impending danger, or even to prepare them for death.

Latter-day Prophets

Many people claim that God no longer appoints prophets to guide His people but that prophets and prophecies ceased with the rise and conquest of Alexander the Great (Judaism), the death of Jesus and his Apostles (Christianity), or the death of Muhammad (Islam). However, the Bible makes no such claim. God always did and will appoint righteous men and women to lead, warn, and prepare His people. Luke 1:70 and Acts 3:21 state that God has called prophets "since the world began." Jesus taught that prophets would continue to teach and prophecy after Him (see Matthew 23:34; Luke 11:49; Acts 13:1). This prophecy was fulfilled in—among others—Paul, Mormon, Moroni, John the Revelator, the Three Nephites, and finally the prophets of the Restoration. In addition, we read in Joel that in the last days, God will "pour out [his] spirit upon all flesh; and your sons and your daughters shall prophesy" (Joel 2:28). The Apostle Paul, as shown above,

28. Waldemar Kaempffert, ed., *A Popular History of American Invention* (Charles Scribner's Sons, 1924), 2:385.

stated that God's people will possess many gifts of the Spirit—the gift of prophecy included. Paul also reminded the Saints that Christ's Church is "built upon the foundation of the apostles and prophets" (Ephesians 2:20). The fact that The Church of Jesus Christ of Latter-day Saints—the only religious group who claim to be the "only *true and living* church upon the face of the whole earth" (Doctrine and Covenants 1:30)—is also the *only* group to claim guidance from living prophets is quite a fascinating phenomenon in Christendom, especially considering the Bible's teachings about prophets and prophecy in the last days.

A traditional "prophet" is one who speaks for God, including predictions of future or past events. A "seer," like a prophet, not only speaks for God but also has the ability to see with spiritual eyes past, present, and future events. The Book of Mormon teaches that "a seer is greater than a prophet" because "a seer is a revelator and a prophet also. . . . A seer can know of things which are past, and also of things which are to come, and by them shall all things be revealed" (Mosiah 8:15–17). Another title usually connected with "prophet," "seer," and "revelator" is "apostle," which comes from the Greek *apostolos*, meaning "one who is sent out." The main duties of an Apostle in Jesus's day and in modern times are to take the gospel message to the entire world and to testify of Christ (see Mark 3:14; John 15:16; Acts 1:21–26). Every member of the Quorum of the Twelve Apostles and First Presidency is an apostle, a prophet, a seer, and a revelator. The President of the Church is the senior Apostle. The primary functions of a prophet, seer, and revelator in this dispensation are to guide the Church—both administratively and spiritually—and to prepare God's children for the Second Coming.

God, therefore, has bestowed upon the prophets, those who "watch over the church," all the spiritual gifts (Doctrine and Covenants 46:27). In the early days of the Church when the original Twelve were called and ordained, Elder Heber C. Kimball reported that they were blessed with "many things," including the "power to heal the sick, cast out devils, raise the dead, give sight to the blind, have power to remove mountains, and all things should be subject to us through the name of Jesus Christ, and angels should minister unto us, and many more things too numerous to mention."[29]

The following chapters illustrate how certain gifts of the Spirit have been displayed in the lives of several prophets of The Church of Jesus Christ of Latter-day Saints as well as how these gifts have assisted the Church through its leaders.

---

29. *Times and Seasons* 6 (1845): 868.

Chapter Two

Manifestations of Jesus the Christ

The gift of the Spirit that every member of the Church should seek after is to come to a knowledge "by the power of the Holy Ghost" that "Jesus Christ is the Son of God, and that he was crucified for the sins of the world" (Moroni 10:7; Doctrine and Covenants 46:13). "Jesus Christ, the Savior of the world," taught President Gordon B. Hinckley, "is the pivotal figure of our theology and our faith. Every Latter-day Saint has the responsibility to know for himself or herself with a certainty beyond doubt that Jesus is the resurrected, living Son of the living God."[30]

One need not talk to Jesus face-to-face or see Him in a vision to know that He is the Messiah, for there is a much stronger witness that every Latter-day Saint can receive, which is through the Holy Ghost. President Joseph Fielding Smith explained that "impressions on the soul that come from the Holy Ghost are far more significant than a vision. When Spirit speaks to spirit, the imprint upon the soul is far more difficult to erase. Every member of the Church should have

30. "Fear Not to Do Good," *Ensign*, May 1983, 80.

impressions that Jesus is the Son of God indelibly pictured on his soul through the witness of the Holy Ghost."[31] The Apostle Paul similarly stated that "no man can say that Jesus is the Lord, but by the Holy Ghost" (1 Corinthians 12:3).

Elder George Q. Cannon once chastised the Saints for not seeking to acquire gifts of the Spirit and for not working and praying to gain a stronger testimony of Jesus: "We find, even among those who have embraced the Gospel, hearts of unbelief. How many of you, my brethren and sisters, are seeking for these gifts that God has promised to bestow? . . . How many of you ask the Father, in the name of Jesus, *to manifest Himself to you* through these powers and these gifts? Or do you go along day by day like a door turning on its hinges, without having any feeling on the subject, without exercising any faith whatever? . . . I say to you, in the name of the Lord, as one of His servants, that you have need to repent of this."[32]

Did Elder Cannon imply that every Latter-day Saint should pray for a vision or a physical manifestation of Christ? Certainly not, for the scriptures state that an "evil and adulterous generation seeketh after a sign" (Matthew 12:39), meaning that sign-seekers are those who succumb to desires of the flesh and who lack faith. For example, on one occasion while Joseph Smith was preaching to a group in Philadelphia, a man interrupted the Prophet and demanded a sign. Joseph told the man to be silent. When the sermon ended, the man once again demanded that the Prophet show him a sign. Joseph recorded, "I told the congregation the man was an adulterer; that a wicked and adulterous generation seeketh after a sign; and that the Lord had said to me in a revelation, that any man who wanted a sign was an adulterous person." Someone in the congregation called out, "It is true for I caught him in the very act." The man later admitted that he had been sexually immoral.[33]

Elder Cannon did not imply that the Saints should pray and seek a physical manifestation of Jesus, but that they should seek a

---

31. Joseph Fielding Smith, "The First Presidency and the Council of the Twelve," *Improvement Era,* Nov. 1966, 979.

32. *Millennial Star* 56 (1894): 260–61.

33. Joseph Smith, in *History of the Church,* 5:268.

manifestation of Jesus through the Holy Ghost. However, even if Elder Cannon was referring to physical manifestations of Jesus, there is a difference between desiring a physical manifestation to strengthen unbelief and living in such a way as to be *worthy* to receive a physical manifestation of Jesus.

Moreover, it is worth noting that, according to Christ, a person will know they are pure if they have seen God: "Blessed are the pure in heart: for they shall see God" (Matthew 5:8). The Savior also revealed to Joseph Smith that "every soul who forsaketh his sins and cometh unto me, and calleth on my name, and obeyeth my voice, and keepeth my commandments, shall see my face and know that I am" (Doctrine and Covenants 93:1). These passages not only refer to those who will live with Christ after Judgment Day but also to those who live on earth before death. The resurrected Messiah also revealed to the Prophet Joseph that "inasmuch as my people build a house unto me in the name of the Lord, and do not suffer any unclean thing to come into it, that it be not defiled, my glory shall rest upon it; Yea, and my presence shall be there, for I will come into it, and all the pure in heart that shall come into it shall see God" (Doctrine and Covenants 97:15–16).

One frequently asked question among the Saints regarding physical manifestations of Jesus is whether prophets are *required* to see Jesus as part of their calling. While there is no definite answer to that question, it is true that special witnesses of Christ (see Doctrine and Covenants 107:23, 26) receive an unmistakable witness of Jesus, whether by a physical manifestation—an appearance, an open vision, or an audible voice—or through the Holy Ghost. In his "general charge to the Twelve" in 1835, Oliver Cowdery told the Brethren, "It is necessary that you receive a testimony from heaven for yourselves; so that you can bear testimony to the truth of the Book of Mormon, and that you have *seen the face of God*. . . . Never cease striving until you have seen God face to face. Strengthen your faith; cast off your doubts, your sins, and all your unbelief; and nothing can prevent you from coming to God."[34]

---

34. *History of the Church*, 2:195–96.

President Joseph Fielding Smith taught that "all men may, by virtue of the priesthood and the gift of the Holy Ghost, become witnesses for Christ. In fact, that is just what every elder in the Church should be, but there is a *special calling* which is given to the Twelve special witnesses that separates them from other elders of the Church in the nature of their calling as witnesses."[35] President Joseph F. Smith stated in general conference that each member of the Twelve is "supposed to be *eye and ear witnesses* of the divine mission of Jesus Christ. It is not permissible for them to say, I believe, simply; I have accepted it simply because I believe it. Read the revelation, the Lord informs us they must *know,* they must get the knowledge for themselves. It must be with them as though they had seen with their eyes and heard with their ears and they know the truth. That is their mission, to testify of Jesus Christ."[36]

Zebedee Coltrin, regarding the School of the Prophets in Kirtland, recorded a relevant account. On March 18, 1833, after the members of the school prayed, Jesus and God the Father walked through the room. The Prophet Joseph subsequently said, "Brethren, now you are prepared to be the apostles of Jesus Christ, for you have seen both the Father and the Son and know that they exist and that they are two separate personages."[37]

Based on these statements, we can certainly conclude that an Apostle—who is also a prophet, seer, and revelator—must receive an unmistakable witness that Jesus is the Messiah. However, based on a September 1859 sermon of Brigham Young, every prophet is not necessarily required to see Jesus to serve as one of His special witnesses. When he delivered this sermon, Brigham was the President of the

---

35. Joseph Fielding Smith, *Doctrines of Salvation, Sermons and Writings of Joseph Fielding Smith,* comp. Bruce R. McConkie (Bookcraft, 1956), 3:146.

36. Conference Report, Apr. 1916, 6.

37. Zebedee Coltrin, Minutes, 3 October 1883, Salt Lake School of Prophets, LDS Church Archives, Salt Lake City, Utah, 56–58; see also Lyndon W. Cook, *The Revelations of the Prophet Joseph Smith* (Deseret Book, 1981), 187–88. In a journal entry dated March 18, 1833, the Prophet Joseph wrote, "Many of the brethren saw a heavenly vision of the Savior, and concourses of angels, and many other things, of which each one has a record of what he saw." *History of the Church,* 1:335.

Church and had been an Apostle for over twenty years; however, he had not yet seen the Savior. "I have flattered myself," stated Brigham, "if I am as faithful as I know how to be to my God, . . . when I have lived to be as old as was Moses when the Lord appeared to him, that perhaps I then may hold communion with the Lord, as did Moses. I am not now in that position, though I know much more than I did twenty, ten, or five years ago."[38]

The accounts below relate the experiences of several prophets who saw Jesus in person or in vision. Latter-day Saints claim that Jesus restored His Church in this dispensation and continues to direct His people. Therefore, it seems fitting that those who lead the Church would *know* Him and see Him, often face-to-face.

Accounts of the Prophets

Melvin J. Ballard

> Away on the Fort Peck Reservation where I was doing missionary work with some of our brethren, laboring among the Indians, seeking the Lord for light to decide certain matters pertaining to our work there, and receiving a witness from him that we were doing things according to his will, I found myself one evening [in May 1917] in the dreams of the night in that sacred building, the temple. After a season of prayer and rejoicing I was informed that I should have the privilege of entering into one of those rooms, to meet a glorious Personage, and as I entered the door I saw, seated on a raised platform, the most glorious Being my eyes have ever beheld, or that I ever conceived existed in all the eternal worlds. As I approached to be introduced, he arose and stepped towards me with extended arms, and he smiled as he softly spoke my name. If I shall live to be a million years old, I shall never forget that smile. He took me into his arms and kissed me, pressed me to his bosom, and blessed me, until the marrow of my bones seemed to melt! When he had finished, I fell at his feet, and, as I bathed them with my tears and kisses, I saw the prints of the nails in the feet of the Redeemer of the world. The feeling that I had in the presence of him who hath all things in his hands, to have his love, his affection, and his

38. *Journal of Discourses*, 7:243.

blessing was such that if I ever can receive that of which I had but a foretaste, I would give all that I am, all that I ever hope to be, to feel what I then felt![39]

Hugh B. Brown

Related by Homer Durham:

Hugh B. Brown, who had served as President McKay's first counselor, resumed his seat as an apostle. A few months later he would confide in his nephew, N. Eldon Tanner, that he missed the intense involvement of the First Presidency. In failing health, he could attend meetings of the Twelve only infrequently, so Eldon became one of his few regular contacts with General Authorities.

Following one visit, President Tanner wrote in his diary, "I am sure it is difficult to adjust after being in the First Presidency." He added an experience related by his uncle that had helped President Brown adjust to these years of declining responsibility. He said it was not a vision, but the Lord appeared to him, very informal, the same as I was sitting talking to him. The Lord said, "You have had some difficult times in your life." Uncle Hugh responded, "Yes, and your life was more difficult than any of us have had." In the conversation Uncle Hugh asked when he would be finished here, and the Lord said, "I don't know and I wouldn't tell you if I did." Then He said, "Remain faithful to the end, and everything will be all right."[40]

George Q. Cannon

I had never been so happy before in all my life as I was then. When I prayed, I could go in faith. He listened to my prayers. He gave

---

39. Bryant S. Hinckley, *Sermons and Missionary Services of Melvin J. Ballard* (Deseret Book, 1949), 156. On another occasion, Ballard said, "I know, as well as I know that I live and look into your faces, that Jesus Christ lives, and he is the Redeemer of the world. . . . For in the visions of the Lord to my soul, I have seen Christ's face, I have heard his voice." Conference Report, Apr. 1920, 40–41.

40. Homer Durham, *N. Eldon Tanner: His Life and Service* (Deseret Book, 1982), 254–56.

me great comfort and joy. He revealed Himself to me as He had never done before, told me that if I would persevere, I should be blessed and be the means of bringing many to a knowledge of the truth and be spared to return home after having done a good work. Many things were revealed to me during these days, when He was the only friend we had to lean upon.[41]

I know that God lives. I know that Jesus lives; for I have seen Him.[42]

Oliver Cowdery

Related by Joseph Smith:

The Lord appeared unto a young man by the name of Oliver Cowdery [in February 1829] and showed unto him the plates in a vision and also the truth of the work and what the Lord was about to do through me his unworthy servant therefore he was desirous to come and write for me and translate.[43]

James E. Faust

Related by Allen Wyatt:

Today is the first day of our stake conference. I am the executive secretary of the Indianapolis Indiana North Stake. Elder James E. Faust is here to replace our stake presidency. I was sitting in the 4:00 priesthood leadership session, and Elder Faust was bearing his testimony. It is, without a doubt, the strongest testimony I have ever heard. He said (paraphrasing) "I have always believed in the Church; I come from good blood. But through thousands of spiritual experiences, so many now that I have at least one a day—we had one earlier today (referring to meeting with the new stake presidency)—I have gained a testimony to the point I can say, as did the brother of Jared, 'I saw the finger of the Lord and the veil could

41. Bryant S. Hinckley, *The Faith of Our Pioneer Fathers* (Deseret Book, 1956), 164–65.

42. George Q. Cannon, *Gospel Truth: Discourses and Writings of President George Q. Cannon*, ed. Jerreld L. Newquist (Deseret Book, 1987), 106.

43. Joseph Smith, *Personal Writings of Joseph Smith*, ed. Dean C. Jessee (Deseret Book, 1984), 8.

not withhold Him from me, therefore I no longer believed, for I had knowledge.' As the brother of Jared stated, so say I—I know that Jesus is the Christ." As Elder Faust spoke, I was hit with the sure and certain knowledge that I truly stood in the presence of an Apostle of the Lord. I had it witnessed to me that Elder Faust had, in truth, beheld the Savior. Here he was, a mere mortal man, who had truly and honestly beheld the Savior.[44]

David B. Haight

Some time ago [in April 1989], as I was convalescing from a serious operation . . . as I lay in the hospital bed, I meditated upon all that had happened to me. . . . I was now in a calm, peaceful setting; all was serene and quiet. I was conscious of two persons in the distance on a hillside, one standing on a higher level than the other. Detailed features were not discernible. The person on the higher level was pointing to something I could not see. I heard no voices but was conscious of being in a holy presence and atmosphere. During the hours and days that followed, there was impressed again and again upon my mind the eternal mission and exalted position of the Son of Man. . . . I was shown a panoramic view of his earthly ministry: his baptism, his teaching, his healing the sick and lame, the mock trial, his crucifixion, his resurrection and ascension. There followed scenes of his earthly ministry to my mind in impressive detail, confirming scriptural eyewitness accounts. I was being taught, and the eyes of my understanding were opened by the Holy Spirit of God so as to behold many things.

The first scene was of the Savior and his apostles in the upper chamber on the eve of his betrayal. Following the Passover supper, he gave instruction and prepared the sacrament of the Lord's Supper for his dearest friends as a remembrance of his coming sacrifice. It was so impressively portrayed to me—the overwhelming love of the Savior for each. I witnessed his thoughtful concern for significant details—the washing of the dusty feet of each apostle, his breaking and blessing of the loaf of dark bread and blessing of the wine, then his dreadful disclosure that one would betray him.

44. Journal entry of Allen Wyatt, Feb. 3, 1990. Used with permission.

He explained Judas's departure and told the others of the events soon to take place. Then followed the Savior's solemn discourse when he said to the eleven: "These things I have spoken unto you, that in me ye might have peace. In the world ye shall have tribulation: but be of good cheer; I have overcome the world" (John 16:33). Our Savior prayed to his Father and acknowledged the Father as the source of his authority and power—even to the extending of eternal life to all who are worthy. . . . When they had sung a hymn, Jesus and the eleven went out to the Mount of Olives. There in the garden, in some manner beyond our comprehension, the Savior took upon himself the burden of the sins of mankind from Adam to the end of the world. . . .

During those days of unconsciousness I was given, by the gift and power of the Holy Ghost, a more perfect knowledge of Jesus' mission. I was also given a more complete understanding of what it means to exercise, in his name, the authority to unlock the mysteries of the kingdom of heaven for the salvation of all who are faithful. My soul was taught over and over again the events of the betrayal, the mock trial, the scourging of the flesh of even one of the Godhead. I witnessed his struggling up the hill in his weakened condition carrying the cross, and his being stretched upon it as it lay on the ground so that the crude spikes could be driven with a mallet into his hands and wrists and feet to secure his body as it hung on the cross for public display. . . .

I testify that our Heavenly Father does answer our righteous pleadings. The added knowledge that has come to me has made a great impact upon my life. The gift of the Holy Ghost is a priceless possession and opens the door to our ongoing knowledge of God and eternal joy. Of this I bear witness.[45]

Heber C. Kimball

I have been at the other side of the veil, in vision, and have seen a degree of its condition with the eyes that God gave me. I have seen it and have seen those that lived in the faith and had the privilege of seeing Jesus, Peter, James, and the rest of the ancient Apostles,

45. David B. Haight, *A Light unto the World* (Deseret Book, 1997), 3–6, 8; see also David B. Haight, "The Sacrament—and the Sacrifice," *Ensign*, Nov. 1989, 59–61.

and of hearing them preach the Gospel. I have also seen those who rebelled against them, and they still had a rebellious spirit, fighting against God and His servants.[46]

David O. McKay

I then fell asleep and beheld in vision something infinitely sublime. In the distance I beheld a beautiful white city. Though far away, yet I seemed to realize that trees with luscious fruit, shrubbery with gorgeously-tinted leaves, and flowers in perfect bloom abounded everywhere. The clear sky above seemed to reflect these beautiful shades of color. I then saw a great concourse of people approaching the city. Each one wore a white flowing robe, and a white headdress. Instantly my attention seemed centered upon their Leader, and though I could see only the profile of his features and his body, I recognized him at once as my Savior! The tint and radiance of his countenance were glorious to behold! There was a peace about him which seemed sublime—it was divine! The city, I understood, was his. It was the City Eternal; and the people following him were to abide there in peace and eternal happiness. But who were they? As if the Savior read my thoughts, he answered by pointing to a semicircle that then appeared above them, and on which were written in gold the words: "These Are They Who Have Overcome The World—Who Have Truly Been Born Again."[47]

Charles C. Rich

Related by the author:

In 1832, Charles C. Rich, future Apostle (ordained in 1849), saw the Savior in a vision. Rich was staying at the home of his uncle, William O'Neal, when he suddenly saw himself standing in a crowd of people surrounding a large house. A man approached Rich and told him that the Savior was inside the house. Rich immediately worked his way through the crowd and entered the building. He found himself on the second floor and in front of a closed door. As he opened the

46. *Journal of Discourses*, 4:274 (given January 25, 1857).

47. Mary Jane Woodger, *The Teachings of David O. McKay* (Deseret Book, 2004), 22–23.

door, he heard Christ's voice instructing the leaders of The Church of Jesus Christ of Latter-day Saints. As Rich entered the room, the Savior looked at him and smiled. "The Savior," recorded Rich, "was so full of the Holy Spirit that I could see it." Rich listened to the Savior's concluding counsel and was subsequently invited to join them in prayer. Rich knelt with the group as the Savior offered the prayer. At this moment, the vision closed and Rich instantly felt that he had control over the "powers of the adversary."[48]

George F. Richards

> Last night [April 9, 1906], I dreamed of seeing the Savior and embracing him. The feelings I cannot describe, but I think it was a touch of heaven. I never expect anything better hereafter. The love of man for woman cannot compare with it. May we be faithful and make every sacrifice necessary . . . to live in his presence forever.[49]

Referring to the same dream, George F. Richards said the following:

> More than forty years ago I had a dream, which I am sure was from the Lord. In this dream I was in the presence of my Savior as he stood in mid-air. He spoke no word to me, but my love for him was such that I have not words to explain. I know that no mortal man can love the Lord as I experienced that love for the Savior unless God reveals it to him. I would have remained in His presence but there was a power drawing me away from him, and as a result of that dream I had this feeling, that no matter what might be required at my hands, what the Gospel might entail unto me, I would do what I should be asked to do, even to the laying down of my life.[50]

---

48. Leonard Arrington, *Charles C. Rich: Mormon General and Western Frontiersman* (Brigham Young University Press, 1974), 22.
49. Lucile C. Tate, *LeGrand Richards: Beloved Apostle* (Bookcraft, 1982), 47.
50. *C*onference Report, Oct. 1946, 139.

Legrand Richards

I had a very beautiful dream last night [May 10, 1926]. I dreamed that while we were met together in priesthood meeting, the Savior appeared [in a pillar of light], and immediately we began to sing "Hosanna, Hosanna, Hosanna to our Lord." It was a most wonderful feeling, and I awakened with the thought that, though the world doubted his coming, I had actually lived to see it. It was a sweet and beautiful climax. I do hope I will be worthy of him when he does appear, for I do know he shall come.[51]

The School of the Prophets

Related by Zebedee Coltrin:

At one of these meetings after the organization of the school, (the school being organized on the 23rd of January, 1833) when we were all together [March 18, 1833], Joseph having given instructions, and while engaged in silent prayer, kneeling, with our hands uplifted each one praying in silence, no one whispered above his breath, a personage walked through the room from east to west, and Joseph asked if we saw him. I saw him and suppose the others did and Joseph answered "that is Jesus, the Son of God, our elder brother." Afterward Joseph told us to resume our former position in prayer, which we did. Another person came through; he was surrounded as with a flame of fire. . . . The Prophet Joseph said this was the Father of our Lord Jesus Christ. I saw Him. . . .

I did not discover his clothing for he was surrounded as with a flame of fire, which was so brilliant that I could not discover anything else but his person. I saw his hands, his legs, his feet, his eyes, nose, mouth, head and body in the shape and form of a perfect man. He sat in a chair as a man would sit in a chair, but this appearance was so grand and overwhelming that it seemed I should melt down in his presence, and the sensation was so powerful that it thrilled through my whole system and I felt it in the marrow of my bones. The Prophet Joseph said: "Brethren, now you are prepared to be the apostles of Jesus Christ, for you have seen both the

51. Tate, *Legrand Richards*, 137.

Father and the Son and know that they exist and that they are two separate personages."[52]

Joseph Smith

Related by Mary E. R. Lightner:

A few evenings after his visit to our house [in 1831], Mother and I went over to the Smith house. There were other visitors. The whole Smith family, excepting Joseph, was there. As we stood talking to them, Brother Joseph and Martin Harris came in, with two or three others. When the greetings were over, Brother Joseph looked around very solemnly. It was the first time some of them had ever seen him. He then said, "There are enough here to hold a little meeting."

A board was put across two chairs to make seats. Martin Harris sat on a little box at Joseph's feet. They sang and prayed; then Joseph got up to speak. He began very solemnly and very earnestly. All at once his countenance changed and he stood mute. He turned so white he seemed perfectly transparent. Those who looked at him that night said he looked like he had a searchlight within him, in every part of his body. I never saw anything like it on earth. I could not take my eyes away from him. He got so white that anyone who saw him would have thought he was transparent. I remember I thought we could almost see the bones through the flesh of his face. I shall remember it and see it in my mind's eye as long as I remain upon the earth.

He stood some moments looking over the congregation, as if to pierce each heart, then said, "Do you know who has been in your midst this night?" One of the Smiths said, "An angel of the Lord." Joseph did not answer. Martin Harris was sitting at the Prophet's feet on a box. He slid to his knees, clasped his arms around the Prophet's knees and said, "I know, it was our Lord and Savior, Jesus Christ."

Joseph put his hand on Martin's head and answered, "Martin, God revealed that to you. Brothers and Sisters, the Savior has been in your midst this night. I want you all to remember it. There is a veil over your eyes, for you could not endure to look upon Him.

---

52. Zebedee Coltrin, Minutes, 56–58.

You must be fed with milk and not strong meat. I want you to remember this as if it were the last thing that escaped my lips. He has given you all to me, and commanded me to seal you up to everlasting life, that where He is there you may be also." . . .

Then he knelt and prayed, and such a prayer I never heard before or since. I felt he was talking to the Lord, and the power rested upon us all. The prayer was so long that some of the people got up and rested, then knelt again.[53]

Joseph Smith

Related by Levi Hancock:

The Fourth of June [1831] came and we all met in a little string of buildings under the hill near Isaac Morley's in Kirtland, Geauga County, Ohio. Then we all went to a school house on the hill about one fourth of a mile ascending nearly all the way. The building was built of logs. It was filled with slab benches, here the elders were seated and the meeting was opened as usual. Joseph Smith began to speak, he said, . . . "Some of you must die for the testimony of this work" and he looked at Lyman White and said to him, "You shall see the Lord and meet him near the corner of the house and laid his hands upon him and blessed him with the visions of heaven." Joseph Smith then stepped out on the floor and said, "I now see God, and Jesus Christ at his right hand, let them kill me, I should not feel death as I am now."[54]

Joseph Smith

I received, by a heavenly vision, a commandment in June [1831] following, to take my journey to the western boundaries of the State of Missouri, and there designate the very spot which was to be the central place for the commencement of the gathering together of those who embrace the fullness of the everlasting Gospel. Accordingly

53. *Diary of Mary Elizabeth Rollins Lightner*; *Young Woman's Journal* 16, no. 12 (Dec. 1905): 556–57.

54. "Autobiography of Levi Ward Hancock (1803–1836)," Typescript, L. Tom Perry Special Collections Library, Harold B. Lee Library, Brigham Young University, Provo, Utah, 33.

I undertook the journey, with certain ones of my brethren, and after a long and tedious journey, suffering many privations and hardships, arrived in Jackson County, Missouri, and after viewing the country, seeking diligently at the hand of God, He manifested Himself unto us, and designated, to me and others, the very spot upon which He designed to commence the work of the gathering, and the up building of an "holy city," which should be called Zion-Zion, because it is a place of righteousness.[55]

Joseph Smith and Sidney Rigdon

By the power of the Spirit our eyes were opened and our understandings were enlightened, so as to see and understand the things of God. . . . And while we meditated upon these things, the Lord touched the eyes of our understandings and they were opened, and the glory of the Lord shone round about. And we beheld the glory of the Son, on the right hand of the Father, and received of his fulness; And saw the holy angels, and them who are sanctified before his throne, worshiping God, and the Lamb, who worship him forever and ever.[56]

Joseph Smith

[On January 21, 1836,] the heavens were opened upon us, and I beheld the celestial kingdom of God, and the glory thereof, whether in the body or out I cannot tell. I saw the transcendent beauty of the gate through which the heirs of that kingdom will enter, which was like unto circling flames of fire; Also the blazing throne of God, whereon was seated the Father and the Son. I saw the beautiful streets of that kingdom, which had the appearance of being paved with gold. I saw Father Adam and Abraham; and my father and my mother; my brother Alvin, that has long since slept.[57]

---

55. *History of the Church*, 2:254.

56. *History of the Church*, 1:247; see also Doctrine and Covenants 76:11–21.

57. *History of the Church*, 2:380; see also Doctrine and Covenants137:1–5.

Joseph Smith

Related by Elder Heber C. Kimball:

[In April 1836, Joseph] saw the Twelve going forth, and they appeared to be in a far distant land. After some time they unexpectedly met together, apparently in great tribulation, their clothes all ragged, and their knees and feet sore. They formed into a circle, and all stood with their eyes fixed upon the ground. The Savior appeared and stood in their midst and wept over them, and wanted to show Himself to them, but they did not discover Him. He [Joseph] saw until they had accomplished their work, and arrived at the gate of the celestial city; there Father Adam stood and opened the gate to them, and as they entered he embraced them one by one and kissed them. He then led them to the throne of God, and then the Savior embraced each one of them in the presence of God. He saw that they all had beautiful heads of hair and all looked alike. The impression this vision left on Brother Joseph's mind was of so acute a nature, that he never could refrain from weeping while rehearsing it.[58]

Joseph Smith and Oliver Cowdery

[On April 3, 1836,] the veil was taken from our minds, and the eyes of our understanding were opened. We saw the Lord standing upon the breastwork of the pulpit, before us; and under his feet was a paved work of pure gold, in color like amber. His eyes were as a flame of fire; the hair of his head was white like the pure snow; his countenance shone above the brightness of the sun; and his voice was as the sound of the rushing of great waters, even the voice of Jehovah, saying: "I am the first and the last; I am he who liveth, I am he who was slain; I am your advocate with the Father. Behold, your sins are forgiven you; you are clean before me; therefore, lift up your heads and rejoice."[59]

---

58. Orson F. Whitney, *Life of Heber C. Kimball*, Collector's Edition (Bookcraft, 1992), 93–94.

59. Joseph Smith, in *History of the Church*, 2:435; see also Doctrine and Covenants 110:1–5.

Lorenzo Snow

I had no sooner opened my lips in an effort to pray [in June 1836] than I heard a sound, just above my head, like the rustling of silken robes, and immediately the Spirit of God descended upon me, completely enveloping my whole person, filling me, from the crown of my head to the soles of my feet, and O, the joy and happiness I felt! No language can describe the almost instantaneous transition from a dense cloud of mental and spiritual darkness into a refulgence of light and knowledge, as it was at that time imparted to my understanding. I then received a perfect knowledge that God lives, that Jesus Christ is the Son of God, and of the restoration of the holy priesthood, and the fullness of the gospel. . . .

That night as I retired to rest . . . the Spirit of the Lord rested mightily upon me—the eyes of my understanding were opened, and *I saw as clear as the sun at noon-day, with wonder and astonishment, the pathway of God and man.* I formed the following couplet which expresses the revelation, as it was shown to me. . . . As man now is, God once was: As God now is, man may be.[60]

Lorenzo Snow

Related by President Snow's son, LeRoi C. Snow:

For some time President Woodruff's health had been failing. Nearly every evening President Lorenzo Snow visited him at his home on South 5th East Street. This particular evening the doctors said President Woodruff was failing rapidly and they feared he would not live much longer. Lorenzo Snow was then President of the Council of Twelve and was greatly worried over the possibility of succeeding President Woodruff, especially because of the terrible financial condition of the Church. Referring to this condition, President Heber J. Grant has said: "The Church was in a financial slough of despond, so to speak, almost financially bankrupt—its credit was hardly good for a thousand dollars without security."

My father went to his room in the Salt Lake Temple, where he was residing at the time. He dressed in his robes of the Priesthood, went into the Holy of Holies, there in the House of the Lord and

60. *Improvement Era* 22, no. 8 (June 1919): 656–57.

knelt at the sacred altar. He plead with the Lord to spare President Woodruff's life, that President Woodruff might outlive him and that the great responsibility of Church leadership would never fall upon his shoulders. Yet he promised the Lord that he would devotedly perform any duty required at his hands. At this time he was in his eighty-sixth year.

Soon after this President Woodruff was taken to California, where he died Friday morning at 6:40 o'clock, September 2, 1898. President George Q. Cannon at once wired the sad information to the President's office in Salt Lake City. Word was forwarded to President Snow who was in Brigham City. The telegram was delivered to him on the street in Brigham. He read it to President Rudger Clawson, then president of the Box Elder Stake, who was with him, went to the telegraph office and replied that he would leave on the train about 5:30 that evening. He reached Salt Lake City about 7:15, proceeded to the President's office, gave some instructions and then went to his private room in the Salt Lake Temple.

President Snow put on his holy temple robes, repaired again to the same sacred altar, offered up the signs of the Priesthood; and poured out his heart to the Lord. He reminded the Lord how he had plead for President Woodruff's life and that his days might be lengthened beyond his own; that he might never be called upon to bear the heavy burdens and responsibilities of Church leadership. "Nevertheless," he said, "Thy will be done. I have not sought this responsibility but if it be Thy will, I now present myself before Thee for Thy guidance and instruction. I ask that Thou show me what Thou wouldst have me do."

After finishing his prayer he expected a reply, some special manifestation from the Lord. So he waited—and waited—and waited. There was no reply, no voice, no visitation, no manifestation. He left the altar and the room in great disappointment. He passed through the Celestial room and into the large corridor leading to his own room where a most glorious manifestation was given President Snow. One of the most beautiful accounts of this experience is told by his granddaughter, Allie Young Pond:

"One evening when I was visiting Grandpa Snow in his room in the Salt Lake Temple, I remained until the doorkeepers had gone and the nightwatchman had not yet come in, so grandpa said he would take me to the main, front entrance and let me out that way. He got his bunch of keys from his dresser. After we left his room and while we were still in the large corridor, leading into the celestial room, I was walking several steps ahead of grandpa when he stopped me, saying: 'Wait a moment, Allie. I want to tell you something. It was right here that the Lord Jesus Christ appeared to me at the time of the death of President Woodruff. He instructed me to go right ahead and reorganize the First Presidency of the Church at once and not wait as had been done after the death of the previous presidents, and that I was to succeed President Woodruff.'

"Then Grandpa came to a step nearer and held out his left hand and said: 'He stood right here, about three feet above the floor. It looked as though he stood on a plate of solid gold.' Grandpa told me what a glorious personage the Savior is and described His hands, feet, countenance and beautiful White Robes, all of which were of such a glory of whiteness and brightness that he could hardly gaze upon Him. Then Grandpa came another step nearer me and put his right hand on my head and said: 'Now, granddaughter, I want you to remember that this is the testimony of your grandfather, that he told you with his own lips that he actually saw the Savior here in the Temple and talked with Him face to face.' Then we went on and Grandpa let me out of the main front door of the Temple."[61]

John W. Taylor

Related by Charles Ora Card:

Although this is the great national day of the U.S. [July 4, 1889], we gathered in fast meeting at 10 A.M. where the brethren and sisters met and joined in asking for rain to moisten the soil as we have only had 2 or 3 light showers for 2 months and much of our crops are dried and parched—also the grass. After the brethren and sisters had testified for a time, Elder J. W. Taylor arose and spoke and bore a powerful testimony stating he had beheld the Savior. Predicted that this would become a fruitful land and yet in time of

61. LeRoi C. Snow, "An Experience of My Father's," *Improvement Era* 36, no. 11 (Sept. 1933): 677–78.

near it would be a haven of rest for those of our people who desire to serve the Lord.[62]

Orson F. Whitney

[In 1876] as I lay upon my bed in the little town of Columbia, Lancaster County, Pennsylvania, I seemed to be in the Garden of Gethsemane, a witness of the Savior's agony. I saw Him as plainly as ever I have seen anyone. Standing behind a tree in the foreground, I beheld Jesus, with Peter, James and John, as they came through a little wicket gate at my right, leaving the three Apostles there, after telling them to kneel and pray, the Son of God passed over to the other side, where He also knelt and prayed. It was the same prayer with which all Bible readers are familiar: "Oh my Father, if it be possible, let this cup pass from me; nevertheless not as I will, but as thou wilt." As He prayed the tears streamed down his face, which was toward me. I was so moved at the sight that I also wept, out of pure sympathy. My whole heart went out to him; I loved him with all my soul, and longed to be with him as I longed for nothing else.

Presently He arose and walked to where those Apostles were kneeling fast asleep! He shook them gently, awoke them, and in a tone of tender reproach, untinctured by the least show of anger or impatience, asked them plaintively if they could not watch with him one hour. . . . All at once the circumstances seemed to change, the scene remaining just the same. Instead of before, it was after the crucifixion, and the Savior, with the three Apostles, now stood together in a group at my left. They were about to depart and ascend into Heaven. I could endure it no longer. I ran from behind the tree, fell at his feet, clasped Him around the knees, and begged Him to take me with Him.

I shall never forget the kind and gentle manner in which He stopped, raised me up, and embraced me. It was so vivid, so real. I felt the very warmth of his body, as He held me in His arms and said in tenderest tones: "No, my son; those have finished their work; they can go with me; but you must stay and finish yours." Still I

---

62. Donald G. Godfrey and Brigham Y. Card, eds., *The Diaries of Charles Ora Card: The Canadian Years, 1886–1903* (University of Utah Press, 1993), 96–97.

clung to Him. Gazing up into His face—for He was taller than I—I besought him fervently: "Well, promise me that I will come to you at the last." Smiling sweetly, He said: "That will depend entirely upon yourself." I awoke with a sob in my throat, and it was morning.[63]

Wilford Woodruff

Related by John Lee Jones:

President Wilford Woodruff told some of the saints that our Savior had appeared to him in the east room in the Holy of Holies [Salt Lake Temple], and told him that he had accepted of the temple and of the dedicatory services, and that the Lord forgave us his saints who had assisted in any manner towards the erection and completion of the Temple—that our sins were forgiven us by the Lord Jesus Christ. He said the light and power of this temple would be felt all over the earth, that our enemies should not have power over his saints. The Lord is going to give his saints the good things of the earth in greater abundance. Seek for the spirit of God and we shall triumph, that if the saints would be faithful their sins should be blotted out. A halo of light was seen hovering around the speaker in the temple. A little boy saw three angels dressed in white and directed his mother's attention to the heavenly vision but she could not see anything.[64]

Notes and Commentary

Many of Christ's attributes are reaffirmed in the aforementioned accounts. The image that comes to mind when thinking of Jesus is His compassionate, peaceful nature. Elder Orson F. Whitney recorded that Jesus approached him in a "gentle manner" and that He "embraced" him. This manifestation was so real to Elder Whitney that he literally felt the warmth of Jesus's body as they embraced. He also

63. Spencer W. Kimball, *Faith Precedes the Miracle* (Deseret Book, 1972), 26–27.

64. *Biography of John Lee Jones*, 147–48, April 6, 1893; as cited in Matthew B. Brown and Paul T. Smith, *Symbols in Stone: Symbols on the Early Temples of the Restoration* (Covenant Communications, 1997), 136.

recorded that Jesus spoke in "tenderest tones" and smiled "sweetly."[65] Elder Melvin J. Ballard's manifestation was similar to Elder Whitney's in that Jesus embraced him, kissed him, and pressed him into His bosom. Jesus smiled at Elder Ballard and softly spoke his name. Elder Ballard commented that he would "never forget that smile."[66]

Hebrews 12:29 describes God as "a consuming fire," and Joseph Smith stated that "God dwells in everlasting burnings."[67] In light of these details, it is worth noting that Elder Ballard explained that the marrow of his bones seemed to melt when he embraced the Savior. Zebedee Coltrin similarly recorded that when God the Father appeared in a March 1833 School of the Prophets meeting, He was "surrounded as with a flame of fire." Coltrin also recalled that the Father's "appearance was so grand and overwhelming that it seemed I should melt down in his presence, and the sensation was so powerful that it thrilled through my whole system and I felt it in the marrow of my bones."[68]

After Joseph Smith saw God's throne in vision on January 21, 1836, he described it as a "blazing throne." He also indicated that the "gate through which the heirs of that kingdom will enter" is "like unto circling flames of fire."[69] Jesus appeared to Joseph and Oliver a few months later, and they recorded that his eyes "were as a flame of fire."[70] In the 1835 account of the First Vision, Joseph explained that the heavenly personages appeared "in the midst of this pillar of flame, which was spread all around and yet nothing consumed."[71] According to Elder Orson Pratt, the Prophet Joseph, "expected to have seen the leaves and boughs of the trees consumed."[72]

---

65. Spencer W. Kimball, *Faith Precedes the Miracle*, 26–27.
66. Hinckley, *Melvin J. Ballard*, 156.
67. *History of the Church*, 6:317.
68. Zebedee Coltrin, Minutes, 56–58.
69. *History of the Church*, 2:380; see also Doctrine and Covenants 137:1–5.
70. *History of the Church*, 2:435; see also Doctrine and Covenants 110:1–5.
71. Milton V. Backman Jr., *Joseph Smith's First Vision: Confirming Evidences and Contemporary Accounts* (Bookcraft, 1980), 158–59.
72. Orson Pratt, *An Interesting Account of Several Remarkable Visions* (Eborn Books, 2000), 5.

Another comparison between Jesus's appearances in this chapter and Joseph's First Vision is the words that Jesus spoke. Joseph related to Warren Cowdery that immediately after God the Father and Jesus appeared to him, the latter said, "Thy sins are forgiven thee."[73] When Jesus appeared to Joseph and Oliver in the Kirtland Temple in 1836, He said—among other things—"Behold, your sins are forgiven you."[74] Similarly, when Jesus appeared to Wilford Woodruff in the Salt Lake Temple, He told President Woodruff that the Saints who assisted in building the temple were forgiven of their sins.[75] It seems that those who dedicate themselves to God's service and who live worthy enough to see Jesus are forgiven and purified.

Perhaps the most powerful of these accounts—Jesus's appearances to Lorenzo Snow and the School of the Prophets—displays a key liturgical theme in temple worship: prayer. In 1 Kings 8, we read concerning the dedication of the temple, recently built under the direction of King Solomon. At this paramount event, Solomon approached the altar at the temple, knelt, and subsequently prayed with uplifted hands (see verses 22 and 54). The account states that God manifested Himself in a cloud at the temple dedication that filled the temple. God's presence overwhelmed the temple priests, and they "could not stand to minister" (verses 10–11).

Similarly, Zebedee Coltrin—in his account of the March 18, 1833, School of the Prophets meeting—recorded that Joseph instructed each man to kneel, raise his hands above his head, and pray in silence. As they prayed, "a personage walked through the room from east to west." Joseph asked the men if they saw the personage and then said, "That is Jesus, the Son of God, our elder brother." The Prophet instructed the group to resume their positions with uplifted hands and to continue in prayer. Immediately, "another person came through; he was surrounded as with a flame of fire. . . . The Prophet Joseph said

---

73. Backman, *First Vision*, 158–59.

74. Joseph Smith, in *History of the Church*, 2:435; see also Doctrine and Covenants 110:1–5.

75. *Biography of John Lee Jones*, 147–48, April 6, 1893; as cited in Brown and Smith, *Symbols in Stone*, 136.

this was the Father of our Lord Jesus Christ."[76] Notice that, just like King Solomon, the members of the School of the Prophets prayed in a precise pattern, which opened the heavens.

In a similar manner, Elder Lorenzo Snow—at a time when he greatly desired divine assistance—"put on his holy temple robes, repaired again to the . . . sacred altar, offered up the signs of the Priesthood; and poured out his heart to the Lord." President Snow's son wrote, "After finishing his prayer he *expected a reply, some special manifestation from the Lord.* So he waited—and waited—and waited. . . . He passed through the Celestial room and into the large corridor leading to his own room where a most glorious manifestation was given President Snow."[77] Notice that Elder Snow, like King Solomon, knelt at the altar, prayed in a certain manner, and received a heavenly manifestation.

Joseph Smith recorded another instance when heavenly manifestations were granted because of prayer. One evening, the Prophet gathered the Twelve and the seven presidents of the Seventy in an upper room of the Kirtland Temple. Joseph instructed them to "call upon God with uplifted hands." Shortly thereafter:

> President Sylvester Smith saw a pillar of fire rest down and abide upon the heads of the quorum, as we stood in the midst of the Twelve. . . . Elder Roger Orton saw a mighty angel riding upon a horse of fire, with a flaming sword in his hand. . . . President William Smith, one of the Twelve, saw the heavens opened, and the Lord's host protecting the Lord's anointed. President Zebedee Coltrin, one of the seven presidents of the Seventy, saw the Savior extended before him, as upon the cross, and a little after, crowned with glory upon his head above the brightness of the sun. After these things were over, and a glorious vision, which I [Joseph Smith] saw, had passed, I instructed the seven presidents to proceed.[78] (See the complete account in chapter four.)

On another occasion, Joseph told the brethren who attended the School of the Prophets to wash, dress in clean clothes, arrive at the

---

76. Zebedee Coltrin, Minutes, 56–58.

77. LeRoi C. Snow, "An Experience of My Father's," 677–78.

78. Joseph Smith, in *History of the Church*, 2:386–87.

school at sunrise, and be prepared to participate in a day of "revelation and vision." After opening with prayer, Joseph instructed the brethren to "kneel and pray with uplifted hands." "Some wished to see an angel," recorded Zebedee Coltrin, "and a number joined in the circle and prayed. When the vision came, two of the brethren shrank and called for the vision to close or they would perish; they were Brothers Hancock and Humphries. When the Prophet came in . . . he said the angel was no further off than the roof of the house, and a moment more he would have been in their midst."[79] Although Jesus did not manifest himself to the group, it is worth noting that the heavens opened after they prayed. In addition, Brothers Hancock and Humphries, like Solomon's temple priests, could not stand the glory of the heavenly personage and even thought that they might perish.

---

79. Zebedee Coltrin, Minutes, 66.

Chapter Three

Manifestations of Satan and Evil Spirits

In the premortal estate, Lucifer—meaning "light bearer" in Latin—was an angel in heaven and even had "authority in the presence of God" (Doctrine and Covenants 76:25). Lucifer presented a plan to the Father and His spirit children that would force redemption for all, thus destroying man's agency. Lucifer said, "Behold, here am I, send me, I will be thy son, and I will redeem all mankind, that one soul shall not be lost, and surely I will do it; wherefore give me thine honor" (Moses 4:1). God rejected Lucifer's plea for total honor; therefore, Lucifer rebelled, along with "a third part of the hosts of heaven" (Doctrine and Covenants 29:36; Revelation 12:4).

Because of pride, Lucifer and his followers were cast out of heaven, thrust down to earth, and denied physical bodies (Revelation 12:9). All of God's spirit children who rejected Satan's plan subsequently wept over the fall and departure of their brothers and sisters (Doctrine and Covenants 76:26). Lucifer "became Satan, yea, even the devil, the father of all lies, to deceive and to blind men, and to lead them captive at his will, even as many as would not hearken unto my voice" (Moses 4:4). "Satan"—meaning to oppose, attack, or accuse—continually wages war with God and the righteous and "stirreth up the children of men unto secret combinations of murder and all manner of secret works of darkness" (2 Nephi 9:9).

Satan and his followers—often called devils, demons, or evil spirits—also seek to possess the bodies of individuals who do not have the Holy Spirit. When this occurs, possessed individuals lose control of their bodies for a time (see Luke 8:30–33). Joseph Smith taught, however, that "all beings who have bodies have power over those who have not. The devil has no power over us only as we permit him; the moment we revolt at anything which comes from God, the devil takes power."[80] Elder Parley P. Pratt discussed evil spirits possessing the bodies of individuals at length as follows:

> [Evil spirits] will sometimes enter human bodies, and will distract them, throw them into fits, cast them into the water, into the fire, etc. They will trouble them with dreams, nightmares, hysterics, fever, etc. They will also deform them in body and in features, by convulsions, cramps, contortions, etc., and will sometimes compel them to utter blasphemies, horrible curses, and even words of other languages. . . . Some of these spirits are adulterous, and suggest to the mind all manner of lasciviousness, all kinds of evil thoughts and temptations.
>
> A person on looking another in the eye, who is possessed of an evil spirit, may feel a shock, a nervous feeling, which will, as it were, make his hair stand on end, in short, a shock resembling that produced in a nervous system by the sight of a serpent. Some of these foul spirits, when possessing a person, will cause a disagreeable smell about the person thus possessed, which will be plainly manifest to the senses of those about him, even though the person thus afflicted should be washed and change his clothes every few minutes.[81]

---

80. *The Words of Joseph Smith: The Contemporary Accounts of the Nauvoo Discourses of the Prophet Joseph,* comp. Andrew F. Ehat and Lyndon W. Cook (Grandin Book Company, 1991), 60.

81. In contrast to the bad smell of evil spirits, Martha Smith Harris, sister of Joseph F. Smith, who saw in vision both her father and mother said, "Their breath smelled like sweet ointment." See "Martha Ann's Vision," in *Joseph Smith, Sr. Family Reunion News* 10, no. 1 (Mar. 5, 1991): 4.

> There are, in fact, most awful instances of the spirit of lust, and of bawdy and abominable words and actions, inspired and uttered by persons possessed of such spirits, even though the persons were virtuous and modest so long as they possessed their own agency. Some of these spirits cause deafness, others dumbness, etc. We can suggest no remedy for these multiplied evils, to which poor human nature is subject, except a good life, while we are in possession of our faculties, prayers and fastings of good and holy men, and the ministry of those who have power given them to rebuke evil spirits, and cast out devils, in the name of Jesus Christ.[82]

Elder Orson Pratt—also discussing the nature of evil spirits—taught:

> If we should inquire what constitutes the misery of the fallen angels, the answer would be, they are destitute of love; they have ceased to love God; they have ceased to have pure love one towards another; they have ceased to love that which is good. Hatred, malice, revenge, and every evil passion have usurped the place of love; and unhappiness, wretchedness, and misery are the results. Where there is no love there will be no desire to promote the welfare of others. Instead of desiring that others may be happy, each desires to make all others miserable like himself; each seeks to gratify that hellish disposition against the Almighty which arises from his extreme hatred of that which is good.[83]

Elder Pratt also taught that those who subject themselves to evil spirits will "have the heavenly principle of love wholly eradicated from their minds, and they will become angels to these infernal fiends, being captivated by them, and compelled to act as they act."[84]

Satan, as displayed below, may also physically attack a righteous person or appear to them with a hateful message when things are not going his way. Fortunately, Satan's power is limited, and he is only permitted to do what God allows. God's power and priesthood is infinitely stronger than Satan's power. An individual who is worthy to

---

82. Parley P. Pratt, *Key to the Science of Theology* (Deseret Book, 1965), 117–20.
83. Orson Pratt, *The Seer, 1853–1854* (Eborn Books, 1990), 156–57.
84. Orson Pratt, *The Seer*, 157.

hold, and who properly exercises the priesthood in God's name, "shall cast out devils" (Doctrine and Covenants 84:67).

Accounts of the Prophets

Ezra T. Benson

Related by the author:

In the late fall of 1840, Elder Ezra T. Benson, the great-grandfather of the future thirteenth president of the Church, Ezra Taft Benson, heard the presence of the devil as he prayed regarding whether or not he should be baptized into The Church of Jesus Christ of Latter-day Saints. "During the winter I took much satisfaction in meeting with the Saints and magnified my calling as well as I could," recalled Benson, "yet I felt my weakness much, and the need of the spirit of God to guide me." Benson decided to retire to a nearby grove of trees where he could pray in private. As he knelt and began to pray in approximately "one foot of snow . . . with a crust which was about half an inch thick," he thought he could hear a "sound as though someone was walking on the frozen snow." Benson sprang to his feet, much like the Prophet Joseph did during the First Vision, and quickly surveyed the area. Not seeing anyone, he continued to pray when he heard "the noise repeated three times." Benson recorded that he saw no individual, nor did he see any signs in the snow of any passersby. "I became satisfied," stated Benson, "[that] it was an opposing power to keep me from praying, and I said, 'Mr. Devil, you may break snow crust, but I will pray,' and when I had so determined, I heard nothing more."[85]

Hugh B. Brown

> In October 1953, I was up in the Canadian Rockies, supervising the drilling of an oil well. Although my family were in good health and good spirits and I was making good money, I was deeply depressed and worried. Early one morning I went up into the mountains and talked with the Lord in prayer. I told Him that although it looked like I was going to become wealthy as a result of my oil ventures, if

---

85. Ezra Taft Benson, "Autobiography," *The Instructor* 80 (1945): 103.

in His wisdom it would not be good for me or my family I hoped He would put an end to it.

That night I drove from the camp up at Rocky Mountain House down to Edmonton still spiritually disturbed and depressed. Without having dinner that night, I went into the bedroom by myself, told my wife that she should stay in the other room as I felt I would have a restless night and did not wish to disturb her. All night I wrestled with the evil spirit. I was possessed with the spirit of wishing that I could be rubbed out of existence. I had no thought of suicide, but wished the Lord would provide a way for me to cease to be. The room was full of darkness and an evil spirit prevailed, so real that I was almost consumed by it. About three o'clock in the morning my wife came in, having heard me moving about the room and asked what was the matter. Upon closing the door, she said, "Oh Hugh, what is in this room?" and I replied, "It is Satan." We spent the balance of the night together, much of it on our knees. The next morning upon going to the office (there was no one there, it being Saturday), I knelt in prayer again and asked for deliverance from this evil spirit. I felt a peaceful spirit come over me and phoned my wife to that effect.

That night, while I was taking a bath about ten o'clock, the telephone rang and she called me and said, "Salt Lake City is calling." Upon going to the phone, I heard a voice which said, "This is David O. McKay calling. The Lord wants you to spend the balance of your life in the service of the Church. The Council of the Twelve have just voted that you should take the place made vacant by the recent death of Stayner Richards, and you are to become an assistant to the Twelve."[86]

Heber C. Kimball

About daybreak [on Sunday, July 30, 1837], Elder Isaac Russell (who had been appointed to preach on the obelisk in Preston Square, that day), who slept with Elder Richards in Wilfred Street, came up to the third story, where Elder Hyde and myself were sleeping, and called out, "Brother Kimball, I want you should get

86. Edwin B. Firmage, "Elder Hugh B. Brown, 1883–1975: In Memorandum," *Ensign*, Jan. 1976, 90–91.

up and pray for me that I may be delivered from the evil spirits that are tormenting me to such a degree that I feel I cannot live long, unless I obtain relief . . ." I immediately arose, slipped off at the foot of the bed, and passed around to where he was. Elder Hyde threw his feet out, and sat up in the bed, and we laid hands on him, I being mouth, and prayed that the Lord would have mercy on him, and rebuked the devil.

While thus engaged, I was struck with great force by some invisible power, and fell senseless on the floor. . . . I then arose and sat up on the bed, when a vision was opened to our minds, and we could distinctly see the evil spirits, who foamed and gnashed their teeth at us. We gazed upon them about an hour and a half (by Willard's watch). We were not looking towards the window, but towards the wall. Space appeared before us, and we saw the devils coming in legions, with their leaders, who came within a few feet of us. They came towards us like armies rushing to battle. They appeared to be men of full stature, possessing every form and feature of men in the flesh, who were angry and desperate; and I shall never forget the vindictive malignity depicted on their countenances as they looked me in the eye; and any attempt to paint the scene which then presented itself, or portray their malice and enmity, would be vain. I perspired exceedingly, my clothes becoming as wet as if I had been taken out of the river. I felt excessive pain, and was in the greatest distress for some time.

I cannot even look back on the scene without feelings of horror; yet by it I learned the power of the adversary, his enmity against the servants of God, and got some understanding of the invisible world. We distinctly heard those spirits talk and express their wrath and hellish designs against us. However, the Lord delivered us from them, and blessed us exceedingly that day."[87]

---

87. Orson F. Whitney, *Life of Heber C. Kimball*, Collector's Edition (Bookcraft, 1992), 129–31. Elder Hyde stated that as the devils were leaving, "the last imp that left turned round to me as he was going out and said, as if to apologize . . . 'I never said anything against you!' I replied to him thus: 'It matters not to me whether you have or have not; you are a liar from the beginning! In the name of Jesus Christ, depart!' He immediately left, and the room was clear." Orson F. Whitney, *Life of Heber C. Kimball*, 131.

Heber C. Kimball

[In June 1839] I was awakened out of my sleep by my wife making a noise as though she was nearly choking to death. I inquired the cause, and she replied that she had dreamed that a personage came and seized her by the throat and was choking her. I immediately lit a candle and saw that her eyes were sunken and her nose pinched in as though she was in the last stage of the cholera. I laid hands upon her and rebuked the evil spirit in the name of Jesus, and by the power of the holy Priesthood commanded it to depart. In a moment afterwards I heard some half a dozen children in different parts of the Bozier house crying as if in great distress. The cattle also began to bellow, the horses neighed, the dogs barked, the hogs squealed, the hens cackled and roosters crowed, and everything around seemed in great commotion. In a few minutes afterwards I was sent for to lay hands upon Sister Patten, the widow of David W. Patten, who was living in the room adjoining mine, and who was seized in a similar manner to my wife.[88]

Spencer W. Kimball

Related by Edward Kimball:

On October 19 [1946], [President Kimball] drove south to a stake conference assignment in Pleasant Grove, Utah, and spent the night with relatives. He awoke in his room alone. There was a strange foreboding feeling. He turned a light on, picked up a book. But he felt something horrible in the room. "I felt almost as if I

---

88. Orson F. Whitney, *Life of Heber C. Kimball*, 258. A short time after this incident, the Prophet Joseph asked Heber to relate to him what had happened that night at the Bozier home. Heber not only related the incident to the Prophet but also the incident that occurred in England two years prior. Heber expressed his concern to the Prophet and asked if he was doing something wrong, to which the Prophet replied, "No, Brother Heber; at that time, when you were in England, you were nigh unto the Lord, there was only a veil between you and Him, but you could not see Him. When I heard of it, it gave me great joy; for I then knew that the work of God had taken root in that land. It was this that caused the devil to make a struggle to kill you." Heber also said that Joseph told him that the "nearer a person approached to the Lord, the greater power would be manifest by the devil to prevent the accomplishment of the purposes of God." Orson F. Whitney, *Life of Heber C. Kimball*, 259.

were being enveloped and taken over." He remembered his grandfather Heber's vision of a great rush of evil spirits "who foamed and gnashed their teeth." Time stopped. As his grandfather had, Spencer broke into a sweat.

"It seemed that an unknown enemy was trying to destroy me. He was unseen but very real. I was not afraid in the ordinary sense of the word. It was a deep fear of the unknown, something or somebody one could not wrestle with. It was bleak and black and fearsome. I sweat and fought and fought and sweat and then remembered the temple program and for the first time in my life invoked the power of the Priesthood in that particular way and relief came to me. As I pondered over it for days and relived it in a measure, I wondered if I was marked for destruction by the enemy of all righteousness—if I might be getting into a program which would upset the plans of the god of this world." He finally fell back asleep, then woke at 7:00 A.M. exhausted, "not wholly my usual self."[89]

Harold B. Lee

I want to bear you my solemn witness that I know there are [evil] forces in the world today. It would seem to me somewhat significant as I have thought about it, that the first and only experience of its kind I ever had, came shortly after I came into the Council of the Twelve [in 1941] when I was asked to administer to a young woman who was possessed of an evil spirit. Seemingly, there might have been a purpose in letting me know that these powers were around. In this experience, as I was challenged by the evil spirit, the hairs on my head felt as though pin pricks were in every hair and coursing down my body. I knew in that experience the power of evil, and I knew again the superior power of the priesthood and the powers of the Living God.[90]

Marriner Wood Merrill

Related by Rudger Clawson:

---

89. Edward L. Kimball and Andrew E. Kimball Jr., *Spencer W. Kimball: Twelfth President of The Church of Jesus Christ of Latter-day Saints* (Bookcraft, 1977), 238.

90. Conference Report, Oct. 1949, 58.

On one occasion [in the late 1880s] I heard the late Apostle Marriner W. Merrill, President of the Logan Temple, relate this extraordinary incident:

He was sitting in his office one morning, he said, when he noticed from the window a company of people coming up the hill to the Temple. As they entered the Temple grounds they presented rather a strange appearance, not only in dress but in their mode of travel. Some were riding on horses, others were in conveyances, and still others were afoot. He wondered who they could be as he was not looking for a company of such size that particular morning. They dismounted from their horses, stepped down from their conveyances, put their animals under the shade and walked about complacently as if they had a perfect right to be there.

A little later a person unknown to Brother Merrill entered the room. Brother Merrill said to him: "Who are you and who are these people who have come up and taken possession of the Temple grounds unannounced?" He answered and said: "I am Satan and these are my people." Brother Merrill then said: "What do you want? Why have you come here?" Satan replied: "I don't like the work that is going on in this Temple and feel that it should be discontinued. Will you stop it?" Brother Merrill answered and said emphatically, "No, we will not stop it. The work must go on." "Since you refuse to stop it, I will tell you what I propose to do," the adversary said. "I will take these people, my followers, and distribute them throughout this Temple district, and will instruct them to whisper in the ears of people, persuading them not to go to the Temple, and thus bring about a cessation of your Temple work." Satan then withdrew.

President Merrill, commenting on this strange interview with the Evil One, said that for quite a period of time the spirit of indifference to Temple work seemed to take possession of the people and very few came to the House of the Lord. The presumption was that Satan had carried out his threat which caused a temporary lull in Temple work. It is not to be wondered at that Satan, who is the enemy of all righteousness, is displeased with Temple work.[91]

91. *Deseret News*, Dec. 12, 1936; see also N. B. Lundwall, *Temples of the Most High*, Collector's Edition (Bookcraft, 1993), 98.

Boyd K. Packer and A. Theodore Tuttle

Related by Lucile Tate:

After Boyd's meetings of the next evening, he returned to his motel at midnight. Without knowing why, he checked out of that motel the next morning and into another before going to his meetings. That night as he opened his motel door the telephone rang. It was Brother Tuttle. "Boyd, I need help!"

"How on earth did you find me?"

"I remembered there is a Utah Motel in Pocatello, so I rang that first." Then he said: "I'm terrified! As I've been praying over what I should do about this man, it is as though all of the hosts of the adversary are working on me. I need your help!"

Promising his best efforts, Boyd hung up, dropped to his knees, and prayed mightily for Ted. "No sooner had I begun to pray than the same heinous power attacked me," he says. "I felt that the room was filled with demons, and I knew that not only Ted's life but mine was in deadly peril."

In faith, he continued to plead with the Lord in their behalf, exercising the power of the priesthood to curb and dispel the dark evil. Finally it left. Anxious about Ted's safety, Boyd joined him as soon as possible. The dread attack upon their persons drew them even closer in spirit. Each had come to know for himself that the power of evil was real.[92]

Sidney Rigdon

Related by Philo Dibble:

I saw Joseph Smith the Prophet when he first came to Kirtland. There was a branch of the Church raised up in Kirtland before he came, and at the time he arrived a variety of false spirits were manifested, such as caused jumping, shouting, falling down, etc. Joseph said, as soon as he came, "God has sent me here, and the devil must leave here, or I will." At this time Sidney Rigdon was left to preside at Kirtland and frequently preached to us. Upon one occasion he said the keys of the kingdom were taken from us. On hearing this,

92. Lucile C. Tate, *Boyd K. Packer: A Watchman on the Tower* (Bookcraft, 1995), 119–20.

many of his hearers wept, and when someone undertook to dismiss the meeting by prayer he said praying would do them no good, and the meeting broke up in confusion. Brother Hyrum came to my house the next morning and told me all about it, and said it was false, and that the keys of the kingdom were still with us. He wanted my carriage and horses to go to the town of Hiram and bring Joseph. The word went abroad among the people immediately that Sidney was going to expose "Mormonism."

Joseph came up to Kirtland a few days afterwards and held a meeting in a large barn. Nearly all the inhabitants of Kirtland turned out to hear him. The barn was filled with people, and others, unable to get inside, stood around the door as far as they could hear. Joseph arose in our midst and spoke in mighty power, saying: "I can contend with wicked men and devils—yes, with angels. No power can pluck those keys from me, except the power that gave them to me; that was Peter, James, and John. But for what Sidney has done, the devil shall handle him as one man handles another."

Thomas B. Marsh's wife went from the meeting and told Sidney what Joseph had said, and he replied: "Is it possible that I have been so deceived? But if Joseph says so, it is so." About three weeks after this [June 1832], Sidney was lying on his bed alone. An unseen power lifted him from his bed, threw him across the room, and tossed him from one side of the room to the other. The noise being heard in the adjoining room, his family went in to see what was the matter, and found him going from one side of the room to the other, from the effects of which Sidney was laid up for five or six weeks.[93]

Joseph Smith Jr.

Amongst those who attended our meetings regularly [in 1830] was Newel Knight, son of Joseph Knight. He and I had many serious conversations on the important subject of man's eternal salvation. We had got into the habit of praying much at our meetings, and

93. "Philo Dibble Autobiography (1806–1843)," in "Early Scenes in Church History," *Eighth Book in the Faith-Promoting Series* (Juvenile Instructor Office, 1882), 80–81; see also Mark L. McConkie, *Remembering Joseph: Personal Recollections of Those Who Knew the Prophet Joseph Smith* (Deseret Book, 2003), 331–32.

Newel had said that he would try and take up his cross, and pray vocally during meeting; but when we again met together, he rather excused himself. I tried to prevail upon him, making use of the figure, supposing that he should get into a mud-hole, would he not try to help himself out? And I further said that we were willing now to help him out of the mud-hole. He replied, that provided he had got into a mud-hole through carelessness, he would rather wait and get out himself, than to have others help him; and so he would wait until he could get into the woods by himself, and there he would pray.

Accordingly, he deferred praying until next morning, when he retired into the woods; where, according to his own account afterwards, he made several attempts to pray, but could scarcely do so, feeling that he had not done his duty, in refusing to pray in the presence of others. He began to feel uneasy, and continued to feel worse both in mind and body, until, upon reaching his own house, his appearance was such as to alarm his wife very much. He requested her to go and bring me to him. I went and found him suffering very much in his mind, and his body acted upon in a very strange manner; his visage and limbs distorted and twisted in every shape and appearance possible to imagine; and finally he was caught up off the floor of the apartment, and tossed about most fearfully.

His situation was soon made known to his neighbors and relatives and in a short time as many as eight or nine grown persons had got together to witness the scene. After he had thus suffered for a time, I succeeded in getting hold of him by the hand, when almost immediately he spoke to me, and with great earnestness requested me to cast the devil out of him, saying that he knew he was in him, and that he also knew that I could cast him out. I replied, "If you know that I can, it shall be done," and then almost unconsciously I rebuked the devil, and commanded him in the name of Jesus Christ to depart from him; when immediately Newel spoke out and said that he saw the devil leave him and vanish from his sight.

As soon as the devil had departed from our friend, his countenance became natural, his distortions of body ceased, and almost immediately the Spirit of the Lord descended upon him, and the visions of eternity were opened to his view. So soon as consciousness returned, his bodily weakness was such that we were obliged to lay him upon his bed, and wait upon him for some time. He afterwards related his experience as follows: "I now began to feel a most pleasing sensation resting on me, and immediately the visions of heaven were opened to my view. I felt myself attracted upward, and remained for some time enwrapt in contemplation, insomuch that I knew not what was going on in the room. By and by, I felt some weight pressing upon my shoulder and the side of my head, which served to recall me to a sense of my situation, and I found that the Spirit of the Lord had actually caught me up off the floor, and that my shoulder and head were pressing against the beams."[94]

Joseph Smith Jr.

Related by Levi Hancock:

The Fourth of June [1831] came and we all met in a little string of buildings under the hill near Isaac Morley's in Kirtland, Geauga County, Ohio. . . . Joseph put his hands on Harvey Whitlock and ordained him to the high priesthood. He turned as black as Lyman was white. His fingers were set like claws. He went around the room and showed his hands and tried to speak; his eyes were in the shape of oval O's. . . . Joseph bowed his head, and in a short time got up and commanded Satan to leave Harvey, laying his hands upon his head at the same time. At that very instant an old man said to weigh two hundred and fourteen pounds sitting in the window turned a complete summersault in the house and came his back across a bench and lay helpless. Joseph told Lyman to cast Satan out. He did. The man's name was [Leman Copley]. . . . The evil spirit left him and as quick lightning Harvey Green fell bound and screamed like a panther. Satan was cast out of him. But immediately entered someone else. This continued all day and the greater part of the night.[95]

---

94. *History of the Church*, 1:82–84; see also William G. Hartley, *Stand By My Servant Joseph: The Story of the Joseph Knight Family and the Restoration* (Deseret Book, 2003), 64–67.

95. "Autobiography of Levi Ward Hancock, 1803–1836," Typescript, L. Tom Perry Special Collections Library, Harold B. Lee Library, Brigham Young University, Provo, Utah, 33–34.

Joseph Smith Jr.

Related by Heber C. Kimball:

I will relate one circumstance that took place at Far West [in 1838], in a house that Joseph had purchased, which had been formerly occupied as a public house by some wicked people. A short time after he got into it, one of his children was taken very sick; he laid his hands upon the child, when it got better; as soon as he went out of doors, the children was taken sick again; he again laid his hands upon it, so that it again recovered. This occurred several times, when Joseph inquired of the Lord what it all meant; then he had an open vision, and saw the devil in person, who contended with Joseph face to face, for some time. He said it was his house, it belonged to him, and Joseph had no right there. Then Joseph rebuked Satan in the name of the Lord, and he departed and touched the child no more.[96]

Joseph Smith Jr.

In the evening meeting [in March 1843] twenty-seven children were blessed, nineteen of whom I blessed myself, with great fervency. Virtue went out of me, and my strength left me, when I gave up the meeting to the brethren. . . . Elder Jedediah M. Grant enquired of me the cause of my turning pale and losing strength last night while blessing children. I told him that I saw that Lucifer would exert his influence to destroy the children that I was blessing, and I strove with all the faith and spirit that I had to seal upon them a blessing that would secure their lives upon the earth; and so much virtue went out of me into the children, that I became weak, from which I have not yet recovered; and I referred to the case of the woman touching the hem of the garment of Jesus. (Luke, 8th chapter). The virtue here referred to is the spirit of life; and a man who exercises great faith in administering to the sick, blessing little children, or confirming, is liable to become weakened.[97]

---

96. Orson F. Whitney, *Life of Heber C. Kimball*, 258–59.

97. *History of the Church*, 5:303.

Joseph F. Smith

Related by President Joseph Fielding Smith:

One night [in Maui in 1854] the wife of the man of the house was suddenly seized with evil spirits. She went through all manner of hideous contortions. Her husband was overcome with fear and crouched in a corner trembling as a leaf in the wind. At first, Joseph F. was also seized with fear at this new and unexpected demonstration of the power from the unseen world of evil spirits. Praying inwardly, he says, the fear suddenly left him and the power of the Spirit of the Lord came upon him in great abundance. He stood upon his feet and faced the writhing, distorted woman and said: "In the name of the Lord Jesus Christ I rebuke you." No sooner had he uttered these words than the woman fell limp to the floor and became as one dead. Her husband then began to wail and pronounced her dead; his actions the youthful missionary rebuked, and the rebuke quieted the husband and restored peace in the home. Presently the woman recovered her strength and her normal attitude and was able to pursue her duties in the home.[98]

Lorenzo Snow

Related by Eliza R. Snow:

Not long after Brother Snow was appointed to preside over the Church in London, a circumstance occurred [in 1840] which plainly illustrated the interference of evil spirits in human affairs, and most strikingly their use as instruments to oppose the progress of the latter-day work. A band of them undertook to frighten him from his post; but Lorenzo Snow is one whom neither favor, fright nor force can move from the post of duty. At the time referred to, he occupied a well-furnished upper room, and directly after his appointment to the presidency, after retiring to bed at night, he was aroused from sleep by the most discordant noises. It seemed as though every piece of furniture in the room was put in motion going . . . back and forth against each other in such terrible fury that sleep and rest were utter impossibilities.

---

98. Joseph Fielding Smith, *The Life of Joseph F. Smith* (Deseret Book, 1938), 180.

He endured the unceremonious visitation for several nights, each night thinking it was the last, that they would leave as unbidden as they came, until the fact forced itself upon his mind that so long as he would tamely submit to their aggressions, so long they would continue to repeat them. Something must be done. He must claim the right of master over his own premises. Accordingly, after a day of fasting and before kneeling to pray, as was his custom before retiring for the night, he read aloud a chapter in the Bible, and then, in the name of Jesus of Nazareth, and by the authority of the Holy Priesthood, rebuked those spirits, and commanded them to leave the house—went to bed and had no more disturbance.[99]

James E. Talmage

I was to be baptized first [in 1873]. As father stood in the water and took my hand, I being on the bank with Ellen and her brother, we were veritably horror-stricken by a combined shriek, yell, scream, I know not how to describe the awful noise—such as none of us had ever heard. It seemed to be a combination of every fiendish ejaculation we could conceive of. I remember how I trembled at the awful manifestation, which had about it the sharpness and volume of a thunderclap followed by an angry roar, which died away as a hopeless groan.

The fearsome sound seemed to come from a point not more than fifty yards from us, near the end of the great bridge. The night was one of bright starlight, and we could have seen anyone on the bridge, which was built of white stone with low walls. Elijah Gilbert, with courage unusual for so young a man, started to investigate, but father called him back. Father, who was also trembling, as were the others, then asked me if I was too frightened to be baptized; I was too much terrified to speak, so I answered by stepping into the water. I was baptized, and Ellen Gilbert was baptized immediately afterward.[100]

---

99. Eliza R. Snow, *Biography and Family Record of Lorenzo Snow* (Deseret News, 1884), 53–54; Francis M. Gibbons, *Dynamic Disciples, Prophets of God: Life Stories of the Presidents of The Church of Jesus Christ of Latter-day Saints* (Deseret Book, 1996), 112–13.

100. James E. Talmage, "An Unusual Accompaniment to a Baptism," *Improvement Era* 25, no. 8 (June 1922): 675.

Wilford Woodruff

April 7th [1837] I spent the day in writing my Journal and when the shades of evening began to appear, I repaired to the house of the LORD in company with Elders Milton Holmes and Joseph B. Nobles for the purpose of worshiping God. We entered one of the stands within the veils and fell upon our knees. Satan appeared also but not to worship God, but to deprive us of the privilege. Satan strove against us with great power by tempting and otherwise he at one time drove me from my stand while I was striving with my brethren to enter into the visions of heaven. . . .

I there [in the outer court] found Elder Freeman Nickerson, an aged father in Israel who was faithful and prayed to God always. I solicited him to join us in prayer that we might gain a victory over Satan and get a blessing at the hand of God. He joyfully accepted the invitation and we again entered the stand being four of us in number of one accord in one place. We had great cause to be united in heart. We all had traveled together about 1,000 miles in the spring of 1834 for the redemption of Zion. We, at that time, offered to lay down our lives and our offering was accepted, as was Abrams. We felt, considering those circumstances, that we could kneel down and unitedly get a blessing by faith through Jesus Christ. We fell upon our Knees and began to cry unto God [and] Satan departed.[101]

Wilford Woodruff

Elder Turley and I went to Manchester [in 1840]; it was the first time I had visited that city. There I met for the first time Elder William Clayton. As soon as I was introduced to him, he informed me that one of the sisters in that place was possessed of a devil. He asked me if I would not go and cast it out of her. He thought one of the Twelve Apostles could do most anything in such a case. I went with him to the house where the woman lay, in the hands of three men, in a terrible rage. She was trying to tear her clothing from her. I also found quite a number of Saints present, and some

101. Dean C. Jessee, "The Kirtland Diary of Wilford Woodruff," *BYU Studies* 12, no. 4 (1971–1972): 392; grammar and some spelling altered for readability.

unbelievers, who had come to see the devil cast out and a miracle wrought.

Had I acted upon my own judgment I should have refrained from administering to her in the company of those present; but as I was a stranger there, and Brother Clayton presided over the branch, I joined with him in administering to the woman. The unbelief of the wicked who were present was so great that we could not cast the devil out of her, and she raged worse than ever; I then ordered the room to be cleared, and when the company, except the few attending her, had left the house, we laid hands upon her head, and in the name of Jesus Christ I commanded the devil to come out of her. The devil left, and she was entirely healed and fell asleep.[102]

Wilford Woodruff

Brothers Heber C. Kimball, George A. Smith and I went to London together in the winter of 1840, being the first Elders who had attempted to establish the gospel in that great and mighty city. As soon as we commenced, we found the devil was manifest; the evil spirits gathered for our destruction, and at times they had great power. They would destroy all the Saints if they were not restrained by the power of God. Brother Smith and I were together, and had retired to our rest, each occupying a cot and but three feet apart.

We had only just lain down, when it seemed as if a legion of devils made war upon us to destroy us, and we were struggling for our lives in the midst of this warfare of evil spirits until we were nearly choked to death. I began to pray the best I could in the midst of this struggle, and asked the Father in the name of Jesus Christ to spare our lives. While thus praying three personages entered the room, clothed in white and encircled with light. They walked to our bedside, laid hands upon our heads and we were instantly delivered; and from that time forth we were no more troubled with evil spirits while in the city of London. As soon as

102. Matthias F. Cowley, *Wilford Woodruff, His Life and Labors* (Deseret News, 1909), 115.

they administered unto us they withdrew from the room, the lights withdrew with them and darkness returned.[103]

Notes and Commentary

In at least three accounts, we learn that Satan is keenly aware of the spirituality of every individual. He tends to rear his ugly head when important events are about to occur. For example, President Hugh B. Brown contended with evil spirits the night before he was called to serve in the Quorum of the Twelve. The presence of evil spirits was so overwhelming that Brother Brown's wife, upon entering the room, said, "Oh Hugh, what is in this room?" to which Brother Brown answered, "It is Satan." He also recorded that, because of Satan's formidable presence, he felt that he might be "rubbed out of existence" and even "wished the Lord would provide a way for me to cease to be."[104] Satan knew that Hugh B. Brown would be called to serve the remainder of his life as a special witness of Jesus Christ and that he would one day see the Savior and speak with Him (see chapter two); therefore, Satan turned his attention to Brother Brown.

One must keep in mind that the Lord will only allow a person to be tempted or tried to an equal degree as the blessing they have received or will soon receive. "When individuals are blessed with visions, revelations, and great manifestations," President Brigham Young taught, "look out, then the devil is nigh you, and you will be tempted in proportion to the vision, revelation, or manifestation you have received. Hence thousands, when they are off their guard, give way to the severe temptations which come upon them, and behold they are gone."[105] Like Brother Brown, Harold B. Lee was "challenged by the evil spirit" following his call to the Twelve, Heber C. Kimball and others were attacked by evil spirits eight days after arriving in England to preach, and Lorenzo Snow wrestled with evil spirits through the night shortly after he was appointed to preside over the Church in London.

---

103. Wilford Woodruff, *Leaves from My Journal* (Covenant Communications, 2005), 173–74.

104. Edwin B. Firmage, "Elder Hugh B. Brown, 1883–1975: In Memorandum," *Ensign*, Jan. 1976, 90–91.

105. *Journal of Discourses*, 3:205–6.

These accounts also reveal that Satan and his followers are literally at war with the Saints, which began in the premortal world. For instance, when evil spirits attacked Heber C. Kimball, Willard Richards, Orson Hyde, and Isaac Russell in England, Elder Kimball recorded that the angry, vindictive devils came in "*legions*, with their *leaders*" and that "they came towards us like *armies rushing to battle*" displaying "enmity against the servants of God."[106] Three years later—when Heber C. Kimball, George A. Smith, and Wilford Woodruff arrived in London to establish the gospel—evil spirits attacked again. Elder Woodruff recorded that "a *legion of devils made war* upon us to destroy us, and we were struggling for our lives in the midst of this *warfare of evil spirits* until we were nearly choked to death." Elder Woodruff also recorded that three heavenly personages entered the room and delivered the elders from this war with evil spirits.[107] Spencer W. Kimball similarly referred to his evil antagonist as an "enemy" who sought to "destroy" him but who was defeated by the power of the priesthood in a particular way as taught in "the temple program."[108]

In the accounts of Ezra T. Benson and James E. Talmage, we learn that Satan does not always seek to attack a righteous individual but may simply attempt to disrupt, terrorize, intimidate, and show disapproval. Ezra Benson, while praying about whether he should be baptized, heard somebody walking on the frozen snow nearby but could not see any mortal being. He concluded that Satan manifested himself to distract him from praying. Similarly, as James Talmage took his father's hand to enter the baptismal pond, everyone present heard a "combined shriek, yell, scream" that "seemed to come from a point not more than fifty yards from us."[109] Perhaps these kinds of experiences are God's way of showing his children firsthand that righteous actions displease Satan.

Some members of the Church have claimed that Satan is not permitted to enter a holy place—a dedicated home or the temple, for example. However, based on Wilford Woodruff's and Marriner

106. Orson F. Whitney, *Life of Heber C. Kimball*, 129–31.

107. Wilford Woodruff, *Leaves From My Journal*, 173–74.

108. Kimball and Kimball, *Spencer W. Kimball*, 238.

109. *Improvement Era* 25, no. 8 (June 1922): 675.

W. Merrill's accounts, this doctrine appears to be false. President Woodruff describes being attacked by Satan while praying in the Kirtland Temple, and Elder Merrill recorded that Satan entered the Logan Temple and spoke to him. On the other hand, at least two individuals claimed they saw heavenly personages guarding the entrance to the temple (see chapter four). It is unclear whether this implies that heavenly beings guard the temple from evil spirits, or from earthly mobs, or both. Regardless of whether Satan or evil spirits can enter a temple or other dedicated buildings, we should not underestimate the power of dedicating our home as a dwelling place for the Holy Spirit.

Regarding this issue, Joseph Smith supposedly taught that "when wicked men and women inhabit a house, invisible spirits congregate there also, that are of the same stamp as the living. Kindred spirits mingle together and the invisible look on, laugh at and enjoy the wicked sports of the living—and when the living, or people in bodies, move away, the others often stay in the house having acquired a sort of right by possession and are the agents by which others that move in are afflicted."[110]

It is also worth noting that Satan and evil spirits have a strong testimony of Jesus; otherwise, they would not be fighting so hard against Him. They know His power. They know His authority. They know His goodness. It is, therefore, not sufficient to only *believe* in Jesus for salvation—as many of our Christian friends teach—for even the devils believe in Jesus.

Satan knows his fate, and he hates to be reminded of it. Satan will never be married, he will never have children, he will never have a resurrected body, and eventually he will be cast out from the presence of God. The prophet Isaiah stated, at least according to Christian interpretation, that when God's children are permitted to look upon Satan and see him in his true form and character, they will be surprised at his pathetic appearance and will say, "Is this the man that made the earth to tremble, that did shake kingdoms; That made the world as a wilderness, and destroyed the cities thereof?" (Isaiah 14:16–17).

---

110. "History of the Life of Oliver B. Huntington, Written by Himself 1878–1990," Typescript, L. Tom Perry Special Collections Library, Harold B. Lee Library, Brigham Young University, Provo, Utah, 17.

Chapter Four

Manifestations Regarding the Temple and Temple Worship

Latter-day Saints are notorious for building temples. The Savior revealed to Joseph in January 1841, "My people are always commanded to build unto my holy name. And verily I say unto you, let this house be built unto my name, that I may reveal mine ordinances therein unto my people" (Doctrine and Covenants 124:39–40). In 1833, three years after the Church was organized, the Latter-day Saints began constructing the first temple (in Kirtland, Ohio). Today, over 190 years later, roughly 350 temples are in operation or in the works.

For the Saints, the temple, along with Christ, is the central focus of *every* aspect of life. The clothes worn, the words said, the activities participated in, the thoughts entertained, the person taken in marriage, and even the business conducted are influenced by what one learns in the temple. The temple is the meeting place between heaven and earth that transcends the carnal, profane, and even the generally "good" activities and passions of life. For the Saints, the temple is everything—it is "a house of prayer, a house of fasting, a house of faith, a house of learning, a house of glory, a house of order, a house of God" (Doctrine and Covenants 109:8). The Prophet Joseph stated, "We need the temple more than anything else."[111]

Because the temple is crucial for learning, for salvation, and for sealing families together, the Lord has revealed much regarding its structure and ritual. The Savior told the Church in a revelation, "And I will show unto my servant Joseph all things pertaining to this house [temple], and the priesthood thereof, and the place whereon it shall be built" (Doctrine and Covenants 124:42). Orson Pratt stated that God revealed everything pertaining to the temple, even the "various courts and apartments, telling the size of the house, the order of the pulpits, and in fact everything pertaining to it was clearly pointed out by revelation. God gave a vision of these things, not only to Joseph, but to several others, and they were strictly commanded to build according to the pattern revealed from the heavens."[112]

As shown in the accounts below, several prophets have received manifestations and revelations regarding the temple and temple worship. Some saw temples in vision before they were built, and others received manifestations regarding temple clothing and rituals. Several accounts also reveal that disembodied spirits are heavily engaged in temple work and are laboring side by side with those who are still living—whether they know it or not.

Accounts of the Prophets

Melvin J. Ballard

Related by Nolan P. Olsen:

> Elder Ballard sat at our baptismal font [in the Logan Utah Temple] one Saturday while nearly a thousand baptisms were performed for the dead. As he sat there, he contemplated on how great the temple ceremonies were, and how we are bringing special blessings to the living and the dead. His thoughts turned to the spirit world, and he

111. Journal History of The Church of Jesus Christ of Latter-day Saints, May 4, 1844, Church History Library, Salt Lake City.

112. *Journal of Discourses*, 13:357–58.

wondered if the people there would accept the work we were doing for them. Brother Ballard said: "All at once a vision opened to me, and I beheld a great congregation of people gathered in the east end of the font room. One by one, as each name was baptized for, one of these people climbed a stairway over the font to the west end of the room. Not one soul was missing, but there was a person for every one of the thousand names done that day."

Brother Ballard said that he had never seen such happy people in all his life, and the whole congregation rejoiced at what was [being] done for them. For the rest of his life, Apostle Ballard preached to the Church in all his travels, that the work we do in the temples is accepted, and that the people themselves are permitted to attend and receive the blessings personally.[113]

Ezra Taft Benson

Soon after retiring [on June 8, 1965,] I had this impressive dream: Karl G. Maeser stood before me. He was tall, dignified yet pleasing, dressed in a dark suit and white shirt, clean shaven with ruddy face and clear blue eyes. He said to me, "Brother Benson, what are you doing to promote the sacred work in the temples for my people of Europe? They are a choice people who have played a major role in building up the Kingdom of God in these last days. The sacred ordinances must be performed for them in the temples in order to permit their progress in the spirit world. Will you please do all you can to help bring this about? They are a choice people of our Heavenly Father." These were his words as nearly as I can recall them. He smiled kindly as he nodded goodbye without further words. The brief message impressed me deeply.[114]

Hugh B. Brown

Related by President Russell M. Nelson:

President Spencer W. Kimball extended an invitation to Elder [Hugh B.] Brown to attend the dedication of [the Washington

113. Nolan P. Olsen, *Logan Temple: The First 100 Years* (Nolan P. Olsen, 1979), 170.

114. Sheri L. Dew, *Ezra Taft Benson: A Biography* (Deseret Book, 1987), 381–82.

D.C.] temple in November 1974. As a physician, I had been invited to accompany Elder Brown, now enfeebled due to advanced age. Months prior to his passing on December 2, 1975, I received his permission to record this experience, from which I quote:

"On the morning of the temple dedication, President Brown greeted me with the news that he had been visited during the night by President Harold B. Lee (President Lee had died the year before). Elder Brown described it as a glorious visit, one that meant much to him, for President Lee had been aware of some of the difficulties encountered by President Brown in the decisions that led to the construction of the temple in Washington, D.C. Later that morning, as we took President Brown to breakfast, Sister Harold B. (Freda Joan) Lee approached us. As we exchanged greetings, President Brown said to her, 'I had a glorious visit with Harold last night. He is just fine. It was so good to visit with him.' This was such a moving experience for us all. We felt the presence of President Lee's spirit in the temple through the witness of President Brown."[115]

George Q. Cannon

There were ten of us, of whom I was the youngest, wind-bound in the Bay of San Francisco, and we had been thus delayed for nearly a week near the Golden Gate in consequence of head winds. I dreamed one night that this party of brethren were heaving at the windlass, having a rope attached to it reaching forward to the anchor at the bow of the vessel. We were working with all our might endeavoring to raise the anchor, but seemingly we made but little progress. While thus engaged I thought the Prophet Joseph came from the after part of the vessel dressed in his temple clothes, and tapping me on the shoulder told me to go with him. I went, and he climbed on to the forecastle which was higher than the main deck and on a level with the bulwarks, and there he knelt down, also telling me to kneel down with him. He prayed according to the order of prayer which is revealed. After prayer, he arose upon his feet. "Now," said he, "George, take hold of that rope—the rope

115. Russell M. Nelson, *The Gateway We Call Death* (Deseret Book, 1995), 100–101.

we had been pulling on with all our might. I took hold of it, and with the greatest ease and without the least effort, the anchor was raised." "Now," said he, "let this be a lesson to you; remember that great things can be accomplished through the power of prayer and the exercise of faith in the right way."[116]

David O. McKay

Related by John L. Hart:

As President [Patrick D.] Dalton (president of the Tonga Nuku'alofa Temple) and his wife travel from one place to another on the main island, they often stop the car to chat or offer rides. "See you at the temple," they say in parting. That phrase is more than a passing expression. The temple has become a gathering place. But it is more than that—the Tonga temple, a symbol of righteousness and a fulfillment of prophecy, has become the spiritual focal point of the island. . . .

Sister Dalton is the one who recorded the temple prophecy made by President David O. McKay in 1955. At that time, she was serving as an education missionary with her husband. She was asked to accompany President McKay as he visited the islands and spoke to various congregations. Her task was to record President McKay's addresses in shorthand. The party traveled to the island of Vava'u where on Jan. 15, the Church president spoke to a group of members. In his address, he said, "Last night in vision I saw a temple in these islands." "I was surprised to hear that," recalled Sister Dalton. "I thought he must be talking about the temple in New Zealand." At the Vava'u meeting, "the people cried," she said. "They had faith all through the years that this [Tonga temple] could happen. They had more faith than I did."[117]

David O. McKay

Related by Allie Howe:

116. *Journal of Discourses*, 22:289–90.

117. "'Friendly Islands' Are Much a Part of Him," *LDS Church News*, Oct. 26, 1991.

The story began when President David O. McKay assigned President Wendell B. Mendenhall of the San Joaquin Stake to a special mission—that of investigating possible temple sites in the lands of the South Seas. President Mendenhall accepted this appointment in the realization that his mission was of a confidential nature. Seeking to acquire property for general Church purposes, he investigated available lands in Auckland, New Zealand, where mission headquarters are located. But the satisfaction of obtaining the proper place for the temple was not experienced.

"Then one day I felt I should go to Hamilton to visit the college" (eighty miles southeast of Auckland), President Mendenhall related to the writer. "While in the car on the way, the whole thing came to me in an instant. The temple should be there by the college. The Church facilities for construction were already there, and that was the center of the population of the mission. Then, in my mind, I could see the area even before I arrived, and I could envision the hill where the temple should stand. As soon as I arrived at the college and drove over the top of the hill, my whole vision was confirmed. In my heart I felt that the Lord had especially made this hill for his temple, everything, about it was so majestic and beautiful."

Without discussing the matter of a temple site with anyone, President Mendenhall investigated the possibility of purchasing this land for an addition to the Church property but received a negative response. This was the only strip of property separating the college grounds from the extensive Church farm lands; if the property could be acquired, it would join the land together into one choice whole. Two weeks later, President McKay arrived late one evening. Being travel weary, he retired at once, and it was not until early the next morning that President Mendenhall greeted him while in the company of three other brethren. Consequently, there could be no mention of a site for the temple. President McKay, President Mendenhall, and the other three brethren drove out to look over the college construction and the farm lands.

"As we drove up the road, there was that noble hill," continued President Mendenhall. "We directed our travel around the back of it to the farm lands. After we stepped from the car and were looking around, President McKay called me to one side. By the way he was looking at the hill, I could tell immediately what was on his mind. I had not said a word to him. He asked, 'What do you think?' I knew what his question implied, and I simply asked in return, 'What do you think, President McKay?' And then in an almost prophetic tone he pronounced 'This is the place to build the temple.' The Lord had again revealed his will unto his servant, a prophet of God." . . .

"Then a week later President McKay came to this beautiful spot," President Mendenhall related, "and I bear witness to you . . . that I saw the prophet of this Church in the spirit of vision, and when he walked away from that hill, he knew the house of the Lord was to be erected upon that particular spot."

President Mendenhall had found that the Murray family, the property owners—three brothers, their mother and a sister—were not willing to sell. But the day President McKay returned to the hill, the three brothers watched as he walked around it. Then as the brethren went to get in the car to leave the hill, one of the three approached President Mendenhall and said they did not want to sell the property, but suggested they discuss the matter after President McKay had finished his tour. As the car drove away, President McKay said in a tone of reassuring confidence, "They will sell it; they will sell it."[118]

Marriner W. Merrill

Related by Nolan P. Olsen:

The Hale family had a week-long reunion in the temple in about 1905, when they completed the last baptism and endowment, and then on Friday afternoon the last sealing was done for the 4,000 family members. As President Merrill neared Smithfield that night on his way to Richmond, he turned to tell the temple good-bye . . . and his heart about jumped out of his body. He could see the temple was on fire, but as he looked at it for a few minutes he was satisfied that there were no red flames licking upwards. The whole temple was filled with light, and the outside of the building shone with a pale pink glow. All the people in the neighborhood gathered to watch the phenomena and said they heard a heavenly choir

---

118. Allie Howe, "A Temple in the South Pacific," *Improvement Era* 58 (Nov. 1955): 811–13.

singing for nearly two hours. Everyone marveled at the sight, for there were no electric lights or other means of lighting the building until ten years later in 1915. The same thing happened the following night, too, with all the rooms in the building lighted, and the heavenly choir singing. President Merrill knew that we had had a very heavenly manifestation. When he reported the incident to President Woodruff, the president asked what special work had been done in the temple. He was told of the unusual activity of the Hale family and how they had accomplished so much in such a little time. President Woodruff said that the Hale and the Boynton families had been permitted to come from the other side to sing and rejoice and celebrate their deliverance in the Logan Temple.[119]

Marriner W. Merrill

Related by Elder Merrill's son Joseph F. Merrill:

My father once asked that question [of why people are sometimes needed more on the other side of the veil] when his oldest son was taken away. The oldest son had the responsibility, in a measure, of looking after father's interests in his home town, taking care of business and economic affairs. But the son was called home leaving a family of small children of his own. Father grieved. He had never grieved so much in his life. It was difficult. How could his son be needed as much on the other side as he was needed at home in Montana?

And father related that one evening as he sat thinking of this matter, he looked up, and there the son stood beside him in spirit form, and speaking to him said, "Father, do not grieve. You want to know why it is so? You know you are doing work for the dead here. You have gathered your genealogy, gotten all possible you could secure from the records, and you can be here doing temple work for those dead. Those dead are not yet converted, and I am engaged in the spirit world preaching the gospel as it was promised me in a patriarchal blessing that I could do. I am very busy. My time is given to that work. You and I are saving our family. You are doing the temple work and I am laboring among them." My father never grieved again, but praised the Lord for this kindness in making it

119. Olsen, *Logan Temple,* 175.

possible for our kindred dead to enjoy the blessings of eternal salvation, because if they accepted, the gates of the Celestial Kingdom would be opened to them.[120]

Parley P. Pratt

I had been on a visit to a singular people called Shakers, at New Lebanon, about seven miles from my aunt Van Cott's, and was returning that distance, on foot, on a beautiful evening of September [1830]. The sky was without a cloud; the stars shone out beautifully, and all nature seemed reposing in quiet, as I pursued my solitary way, wrapt in deep meditations on the predictions of the holy prophets; the signs of the times; the approaching advent of the Messiah, to reign on the earth, and the important revelations of the Book of Mormon; my heart filled with gratitude to God that He had opened the eyes of my understanding to receive the truth, and with sorrow for the blindness of those who lightly rejected the same, when my attention was aroused by a sudden appearance of a brilliant light which shone around me, above the brightness of the sun.

I cast my eyes upward to inquire from whence the light came, when I perceived a long chain of light extended in the heavens, very bright, and of a deep fiery red. It at first stood stationary in a *horizontal position*; at length bending in the center, the two ends approached each other with a rapid movement, so as to form an *exact square*. In this position it again remained stationary for some time, perhaps a minute, and then again the ends approached each other with the same rapidity, and again ceased to move, remaining stationary, for perhaps a minute, in the form of a *compass*; it then commenced a third movement in the same manner, and closed like the closing of a compass, the whole forming a *straight line* like a chain doubled. It again remained stationary for a minute, and then faded away. I fell upon my knees in the street, and thanked the Lord for so marvelous a sign of the coming of the Son of Man.

Some persons may smile at this, and say that all these exact movements were by chance; but, for my part, I could as soon believe

120. Remarks are from a transcript of the funeral services; cited in Duane S. Crowther, *Life Everlasting* (Deseret Book, 1967), 206.

that the letters of the alphabet would be formed by chance, and be placed so as to spell my name, as to believe that these *signs (known only to the wise)* could be formed and shown forth by chance.[121]

Franklin D. Richards

When we dedicated the Temple at Manti, many of the brethren and sisters saw the presence of spiritual beings, discernible only by the inward eye. The Prophets Joseph, Hyrum, Brigham and various other Apostles that have gone were seen and not only this, but the ears of many of the faithful were touched, and they heard the music of the heavenly choir.[122]

The Kirtland Saints

Related by Prescindia Huntington:

In Kirtland we enjoyed many very great blessings, and often saw the power of God manifested. On one occasion I saw angels clothed in white walking upon the temple. It was during one of our monthly fast meetings, when the saints were in the temple worshipping. A little girl came to my door and in wonder called me out, exclaiming, "The meeting is on the top of the meetinghouse!" I went to the door, and there I saw on the temple angels clothed in white covering the roof from end to end. They seemed to be walking to and fro;

---

121. *Autobiography of Parley P. Pratt*, ed. Facer Proctor and Maurine Jensen Proctor (Deseret Book, 2000), 42; emphasis added. Parley saw the symbols of the temple and the garments of the priesthood in the heavens.

122. *Genealogical Magazine* 15: 148; as cited in N. B. Lundwall, *Temples of the Most High,* Collector's Edition (Bookcraft, 1993), 116. It is interesting that Franklin D. Richards recorded that music was heard at the dedication. Similarly, Nancy N. Tracy recorded hearing heavenly music coming from the temple in Nauvoo: "About the last of May [1846], previous to our departure from Nauvoo, I was aroused from my slumbers on [that] night, hearing such heavenly music as I had never heard before. Everything was so still and quiet when it burst upon my ear that I could not imagine where it came from. I got up and looked out of the window. The moon shone bright as I looked over at the Temple from whence the sound came. There on the roof of the building heavenly bands of music had congregated and were playing most beautifully. The music was exquisite!" Carol Cornwall Madsen, *Journey to Zion* (Deseret Book, 1997), 405.

they appeared and disappeared. The third time they appeared and disappeared before I realized that they were not mortal men. Each time in a moment they vanished, and their reappearance was the same. This was in broad daylight, in the afternoon. A number of the children in Kirtland saw the same. When the brethren and sisters came home in the evening, they told of the power of God manifested in the temple that day, and of the prophesying and speaking in tongues. It was also said, in the interpretation of tongues, "That the angels were resting down upon the house."

At another fast meeting I was in the temple with my sister Zina. The whole of the congregation were on their knees, praying vocally, for such was the custom at the close of these meetings when Father Smith presided; yet there was no confusion; the voices of the congregation mingled softly together. While the congregation was thus praying, we both heard, from one corner of the room above our heads, a choir of angels singing most beautifully. They were invisible to us, but myriads of angelic voices seemed to be united in singing some song of Zion, and their sweet harmony filled the temple of God.

We were also in the temple at the pentecost. In the morning Father Smith prayed for a pentecost, in opening the meeting. That day the power of God rested mightily upon the saints. There was poured out upon us abundantly the spirit of revelation, prophesy and tongues. The Holy Ghost filled the house; and along in the afternoon a noise was heard. It was the sound of a mighty rushing wind. But at first the congregation was startled, not knowing what it was. To many it seemed as though the roof was all in flames. Father Smith exclaimed, "Is the house on fire!" "Do you not remember your prayer this morning, Father Smith?" inquired a brother. Then the patriarch, clasping his hands, exclaimed, "The spirit of God, like a mighty rushing wind!"

At another time a cousin of ours came to visit us at Kirtland. She wanted to go to one of the saints' fast meetings, to hear someone sing or speak in tongues, but she said she expected to have a hearty laugh. Accordingly we went with our cousin to the meeting, during which a Brother McCarter rose and sang a song of Zion in tongues; I arose and sang simultaneously with him the same tune and words, beginning and ending each verse in perfect unison, without varying a word. It was just as though we had sung it together a thousand times. After we came out of meeting, our cousin observed, "Instead of laughing, I never felt so solemn in my life."[123]

The Prophets in Kirtland

Related by Joseph Smith:

In the evening met the quorum of High Priests, in the west room of the upper loft of the Lord's house, and, in company with my counselors, consecrated and anointed the counselors of the presidents of the High Priests' quorum, and, having instructed them and set the quorum in order, I left them to perform the holy anointing, and went to the quorum of Elders at the other end of the room. I assisted in anointing the counselors of the president of the Elders, and gave the instruction necessary for the occasion, and left the president and his counselors to anoint the Elders while I should go to the adjoining room, and attend to organizing and instructing the quorum of the Seventy.

I found the Twelve Apostles assembled with this quorum, and I proceeded, with the quorum of the Presidency, to instruct them, and also the seven presidents of the Seventy Elders, to call upon God with up-lifted hands, to seal the blessings which had been promised to them by the holy anointing. As I organized this quorum, with the presidency in this room, President Sylvester Smith saw a pillar of fire rest down and abide upon the heads of the quorum, as we stood in the midst of the Twelve.

When the Twelve and the seven presidents were through with their sealing prayer, I called upon President Sidney Rigdon to seal them with uplifted hands; and when he had done this, and cried hosanna, that all the congregation should join him, and shout hosanna to God and the Lamb, and glory to God in the highest. It was done so, and Elder Roger Orton saw a mighty angel riding upon a horse of fire, with a flaming sword in his hand, followed by five others, encircle the house, and protect the Saints, even the Lord's anointed, from the power of Satan and a host of evil spirits, which were striving to disturb the Saints.

---

123. Edward W. Tullidge, *The Women of Mormondom* (Tullidge & Crandall, 1877), 207–9.

President William Smith, one of the Twelve, saw the heavens opened, and the Lord's host protecting the Lord's anointed. President Zebedee Coltrin, one of the seven presidents of the Seventy, saw the Savior extended before him, as upon the cross, and a little after, crowned with glory upon his head above the brightness of the sun. After these things were over, and a glorious vision, which I saw, had passed, I instructed the seven presidents to proceed and anoint the Seventy, and returned to the room of the High Priests and Elders, and attended to the sealing of what they had done, with up-lifted hands.[124]

George Albert Smith

Related by W. Aird Macdonald:

Forty years ago this summer, in 1924, the late President George Albert Smith, then a member of the Council of the Twelve, was in San Francisco attending regional Boy Scout meetings. As the president of the little Oakland Branch of the California Mission, I was invited to meet him at the Fairmont Hotel, high atop Nob Hill. We sat on the roof terrace facing the East Bay, discussing affairs concerning the little church organization across the bay. From the Fairmont terrace we had a wonderful panorama of the great San Francisco Bay, nesting at our feet. The setting sun seemed to set the whole eastern shore afire, until the Oakland hills were ablaze with golden light. As we admired the beauty and majesty of the scene, President Smith suddenly grew silent, ceased talking, and for several minutes gazed intently toward the East Bay hills.

"Brother Macdonald, I can almost see in vision a white temple of the Lord high upon those hills," he exclaimed rapturously, "an ensign to all the world travelers as they sail through the Golden Gate into this wonderful harbor." Then he studied the vista for a few moments as if to make sure of the scene before him. "Yes, sir, a great white temple of the Lord," he confided with calm assurance, "will grace those hills, a glorious ensign to the nations to welcome our Father's children as they visit this great city."[125]

---

124. *History of the Church,* 2:386–87.

125. Harold W. Burton and W. Aird MacDonald, "The Oakland Temple," *Improvement Era* 67 (May 1964): 380–81.

Joseph Smith Jr. and His Counselors

Related by Truman O. Angell:

About this time [June 1833] Frederick G. Williams, one of President Smith's counselors, came into the temple when the following dialogue took place in my presence: Carpenter Rolph said, "Doctor, what do you think of the House?" He answered, "It looks to me like the pattern precisely." He then related the following: "Joseph received the word of the Lord for him to take his two counselors, [Frederick G.] Williams and [Sidney] Rigdon, and come before the Lord and He would show them the plan or model of the house to be built. We went upon our knees, called on the Lord, and the building [the Kirtland Temple] appeared within viewing distance. I being the first to discover it. Then all of us viewed it together. After we had taken a good look at the exterior, the building seemed to come right over us, and the makeup of this hall seemed to coincide with what I there saw to a minutia."[126]

Joseph Smith Jr. and the Brethren

Related by Truman O. Angell:

When about midway during the prayer, there was a glorious sensation passed through the house [the Kirtland Temple]; and we, having our heads bowed in prayer, felt a sensation very elevating to the soul. At the close of the prayer, F. G. Williams being in the upper east stand—Joseph being in the speaking stand next below—rose and testified that midway during the prayer an holy angel came and seated himself in the stand. When the afternoon meeting assembled, Joseph, feeling very much elated, arose the first thing and said the personage who had appeared in the morning was the Angel Peter come to accept the dedication.[127]

Joseph Smith Jr. and Oliver Cowdery

Related by the author:

---

126. *Improvement Era* 14, no. 10 (Oct. 1942): 630.

127. Kate B. Carter, comp., *Our Pioneer Heritage* (Daughters of the Pioneers, 1961), 10:198.

Ora H. Barlow, regarding Israel Barlow, one of Joseph Smith's bodyguards, recorded an interesting account concerning the many visions seen in the Kirtland Temple. She recorded that three days following the temple dedication (March 30, 1836), Israel was passing by the temple on his horse when the Prophet Joseph and Oliver Cowdery exited the temple and proceed down the east walkway. Israel thought he saw Joseph wearing a white suit, but as he approached them, he discovered that the Prophet's suit was black. Oliver looked extremely pale and weak as Joseph assisted him toward the gate. Joseph said, "Brother Barlow, Oliver has just been blessed with a great manifestation and he is not as used to this as I am, so it has been almost too much for him." Joseph also said, because of what they saw, he would deliver the "greatest sermon" of his life the next Sunday, April 3, 1836. [128] This day is well known as the day in which Joseph and Oliver were visited by Christ, Elijah, Elias, and Moses.

Joseph Smith Jr.

> In the afternoon, Elder William Weeks (whom I had employed as architect of the [Nauvoo] Temple), came in for instruction. I instructed him in relation to the circular windows designed to light the offices in the dead work of the arch between stories. He said that round windows in the broad side of a building were a violation of all the known rules of architecture, and contended that they should be semicircular—that the building was too low for round windows. I told him I would have the circles, if he had to make the Temple ten feet higher than it was originally calculated; that one light at the center of each circular window would be sufficient to light the whole room; that when the whole building was thus illuminated, the effect would be remarkably grand. "I wish you to carry out my designs. I have seen in vision the splendid appearance of that building illuminated, and will have it built according to the pattern shown me."[129]

---

128. Ora Haven Barlow, *The Israel Barlow Story and Mormon Mores* (Publishers Press, 1968), 113–14.

129. *History of the Church,* 6:196–97.

Joseph Smith Jr.

Related by Truman O. Angell:

Joseph came into the hall. The leading mechanic, John Carl, by profession a carriage builder, wanted to seat the house contrary to what Joseph had proposed. *Joseph answered him that he had seen the inside of every building that had been built unto the Lord upon this earth* and he hated to have to say so. Under such childlike feeling, they prepared to dedicate the lower hall. The hall was filled at an early hour in the afternoon, I being present among the rest. The dedicatory prayer was offered, Sidney Rigdon being mouth.[130]

Joseph Smith Jr.

Related by Elizabeth A. Whitney:

It was during the time we lived at the brick store that Joseph received the revelation pertaining to celestial marriage [Doctrine and Covenants 132]; also concerning the ordinances of the house of the Lord. He had been strictly charged by the angel who committed these precious things into his keeping that he should only reveal them to such persons as were pure, full of integrity to the truth, and worthy to be entrusted with divine messages; that to spread them abroad would only be like casting pearls before swine, and that the most profound secrecy must be maintained, until the Lord saw fit to make it known publicly through His servants.[131]

Joseph Smith Jr.

I know not why; but for some reason I am constrained to hasten my preparations, and to confer upon the Twelve all the ordinances, keys, covenants, endowments, and sealing ordinances of the

---

130. Carter, *Our Pioneer Heritage*, 10:198–99; see also Lyndon W. Cook, *The Revelations of the Prophet Joseph Smith* (Deseret Book, 1981), 198; emphasis added.

131. "Elizabeth Ann Whitney, Autobiography," *Woman's Exponent* 7 (1878): 105; see also Carol Cornwall Madsen, ed., *In Their Own Words: Women and the Story of Nauvoo* (Deseret Book, 1994), 201.

priesthood, and so set before them a pattern in all things pertaining to the sanctuary and the endowment therein. . . .

The Lord is about to lay the burden on your shoulders and let me rest awhile; and if they kill me, the kingdom of God will roll on, as I have now finished the work which was laid upon me, by committing to you all things for the building up of the kingdom according to the heavenly vision, and the pattern shown me from heaven.[132]

John Taylor

[On June 18, 1845,] I dreamt that I stood by the [New Jerusalem] Temple and looked up, and saw that it was finished. I admired the elegance and symmetry of the building, and felt animated in my spirits and rejoiced to see the building finished. I remarked to a person standing by, what a beautiful structure this is, how elegant the design, and how well it is executed. I then said it is only a very short time since we laid the topstone; and now it is finished. I knew that a great deal of the wood work was prepared, but did not anticipate that the building would be so soon completed. I felt at the same time filled with the spirit of God, and my heart rejoiced before the Lord.

While I stood gazing with pleasure at the Temple, I saw another tower rising like unto the one that is on the west end of the Temple, and immediately exclaimed to the person that I had before conversed with, why there is another tower, and said I pointing my finger, still further there is another, and yet another; we have not yet began to see the whole; the scenery gradually changed, and a temple very much larger in dimensions, than the one which we are building, stood before me; there were a number of towers, placed apparently at equal distances on the outside, each of which were supported by buildings as large as this temple, and yet were united with, and were a part of the great temple; they were of as large dimensions as that which is on this Temple, from the midst of these towers and in the center of the building arose in majestic grandeur an immense large dome, that seemed to tower as high above the towers, as the towers were from the earth; it was not quite finished

132. *Millennial Star* 5, no. 10 (Mar. 1845): 151.

at the top, and there were some workmen employed near the top of the dome, who in consequence of the extreme height of the building appeared very small.[133]

Wilford Woodruff

The last time I saw [Joseph Smith] was in heaven. In the night vision I saw him at the door of the Temple in heaven. He came and spoke to me. He said he could not stop to talk to me because he was in a hurry. The next man I met was Father Smith; he couldn't talk to me because he was in a hurry. I met a half a dozen brethren who held high positions on earth, and none of them could stop to talk with me because they were in a hurry. I was much astonished. By and by I saw the Prophet again, and I got the privilege to ask him a question. "Now," said I, "I want to know why you are in a hurry? I have been in a hurry all my life, but I expected my hurry would be over when I got into the Kingdom of Heaven, if I ever did."

Joseph said, "I will tell you, Brother Woodruff, every dispensation that has had the priesthood on earth and has gone into the celestial kingdom, has had a certain amount of work to do to prepare to go to the earth with the Savior when he goes to reign on earth. Each dispensation has had ample time to do this work. We have not. We are the last dispensation, and so much work has to be done and we need to be in a hurry in order to accomplish it." Of course, that was satisfactory with me, but it was new doctrine to me.[134]

Wilford Woodruff

When in the western country, many years ago, before we came to the Rocky Mountains, I had a dream. I dreamed of being in these mountains, and of seeing a large fine looking temple erected in one of these valleys which was built of cut granite stone, I saw that temple dedicated, and I attended the dedicatory services, and I saw a good many men that are living to-day in the midst of this people.

133. "The John Taylor Nauvoo Journal," *BYU Studies* 23, no. 2 (1983): 238.

134. *The Discourses of Wilford Woodruff*, ed. G. Homer Durham (Bookcraft, 1946), 288.

And I saw them called of God and sent forth unto the United States and to Babylon, or what is called the Christian world, to bind up the law and seal up the testimony against the nations of the earth, because they had rejected the testimony of Jesus, and of the establishment of the kingdom of God upon the earth.

When the foundation of that temple was laid I thought of my dream and a great many times since. And whenever President Young held a council of the brethren of the Twelve and talked of building the temple of adobe or brick, which was done I would say to myself, "No, you will never do it;" because I had seen it in my dream built of some other material. I mention these things to show you that things are manifested to the Latter-day Saints sometimes which we do not know anything about, only as they are given by the Spirit of God.[135]

Wilford Woodruff

I dreamed last night [May 13, 1847] we had arrived at our journey's end where we built up a stake of Zion. As we came onto the place there was an open vision of the temple presented before me. I asked some brethren that stood by me if they saw it. They said they did not. I gazed upon it and it was glorious. It appeared as though it was built of white and blue stone. The sight of it filled me with joy and I awoke and behold it was a dream.[136]

Wilford Woodruff

I had one of the most interesting dreams of my life during the night [March 5, 1848]. Most of it was taken from me when I awoke. I flew through the air from state to state & escaped from the hand of my enemies. I went to HEAVEN and saw the Saints in their employment. I saw Joseph & Hiram Smith & many others who had died of the Latter Day Saints. The innumerable company of Saints which I saw seemed to be preparing for some grand & important event which I could not understand. Many were busily engaged in

---

135. *Journal of Discourses,* 21:300; sermon given in August 1880.

136. *Wilford Woodruff's Journal,* ed. Scott G. Kenney (Signature Books, 1983), 3:175.

making Crowns for the Saints. One crown did not suit the artist so they cut it in to the middle to make it over new. The saints were all dressed in white robes both male and female. My soul was filled with Joy & glory while I gazed upon the scenery that surrounded me but I awoke and behold it was a dream.[137]

Wilford Woodruff related this vision again on October 20, 1850:

Was Called upon to Address the meeting. I gave An account of my mission to the East. I spoke of my dream I dreamed of dying & going to the place of the departed spirits. I saw Brother Joseph & Hyram Smith & many of the Saints who had died. They all appeared to be in a Hurry. I thought Strange to find them in A Hurry And I enquired the Cause. They informed me that the time was set for Christ to Come as the great Bridegroom to the Earth to meet the Bride the Lambs wife & they had not had time to prepare as those of other dispensations & Had to be in a Hurry in order to get ready. And when I awoke I was overwhelmed with a peculiar sensation at the view of the work the Latter Day Saints Had to perform in order to prepair the Bride for to meet the Bridegroom.[138]

Wilford Woodruff

[On December 16, 1877,] I saw a short distance from the Missouri River, where I stood, twelve men dressed in the robes of the Temple. They stood in a square nearby and I was given to understand that they represented the twelve gates of the New Jerusalem. Their hands were uplifted while they were consecrating the ground; and later they laid the corner-stones of the house of God. I saw myriads of angels hovering over them, and above their heads there was a pillar-like cloud. I heard the most beautiful singing in the words: "Now is established the Kingdom of our God and His Christ, and He shall reign forever and forever, and the Kingdom shall never be thrown down, for the Saints have overcome." I saw people coming from the river and from distant places to help build the Temple. It seemed as though there were hosts of angels helping to bring

137. *Wilford Woodruff's Journal*, 3:327–28.

138. *Wilford Woodruff's Journal*, 3:578–79.

material for the construction of that building. Some were in Temple robes, and the pillar-like cloud continued to hover over the spot.[139]

Wilford Woodruff

I dreamed last night [March 12, 1887] that the Latter-day Saints were holding a great conference in the Salt Lake Temple. I saw a great rush to finish the Temple. I was called upon to open the conference, and I was given the keys of the Temple to open it. I saw thousands assembling and I met President Young, who asked me what was the matter with the great multitude at the door. Someone answered that the elders did not want to let the people into the Temple. He exclaimed, "Oh, oh, oh;" he then leaned over to me and said, "Let all come into the Temple who seek salvation." I saw several who were dead, among them my wife, Phoebe. I believe there is some special meaning in this dream.[140]

Wilford Woodruff

I am going to bear my testimony to this assembly, if I never do it again in my life, that those men who laid the foundation of this American Government and signed the Declaration of Independence were the best spirits the God of Heaven could find on the face of the earth. They were choice spirits, not wicked men. General Washington and all the men that labored for the purpose were inspired of the Lord. Another thing I am going to say here, because I have a right to say it. Every one of those men that signed the Declaration of Independence with General Washington called upon me, as an Apostle of the Lord Jesus Christ, in the Temple at St. George two consecutive nights, and demanded at my hands that I should go forth and attend to the ordinances of the house of God for them. Men are here, I believe, that know of this—Brothers J. D. T. McAllister, David H. Cannon and James C. Bleak. Brother McAllister baptized me for all these men, and I then told these brethren that it was their duty to go into the Temple and labor until

139. Matthias F. Cowley, *Wilford Woodruff, His Life and Labors* (Deseret News, 1909), 505.

140. Cowley, *Wilford Woodruff*, 562.

> they got endowments for all of them. They did it. Would those spirits have called upon me, as an Elder in Israel, to perform that work if they had not been noble spirits before God? They would not. I bear this testimony because it is true.[141]

On another occasion, President Wilford Woodruff talked about this experience:

> The dead will be after you, they will seek after you as they have after us in St. George. They called upon us, knowing that we held the keys and power to redeem them. I will say here, before closing, that two weeks before I left St. George, the spirits of the dead gathered around me, wanting to know why we did not redeem them. Said they: "You have had the use of the Endowment House for a number of years and yet nothing has ever been done for us. We laid the foundation of the government you now enjoy, and we never apostatized from it, but we remained true to it and were faithful to God." These were the signers of the Declaration of Independence, and they waited on me for two days and two nights.
>
> I thought it very singular that notwithstanding so much work had been done, and yet nothing had been done for them. The thought never entered my heart from the fact, I suppose, that heretofore our minds were reaching after our more immediate friends and relatives. I straightway went into the baptismal font and called upon Brother McAllister to baptize me for the signers of the Declaration of Independence, and fifty other eminent men, making one hundred in all, including John Wesley, Columbus, and others; I then baptized him for every President of the United States except three; and when their cause is just, somebody will do the work for them.[142]

---

141. Conference Report, Apr. 1898, 89–90.

142. *Journal of Discourses*, 19:229. Among these individuals were the first seventeen presidents of the United States of America except for two (Martin Van Buren and James Buchanan). The "fifty eminent" individuals world included kings, queens, emperors, diplomats, politicians, authors, novelists, poets, religious reformers, scientists, military commanders, actors, historians, artists, and members of their families. See Vicki Jo Anderson, *The Other Eminent Men of Wilford Woodruff* (Nelson Books, 2000).

Wilford Woodruff

[On March 19, 1894,] I spent some time with [Benjamin Franklin] and we talked over our Temple ordinances which had been administered for Franklin and others. He wanted more work done for him than had already been done. I promised him it should be done. I awoke and then made up my mind to receive further blessings for Benjamin Franklin and George Washington.[143]

Brigham Young and Truman O. Angell

Related by President Wilford Woodruff:

President Brigham Young related the circumstances of their seeing a circle of about 40 persons dressed in white robes and caps in the upper story of the Temple in Kirtland during the spring of [1836] after the Endowments. There was no person in that room at the time that was mortal, yet the room was filled with light and many personages did appear clothed in white and frequently went to the windows and looked out so that the Brethren in the street could see them plainly. Brother Young and Truman Angell stood together in the street and looked at them a long time. W. W. Phelps says he saw them for three hours. They were visible by all the Brethren present. Brother Angell said they must have stood some two feet from the floor. If they were only the size of common men they could not have been seen from the place where they stood except it should be the head, and those personages appeared nearly down to the waist as they looked out of the window with a front view.[144]

Brigham Young

This I do know—there should be a temple built here (Salt Lake City). I do know it is the duty of this people to commence to build a temple. Now, some will want to know what kind of a building it will be. Wait patiently, brethren, until it is done, and put forth your hands willingly to finish it. I know what it will be. I scarcely ever say much about revelations, or visions, but suffice it to say, five

---

143. Cowley, *Wilford Woodruff*, 586–87.

144. *Wilford Woodruff's Journal*, 5:120.

years ago last July I was here, and saw in the spirit the temple not ten feet from where we have laid the chief cornerstone. I have not inquired what kind of a temple we should build. Why? Because it was represented before me. I have never looked upon that ground, but the vision of it was there. I see it as plainly as if it was in reality before me. Wait until it is done. I will say, however, that it will have six towers, to begin with, instead of one. Now do not any of you apostatize because it will have six towers, and Joseph only built one. It is easier for us to build sixteen, than it was for him to build one. The time will come when there will be one in the center of temples, we shall build, and, on the top, groves and fish ponds. But we shall not see them here, at present.[145]

Brigham Young

Related by D. D. MacArthur:

President Brigham Young, with a shovel in his hand, marked the ground where the southeast cornerstone would be laid, and where the records of the [St. George] Temple would be deposited, as also in the capstone, directly over it. He then said: "We will now break ground, praying that our enemies may never hinder this work, but that a Temple may be reared to administer the ordinances for the living and the dead." Then breaking ground by throwing out a few shovelfuls of the soil, he handed the shovel to President George A. Smith, who did the same. . . .

President E. Snow spoke briefly, referring to those who came here with him in December, 1862, as pioneers of the Southern

145. *Journal of Discourses*, 1:133; sermon given April 6, 1853. Speaking of Brigham's vision and description of temples, Elder John A. Widtsoe said in 1916, "Evidently the people of that day [1850s] had also been asking questions about temple architecture and the President virtually declared that there is no set type. Moreover, he intimated that the Salt Lake Temple had been shown him in a vision, and that he knew just how it was to look. Further, he made it clear that, in vision, he had also seen other temples, which would be built later and elsewhere, some of which would have one central tower, and 'groves and fish ponds' on the roofs. President Young's description of the coming temple fits with singular exactness, the architecture of the temple in Hawaii. He speaks of a tower placed in the centre of the temple. The upper room of the Hawaiian temple is the exact centre of the building, and forms a truncated or blunt tower." *Improvement Era* 19, no. 11 (Sept. 1916).

Mission, and who have been faithful to their calling; also to the prospect of an early completion of the handsome Tabernacle now in progress. He was reminded of the vision of President Young in regard to seeing a beautiful city, with its Temple towering to the heavens, where St. George now stands, and hoped to see it rapidly pushed forward and accomplished.[146]

Brigham Young and Truman O. Angell

Related by Truman O. Angell:

After the building was dedicated, a few of us, some six or eight, having Patriarch Joseph Smith, Sr., in company, went morning and evening to pray, entering at the west end of the [Kirtland] Temple and going clear through to the east stand. This we enjoyed very much. The stand being enclosed by curtains or veils made it quite by itself and a good place to pray with none to molest. One evening, having been in the country, I was too late to enter with the brethren. The company would not emerge till quite dark. I had tried the door and knew they were at prayer. I felt out of place and went to my house, but soon came out and met Brother Brigham Young, inquiring for Oliver Cowdery. I said I had not seen him.

We walked out towards the Temple, approaching the building on the side which was used for the Prophet Joseph and his counselors, a portion of the attic on the east being especially appropriated to their use. In the said attic, and right over the stand where the brethren were praying in the hall below were two windows in the gable end to help give light to his compartment or room, the windows being 12 or 14 feet apart, and unusually high from the floor; being nearly 4 feet to the bottom of the lower sash.

When about ten rods distant we looked up and saw two personages; before each window, leaving and approaching each other like guards would do. This continued until quite dark. As they were walking back and forth, one turned his face to me for an instant; but while they walked to and fro, only a side view was visible. I have

146. Preston Nibley, *Brigham Young: The Man and His Work* (Deseret Book, 1936), 476.

no doubt that the house was guarded, as I have had no other way to account for it.[147]

Notes and Commentary

A few important details are emphasized from the accounts concerning departed spirits: (1) spirits in the spirit world assist the Saints on this side of the veil with their temple work, and (2) departed spirits are often present when their temple ordinances are being performed. For instance, in 1965, Karl G. Maeser appeared to Ezra Taft Benson and asked him to promote the temple ordinances for his people, the Europeans. Maeser said that departed spirits cannot progress in the spirit world until their ordinances have been performed.[148]

President Wilford Woodruff experienced a similar manifestation when hundreds of people appeared to him in the St. George Temple regarding their ordinances. These individuals—including former US presidents, signers of the Declaration of Independence, and many other noble men and women—asked President Woodruff why he had not performed their temple ordinances. They rebuked him, saying, "You have had the use of the Endowment House for a number of years and yet nothing has ever been done for us. We laid the foundation of the government you now enjoy, and we never apostatized from it, but we remained true to it and were faithful to God."[149] Benjamin Franklin appeared to President Woodruff on another occasion and "wanted more work done for him than had already been done."[150] Departed spirits are anxious to receive their own temple blessings, and the Lord will occasionally allow them to appear to individuals on this side of the veil to assist them with temple work.

On another occasion, President Woodruff saw Joseph Smith and several other men at the temple in vision. These men were all rushing around. President Woodruff finally stopped the Prophet Joseph and asked why everyone was in a hurry. Joseph told Elder Woodruff,

147. Carter, *Our Pioneer Heritage*, 202.

148. Dew, *Ezra Taft Benson*, 381–82.

149. *Journal of Discourses*, 19:229.

150. Cowley, *Wilford Woodruff*, 586–87.

"Each dispensation has had ample time to do [the work of the Lord]. We have not. We are the last dispensation, and so much work has to be done and we need to be in a hurry in order to accomplish it."[151]

Marriner W. Merrill recorded seeing numerous heavenly personages on the Logan Temple grounds one day, which caused the temple to appear on fire. When President Woodruff received word of Elder Merrill's manifestation, he said that the "Hale and the Boynton families had been permitted to come from the other side to sing and rejoice and celebrate their deliverance in the Logan Temple."[152] On another occasion, Marriner Merrill's deceased son appeared and talked to him at length about temple work. He told Brother Merrill not to grieve over his death and to continue working at the temple. Like Wilford Woodruff's visionary experience with the Prophet Joseph at the temple, Elder Merrill's son told him that he was very busy preparing those in the spirit world to receive their temple blessings.[153] Elder Woodruff's and Elder Merrill's accounts reveal that departed spirits not only appear to individuals concerning temple work but are extremely busy in the spirit world, teaching the gospel to prepare others to receive their temple blessings when they are performed by the living on this side of the veil.

Elder Melvin J. Ballard's account—providing many details—indicated that he saw many departed spirits who had gathered in "the east end of the font room" in the Logan Temple while their temple work was being finished. "One by one," recorded Elder Ballard, "as each name was baptized for, one of these people climbed a stairway over the font to the west end of the room. Not one soul was missing, but there was a person for every one of the thousand names done that day."[154]

Several accounts in this chapter—and throughout this book—also emphasize that heavenly messengers wear vestments similar to those worn in Latter-day Saint temples. For example, when Joseph Smith appeared to Elder George Q. Cannon, he was "dressed in his

---

151. *Discourses of Wilford Woodruff*, 288.

152. Olsen, *Logan Temple*, 175.

153. Crowther, *Life Everlasting*, 206.

154. Olsen, *Logan Temple*, 170.

temple clothes."[155] In Wilford Woodruff's vision on March 5, 1848, he saw Joseph, Hyrum, and other heavenly beings dressed in "white robes" making crowns for the Saints.[156] President Brigham Young and Truman O. Angell saw forty angelic personages in the Kirtland Temple "dressed in white robes and caps."[157] Before the Saints built the temple in Nauvoo, a woman named Elizabeth Tyler claimed that she had seen an angel but did not know if it was from God or Satan. When she told Joseph about the manifestation, he asked her to explain the clothing that the angel was wearing. She said that he wore "white from head to foot" and "a peculiar cap," different from any she had ever seen. The angel also wore "a white robe, underclothing, and moccasins."[158] Joseph said that it was a true vision and that he had seen the same angel many times, the angel being Adam. On one occasion, Joseph Smith, Zebedee Coltrin, and Oliver Cowdery saw Adam and Eve in vision wearing "white garments."[159] In 1823, the angel Moroni appeared to Joseph Smith wearing a garment that "was perfectly white and had the appearance of being without seam."[160] Moroni also wore a sash "about his waist."[161] Similarly, during the Kirtland Temple dedicatory sessions in March 1836, a heavenly messenger appeared and sat down in the vacant seat between Fredrick G. Williams and Joseph Smith Sr. Brother Williams recorded that the robe worn by the personage—similar to Moroni's garment—was "without seam."[162] We also read that the robe Jesus wore during His ministry was "without seam" (John 19:23). One Latter-day Saint scholar suggested that a seamless robe is "frequently seen as having been typified by the robe of the Mosaic high priest."[163]

---

155. *Journal of Discourses*, 22:289–90.

156. *Wilford Woodruff's Journal*, 3:327–28.

157. *Wilford Woodruff's Journal*, 5:120.

158. *The Juvenile Instructor* 27 (Feb. 1, 1892): 93–95.

159. Zebedee Coltrin, "High Priest Minutes, Spanish Fork, Utah, February 5, 1870," LDS Church Archives, Salt Lake City, Utah.

160. *Messenger and Advocate* 1, no. 5 (Oct. 1834–Sept. 1835): 79.

161. *Kansas City Times*, Apr. 11, 1895.

162. *Journal of Discourses*, 11:10.

163. Alonzo L. Gaskill, *The Lost Language of Symbolism* (Deseret Book, 2003), 74.

Chapter Five

Manifestations of Heavenly Intervention

One of the gifts of the Spirit is the "beholding of angels and ministering spirits" (Moroni 10:14). Concerning this gift, Elder Jedediah M. Grant of the First Presidency taught, "Latter-day Saints believe differently from other folks. . . . The Lord God has spoken to us from the heavens and commanded us to gather. . . . The Latter-day Saints try to live their religion, that they may converse with angels [and] receive the administration of holy messengers from the throne of God."[164]

When a man receives the Aaronic Priesthood, he receives—among other things—"the key of the ministering of angels" (Doctrine and Covenants 84:26). "The Lord revealed it to be the privilege of those holding the keys of the Aaronic Priesthood," explained President Joseph Fielding Smith, "to have the visitation and ministering of angels if the occasion should arise, in relation to the temporal matters of

164. *Journal of Discourses*, 2:279.

the Church."[165] The Savior told the Saints through Joseph Smith that for all who are righteous, "I will go before your face. I will be on your right hand and on your left, and my Spirit shall be in your hearts, and mine angels round about you, to bear you up" (Doctrine and Covenants 84:88). When Joseph Smith organized the Relief Society in 1842, he counseled them, saying, "If you live up to these principles, how great and glorious will be your reward in the celestial kingdom! If you live up to your privileges, the angels cannot be restrained from being your associates."[166]

Occasionally, angels will minister to individuals without revealing themselves. Other situations, however, require the physical appearance of a heavenly messenger. Angels may also minister to an individual by opening dreams and visions to them. Elder John A. Widtsoe taught the Saints that the duties of heavenly messengers are "many and varied, as set forth in Holy Writ. They may announce the truths of the gospel or convey special messages to individuals or nations. They may act as guardians to protect the righteous, or agents to inflict divine penalties upon the wicked. They may come, as at the beginning of a dispensation, with authority to bestow the Priesthood or to help in the development of the organized Church. In short, they go and do as they are bidden."[167] Elder Parley P. Pratt similarly taught that the business of an angel is to "comfort and instruct individual members of the Church, . . . to heal them by the laying on of hands in the name of Jesus Christ, or to tell them what means to use in order to get well; to teach them good things, to sing them a good song, to warn them of approaching danger, or to deliver them from prison or from death."[168]

The accounts in this chapter describe occasions when heaven intervened on behalf of the prophets. Sometimes angels were not present. On other occasions, angels ministered to the prophets directly. Several accounts describe the presence of heavenly personages (deceased family members) who came to assist with a concern or an administrative

---

165. Joseph Fielding Smith, *Answers to Gospel Questions* (Deseret Book, 1998), 1:116.

166. *History of the Church*, 4:605.

167. John A. Widtsoe, *Evidences and Reconciliations* (Bookcraft, 1960), 108.

168. Parley P. Pratt, *Key to the Science of Theology* (Deseret Book, 1965), 113.

issue. Others received a vision or dream from an unseen angel or were even directly protected or healed by a heavenly personage.

Accounts of the Prophets

Heber J. Grant

I can truthfully say that from October, 1882, until February, 1883, that spirit followed me day and night telling me that I was unworthy to be an Apostle of the Church, and that I ought to resign. When I would testify of my knowledge that Jesus is the Christ, the Son of the Living God, the Redeemer of mankind, it seemed as though a voice would say to me: "You lie! You lie! You have never seen Him."

While on the Navajo Indian reservation with Brigham Young, Jr., and a number of others, six or eight, on horseback, and several others in "white tops"—riding along with Lot Smith at the rear of that procession, suddenly the road veered to the left almost straight, but there was a well beaten path leading ahead. I said: "Stop, Lot, stop. Where does this trail lead? There are plenty of foot marks and plenty of horses' hoof marks here." He said, "It leads to an immense gulley just a short distance ahead, that it is impossible to cross with a wagon. We have made a regular 'Muleshoe' of miles here to get on the other side of the gulley. . ." I said, "Lot, is there any danger from Indians?" "None at all." "I want to be all alone. Go ahead and follow the crowd." I first asked him if I allowed the animal I was riding to walk if I would reach the road on the other side of the gulley before the horsemen and the wagons, and he said, "Yes."

As I was riding along to meet them on the other side I seemed to see, and I seemed to hear, what to me is one of the most real things in all my life, I seemed to see a Council in Heaven. I seemed to hear the words that were spoken. I listened to the discussion with a great deal of interest. The First Presidency and the Council of the Twelve Apostles had not been able to agree on two men to fill the vacancies in the Quorum of the Twelve. There had been a vacancy of one for two years, and a vacancy of two for one year, and the Conference had adjourned without the vacancies being filled. In this Council the Savior was present, my father was there, and the Prophet Joseph Smith was there. They discussed the question that a mistake had been made in not filling those two vacancies and that in all probability it would be another six months before the Quorum would be completed, and they discussed as to whom they wanted to occupy those positions, and decided that the way to remedy the mistake that had been made in not filling these vacancies was to send a revelation. It was given to me that the Prophet Joseph Smith and my father mentioned me and requested that I be called to that position.

I sat there and wept for joy. It was given to me that I had done nothing to entitle me to that exalted position, except that I had lived a clean, sweet life. It was given to me that because of my father having practically sacrificed his life in what was known as the great Reformation, so to speak, of the people in early days, having been practically a martyr, that the Prophet Joseph and my father desired me to have that position, and it was because of their faithful labors that I was called, and not because of anything I had done of myself or any great thing that I had accomplished. It was also given to me that that was all these men, the Prophet and my father, could do for me; from that day it depended upon me and upon me alone as to whether I made a success of my life or a failure.[169]

Jedediah M. Grant

In the year 1834, when Zion's camp was moving from Kirtland to Missouri, one day I left the camp and went out to hunt in the woods of Ohio, and strayed away from the camp some 10 or 11 miles. The camp kept moving on all the time, and I entirely lost the track, and having no compass, I knew not towards what point I should travel. I kept traveling on till the after part of the day; I then concluded I would pray, but I could not get any impression where the camp was. However, I soon after received an impression from the Spirit, the same Spirit we had in Kirtland, and the same Spirit we enjoy in this place; and immediately after receiving the impression, I looked before me, and there was the camp moving on in regular order. I could see it just as clear as I did in the morning; there were the people, the wagons and horses, all in their places as I left them in the fore part of the day, and I supposed they were

169. Conference Report, Apr. 1941, 4–5.

not more than 80 rods off. But after turning away for a moment, I again looked in the same direction, but all was gone. Still the Spirit told me to travel on in the same direction I had seen the camp; I did so, and after traveling some 8 or 10 miles, came up with them, and when they first came in sight, they looked just as I saw them in the vision.[170]

Alonzo A. Hinckley

Related by Bryant S. Hinckley:

Shortly before Elder Hinckley's death, his daughter, Afton, was with him in his home in Salt Lake City. The family had gone out. Everything was quiet, there was an indescribably sweet influence in the house. She supposed her father was asleep and after some little time she went to his room. When she appeared at the door, she said, "Come in, I have had a wonderful afternoon. Three heavenly messengers dressed in the robes of the Holy Priesthood had been my visitors." He spoke of them teaching him to sing a hymn. At that juncture, the family began to appear and he never mentioned the matter again.[171]

Alonzo A. Hinckley

Related by Bryant S. Hinckley:

Shortly before Alonzo died, he went to Southern California hoping that a change in climate might help him. While there on one occasion, he was pondering the fact that his health had not permitted him to discharge his duties as an apostle in a way that was satisfactory to him. While in this mood, his father, Ira N. Hinckley, who had been dead for more than thirty years, appeared to him and told him that he greatly needed his assistance on the other side of the veil, that he had more work than he could possibly do, and really needed him. Alonzo explained that there was so much here to do, that his health had retarded him, and he would like to stay and finish it. And so they talked face to face with one another.

---

170. *Journal of Discourses*, 3:9–10.

171. Bryant S. Hinckley, *The Faith of Our Pioneer Fathers* (Deseret Book, 1959), 236.

The experience was repeated the second time, and with the same results. Then his father appeared for the third time, and told him he would have to have him. That was the final word. Soon after, Alonzo returned to Salt Lake City, and died, but not until after he had fought a brave and gallant fight for his life, did he pass away in peace to his great reward.[172]

Orson Hyde

While I remained at Nauvoo, I urged the brethren to get ready and start [for the West] as early as possible; and those who could not prepare to go on and overtake the first company to start and go as far as they could, and then stop in the Settlements in Iowa and go to work; and be sure and not wander off the main thoroughfare of the Saints, but remain on the track, and work to keep themselves, praying to God to help them, and watch for those who were passing that peradventure someone might pass with extra teams and hitch on to them and take them along, whereas if they should wander away from the main track such opportunities would escape their notice, and they still be left.

Almon W. Babbitt, one of the Trustees of the Church, was very anxious that I should exert an influence to have the Saints stay in Nauvoo for his protection against the mob until he and his associates could settle up the business. I told him that I could not do it; and assured him that his safety was in his weakness, and not in his strength or numbers. Still, he would persevere to get me to use an influence to have a good many families remain in Nauvoo for the protection of the committee of trustees. About this time an Angel of the Lord appeared to me in a night vision and spoke these words to me: "This people cannot stay here."[173]

Spencer W. Kimball

Related by Elder Francis M. Gibbons:

---

172. Hinckley, *The Faith of Our Pioneer Fathers*, 238–39.

173. Elden Jay Watson, ed., *Manuscript History of Brigham Young 1846–1847* (Elden Jay Watson, 1971), 187–88.

When the reorganization of the First Presidency took place on December 30, 1973, in the upper room of the temple, President Kimball was ordained and set apart as the twelfth President of the Church. He selected N. Eldon Tanner and Marion G. Romney as his counselors. President Ezra Taft Benson became the president of the Quorum of the Twelve. At the press conference the next day, President Kimball gave no hint of the determined action he would take later to advance the Church and motivate its members. He endorsed the work of his predecessors and said he would emphasize the home, the family, and the training of youth, while promoting missionary service. Questioners were told that he was in relatively good health, that women who could do so should give priority to child rearing, and that the Church policy on priesthood would not change unless by revelation.

President Kimball found his new duties more demanding than he expected. The enormous volume of meetings, correspondence, invitations to speak, and requests for interviews was burdensome. Many issues came to him for final decision, and the fact that he was the final arbiter created a sense of isolation and aloneness. It also increased his dependence on divine direction and sharpened his spiritual sensitivities. One night his father appeared to him in a dream or a vision. Another time he awoke with a sense that President Harold B. Lee was in the room. Both experiences gave him feelings of comfort and an assurance that he was not alone.[174]

Harold B. Lee

May I impose upon you for a moment to express appreciation for something that happened to me some time ago? I was suffering from an ulcer condition that was becoming worse and worse. We had been touring a mission; my wife, Joan, and I were impressed the next morning that we should get home as quickly as possible, although we had planned to stay for some other meetings.

On the way across the country, we were sitting in the forward section of the airplane. Some of our Church members were in the next section of the airplane. As we approached a certain point en

174. Francis M. Gibbons, *Spencer W. Kimball: Resolute Disciple, Prophet of God* (Deseret Book, 1995), 274–75.

route, someone laid his hand upon my head. I looked up; I could see no one. That happened again before we arrived home, again with the same experience. Who it was, by what means or what medium, I may never know, except I knew that I was receiving a blessing that I came a few hours later to know I needed most desperately.

As soon as we arrived home, my wife very anxiously called the doctor. It was now about 11 o'clock at night. He called me to come to the telephone, and he asked how I was; and I said, "Well, I am very tired. I think I will be all right." But shortly thereafter, there came massive hemorrhages which, had they occurred while we were in flight, I wouldn't be here today talking about it.[175]

Amasa M. Lyman

When we were in Nauvoo, at the beginning of the last winter we spent in Illinois, about the time the clouds were gathering so thick, and the last storm began to break upon us, we heard the thunders and threatenings of our enemies wherein they stated that we were to be driven away. At that time I was confined to my bed with sickness, but I heard the report of the proceedings day after day; but I could not come out to see the face of the heavens, to judge what the issues would be. To get away was impossible with me at that time, and we knew that the longer we stayed the more we should be oppressed by our enemies.

After I had commenced to recover my health, one morning, while lying in my bed in open day, as wakeful as I am at this moment, the surrounding objects which I could see when in my natural condition all in an instant disappeared, and, instead of appearing to keep my bed, I found myself standing in a place where those acquainted with Nauvoo and the location of the Printing Office, subsequent to the death of the Prophets, will remember. There was a vacant lot in front of the Printing Office; I stood there, and I heard a rumbling noise something like that which attends the moving of a mass of people. I turned round to look in the direction of Main Street, and behold! The whole country was filled with one moving mass of people that seemed to be traveling directly to the point where I stood.

175. Harold B. Lee, *Stand Ye in Holy Places* (Deseret Book, 1974), 187–88.

As they approached somewhat nearer, they seemed not to be traveling on the ground, but somewhat near the altitude of the tops of the buildings. At the head of the company were three personages clothed with robes of white, something like those which many of us are acquainted with. Around their waist was a girdle of gold, and from this was suspended the scabbard of a sword, the sword being in the hand of the wearer. They took their places with their faces directly west; and as they stopped, the individual in advance turned and looked over his shoulder to me with a smile of recognition. It was Joseph; and the others were his two brothers, Hyrum and Carlos. . . . After contemplating the scene a few moments, I was again in my bed as before, and the vision had disappeared. This was my assurance, in the commencement of our troubles there, that I received of the guardianship that was around us and the protection that we were receiving from the hosts of heaven.[176]

Parley P. Pratt

Having rested myself a few days [in June 1833], I now commenced again to cultivate the earth. I plowed about six acres of ground for wheat, and was busy from day to day in the woods, preparing timber to fence the same, when the following dream, or night vision, was given me: A man came to me and called me with a loud voice: "Parley, Parley." I answered, "Here am I." Said he, "Cease splitting rails, for the Lord has prepared you for a greater work." I answered, "Whereby shall I know that this message is from the Lord?" He replied, "Follow me, and I will show you."

I followed him for some distance along a long path, and at last came to a place of ancient sepulchers, where many of the Nephites of old had been buried. One of these opened—the flesh of the man withered away; he became like a skeleton, and passed down into the grave. I understood and knew by the spirit, that this signified that it was the voice of one from the dead which had spoken to me. I therefore exclaimed, "It is enough; I know the message is of the Lord; return unto me, that we may converse together." He then

176. *Journal of Discourses*, 5:59.

came forth out of the grave, was again clothed upon with a body like a man, and he talked with me, and told me many things.[177]

Parley P. Pratt

In the winter months of 1839, Parley P. Pratt, King Follett, and others were taken to the Richmond Jail. They were separated from Joseph, Hyrum, and Sidney, along with about seventeen other men who were taken to the Liberty Jail. Parley spent close to eight months in prison with Morris Phelps, Luman Gibbs, Darwin Chase, Norman Shearer, and King Follett.

> Under these circumstances [March 1839 in the Richmond Jail], and half way between hope and despair, I spent several days in fasting and prayer, during which one deep and all absorbing inquiry, one only thought, seemed to hold possession of my mind. It seemed to me that if there was a God in Heaven who ever spake to man on earth I would know from him the truth of this one question. It was not how long shall I suffer; it was not when or by what means I should be delivered; but it was simply this: Shall I ever, at any time, however distant it may be, or whatever I may suffer first; shall I ever be free again in this life, and enjoy the society of my dear wife and children, and walk abroad at liberty, dwell in society and preach the gospel, as I have done in bygone years? Let me be sure of this and I care not what I suffer. To circumnavigate the globe, to traverse the deserts of Arabia, to wander amid the wild scenes of the Rocky Mountains to accomplish so desirable an object, would seem like a mere trifle if I could only be sure at last.
>
> After some days of prayer and fasting, and seeking the Lord on the subject, I retired to my bed in my lonely chamber at an early hour, and while the other prisoners and the guard were chatting and beguiling the lonesome hours in the upper apartment of the prison, I lay in silence, seeking and expecting an answer to my prayer, when suddenly I seemed carried away in the spirit, and no longer sensible to outward objects with which I was surrounded. A heaven of peace and calmness pervaded my bosom; a personage from the world of spirits stood before me with a smile of compassion

---

177. *Autobiography of Parley P. Pratt*, ed. Facer Proctor and Maurine Jensen Proctor (Deseret Book, 2000), 109–110.

in every look, and pity mingled with the tenderest love and sympathy in every expression of the countenance. A soft hand seemed placed within my own, and a glowing cheek was laid in tenderness and warmth upon mine. A well known voice saluted me, which I readily recognized as that of the wife of my youth, who had for near two years been sweetly sleeping where the wicked cease from troubling and the weary are at rest. I was made to realize that she was sent to commune with me, and answer my question.

Knowing this, I said to her in a most earnest and inquiring tone: Shall I ever be at liberty again in this life and enjoy the society of my family and the Saints, and preach the gospel as I have done? She answered definitely and unhesitatingly: "YES!" I then recollected that I had agreed to be satisfied with the knowledge of that one fact, but now I wanted more. Said I: "Can you tell me how, or by what means, or when I shall escape?" She replied: "THAT THING IS NOT MADE KNOWN TO ME YET." I instantly felt that I had gone beyond my agreement and my faith in asking this last question, and that I must be contented at present with the answer to the first. Her gentle spirit then saluted me and withdrew. I came to myself. The doleful noise of the guards, and the wrangling and angry words of the old apostate again grated on my ears, but Heaven and hope were in my soul.[178]

Parley P. Pratt

After a wearisome journey and various toils and dangers . . . [Mrs. Pratt] at length arrived at Quincy, Illinois, where [she] rented a small house, and by the sale of a few books, with the use of her two cows, which some of the brethren had brought from Missouri for her, she was making shift to live from day to day. She still expressed some faint hopes of seeing her husband again in a land of liberty, although at present there was little ground to hope, and she was sometimes nearly in despair.

Such was the news brought us by the arrival of our friends in the prison at Columbia on the 1st of July, 1839, after eight months of weary confinement. Previous to their arrival the Lord had shown me in a vision of the night the manner and means of escape. And,

178. *Autobiography of Parley P. Pratt*, 295–97.

like Pharaoh's dream, the thing had been doubled—that is shown to me on two occasions in the same manner.

Mrs. Phelps had the same thing shown to her in a vision previous to her arrival; my brother, Orson Pratt, also came to us with a firm impression that we were about to be delivered. He even predicted that we should go to Illinois, when he should return there. As we sat pondering upon these things, and comparing our visions and manifestations of the spirit on this subject, my brother Orson opened the Book of Mormon, when the first sentence that caught his eye was the words of Ammon to King Lamoni: "Behold, my brother and my brethren are in prison, in the land of Middoni, and I go to deliver them!" This was indeed a similar instance to ours. Ammon, on that occasion had an own brother in prison, and also brethren in the ministry, and did deliver them. Our case was exactly similar, not in Middoni, but in Missouri. And, what was still more strange, in a book of six hundred pages, this was the only sentence which would have fitted our case.

He now began in earnest to make arrangements for our escape. If there had been no strong bolts and bars to overcome, still there was one serious obstacle which a miracle alone could immediately remove, which was this: I was then very sick and scarcely able to stand on my feet, or to go up and down from the upper room, where we were in the day time, to the dungeon where we slept.

It was the second of July, and our friends could only make an excuse for staying to spend the great national holiday with us (the 4th) before they must leave or excite the suspicions and ill will of the people; and, as that day had been a lucky one for our fathers and our nation, we had determined on that time as the proper one to bid farewell to bondage and gain our liberty. In short, we had determined to make that notable day a jubilee to us, or perish in the attempt. We, therefore, prayed earnestly to the Lord, that if he had determined to favor our plan, he would heal and strengthen me, and give us all courage to act well our part. Through the ministration of the ordinance appointed for healing, I was instantly healed, and from that moment began to feel as strong and fearless as a lion.

Our plan was this: My brother, Orson Pratt, was to wait on the Judge and Attorney, and obtain various papers and arrangements for summoning witnesses from Illinois to attend our trial, which had just been adjourned for some months to come. He was also to procure an order from the Court to take affidavits in Illinois, in case the witnesses should object to come to the State from which they had been banished, in order to attend the trials.

These active preparations on our part to defend our case, together with engaging a lawyer or two, and paying a part of their fees beforehand, served as a sufficient blindfold to cover our real intentions. This done, and the papers all prepared in the hands of my brother, he and Mrs. Phelps and her brother were to stay with us until the 4th, and after celebrating the day with a dinner in the prison (which we obtained leave to do), he and the young Mr. Clark were to take leave with their horses, and also with the horse and saddle on which Mrs. Phelps had ridden, on pretence of taking him home with them to Illinois, while she stayed with her husband a few weeks in the prison; in the meantime engaging her board in the family of the keeper, who occupied part of the building in connection with the prison.

This measure, on the part of Mrs. Phelps, served the double purpose of lulling them into serenity, and also of furnishing a third horse; as there were three of us. These three horses were to be stationed in a thicket, or forest, about half a mile from the prison, and there the two friends were to await, in readiness for us to mount, should we be so fortunate as to reach the thicket alive. Sundown, on the evening of the fourth, was the moment agreed upon, and if we did not then appear they were to give us up for lost, and make the best of their way to Illinois and inform our friends that we had gone to Paradise in attempting to come to them. The reason for appointing this hour was this: Our door would be opened at sundown to hand in our supper, and we must then make the attempt as our only chance; for it was customary to lock us up in the lower dungeon as soon as the shades of evening began to appear.[179]

LeGrand Richards

Related by Elder Francis M. Gibbons:

President Kimball had begun to discuss the priesthood question with his brethren and to pray for spiritual direction. This included fervent and frequent prayers alone in the Salt Lake Temple. On

179. *Autobiography of Parley P. Pratt*, 301–2.

March 23, 1978, President Kimball advised his counselors that he had had a wakeful night struggling with the question of priesthood restrictions and felt they should be lifted. No action was taken at the time. On April 20, 1978, the prophet advised the Twelve of his prayerful efforts to receive divine guidance on the issue and asked them to join him and his counselors in their prayers to that end. There followed personal interviews between President Kimball and members of the Twelve to discuss the matter. President Kimball continued to spend many hours alone in the temple, imploring the Lord for guidance.

On May 4, 1978, following a council meeting, Elder LeGrand Richards asked President Kimball for the privilege of saying a few words. He told the Brethren that during the meeting, he had seen a personage seated in a chair on the organ. He said he thought it was President Wilford Woodruff. The significance and timing of this appearance are apparent. Here, appearing through the veil in the upper room of the temple, was the prophet who, almost a hundred years before, had wrestled with a critical problem, plural marriage, which was resolved by revelation, the same way the problem President Kimball faced would be resolved.[180]

LeGrand Richards explains what he saw as follows:

"Brethren, I have something to tell you. A little while ago, I saw a man seated above the organ there and he looked just like that [pointing to a portrait of Wilford Woodruff]. . . . I saw him just as clearly as I see any of you Brethren. . . . He was dressed in a white suit and was seated in an armchair." I thought at the time that the reason I was privileged to see him was probably that I was the only one there who had ever seen President Woodruff while he was upon the earth. I had heard him dedicate the Salt Lake Temple and I had heard him give his last sermon in the Salt Lake Tabernacle before he died. I thought it wonderful that the Lord could project, without mechanical means, the likeness of a man long since dead.[181]

Hyrum Smith

Related by Joseph and Hyrum to Lucy Mack Smith:

---

180. Gibbons, *Spencer W. Kimball*, 294–95.

181. Lucile C. Tate, *LeGrand Richards: Beloved Apostle* (Bookcraft, 1982), 291–92.

Soon after arriving at the point of destination [in 1834], the cholera broke out among us, and the brethren [Zion's Camp] were so violently attacked that it seemed impossible to render them any assistance. They immediately sent for us to lay hands on them, but we soon discovered that this also was the judgment of the Almighty, for when we laid our hands upon them in the name of the Lord in order that they might be healed, the disease instantly fastened itself upon us. And in a few minutes we were in awful distress. We made mute signals to each other and left the house for the purpose of going into some secluded place to join in prayer that God would deliver us from this awful influence; but before we could get a sufficient distance to be secure from interruption, we were scarcely able to stand upon our feet and we were greatly alarmed, fearing that we should die in this western wilderness so far from our families, without even the privilege of blessing our children or giving them one word of parting counsel. Hyrum cried out, "Joseph, what shall we do? Must we be cut off from the face of the earth by this horrid curse?"

"Let us," said Joseph, "get down upon our knees and pray to God to remove the cramp and other distress and restore us to health, that we may return to our families." We did so but without receiving any benefit, but still grew worse. We concluded, however, to make a second effort, and when we kneeled again, the cramp seized the calves of Joseph's legs, gathering the cords into bunches, and then the operation extended in like manner all over his system. He cried heartily unto God, but the heavens seemed sealed against us and every power that could render us any assistance shut within its gates. The universe was still. "When we arose again," said Joseph, "I found Hyrum was in the same situation with myself."

We soon came to the resolution of appealing again to God for mercy, and not to rise from our knees until one or the other got a testimony that we should be healed, and he who received the first intimation from the Spirit should inform the other of the same. We prayed some time, first one and then the other, and soon perceived that the cramp began to loose its hold. In a short time Hyrum sprang to his feet and exclaimed, "Joseph, we shall return, for I have seen an open vision in which I saw Mother on her knees under an apple tree praying for us, and she is even now asking God, in tears, to spare our lives, that she may behold us again in the flesh. The

Spirit testifies to me that her prayers and ours shall be heard"—and from that moment we were healed and went on our way rejoicing.[182]

Joseph Smith Jr.

Early in the month of August [1830] Newel Knight and his wife paid us a visit at my place in Harmony, Pennsylvania; and as neither his wife nor mine had been as yet confirmed, it was proposed that we should confirm them, and partake together of the Sacrament, before he and his wife should leave us. In order to prepare for this I set out to procure some wine for the occasion, but had gone only a short distance when I was met by a heavenly messenger, and received the following revelation: "Listen to the voice of Jesus Christ, your Lord, your God, and your Redeemer, whose word is quick and powerful. For, behold, I say unto you, that it mattereth not what ye shall eat, or what ye shall drink, when ye partake of the sacrament, if it so be that ye do it with an eye single to my glory—remembering unto the Father my body which was laid down for you, and my blood which was shed for the remission of your sins"[183]

Joseph Smith Jr. and Mary E. R. Lightner

Related by Mary Lightner:

Well, I talked with [Joseph] for a long time and finally I told him I would never be sealed to him until I had a witness. Said he, "You shall have a witness." Said I, "If God told you that, why does he not tell me? . . ." "Well," said he, "pray earnestly for the angel said to me you should have a witness." Well, Brigham Young was with me. He said if I had a witness he wanted to know it. "Why should I tell you?" said I. "Well," said he, "I want to know for myself." Said he, "Do you know what Joseph said? Since we left the office the angel appeared to him and told him he was well pleased with him and that you should have a witness."

I made it a subject of prayer and I worried about it because I did not dare to speak to a living being except Brigham Young. I

182. Lucy Mack Smith, *Lucy's Book: A Critical Edition of Lucy Mack Smith's Family Memoir*, ed. Lavina Fielding Anderson (Signature Books, 2001), 576–77.

183. *History of the Church*, 1:106–7; see also Doctrine and Covenants 27.

went out and got between three haystacks where no one could see me. . . . I knelt down and if ever a poor mortal prayed, I did. A few nights after that an angel of the Lord came to me and if ever a thrill went through a mortal, it went through me. I gazed upon the clothes and figure but the eyes were like lightning. They pierced me from the crown of my head to the soles of my feet. I was frightened almost to death for a moment. I tried to waken my aunt, but I could not. The angel leaned over me and the light was very great, although it was night. When my aunt woke up she said she had seen a figure in white robes pass from our bed to my mother's bed and pass out of the window.

Joseph came up the next Sabbath. He said, "Have you had a witness yet?" "No." "Well," said he, "the angel expressly told me you should have." Said I, "I have not had a witness, but I have seen something I have never seen before. I saw an angel and I was frightened almost to death. I did not speak." He studied a while and put his elbows on his knees and his face in his hands. He looked up and said, "How could you have been such a coward?" Said I, "I was weak . . ." "He came to you with more knowledge, intelligence, and light than I have ever dared to reveal." I said, "If that was an angel of light, why did he not speak to me?" "You covered your face and for this reason the angel was insulted." Said I, "Will it ever come again?" He thought a moment and then said, "No, not the same one, but if you are faithful you shall see greater things than that." And then he gave me three signs of what would take place in my own family. . . . Every work came true. I went forward and was sealed to him.[184]

Joseph Smith Jr.

Related by Martha C. Cox:

Allen Stout . . . used to come to live with us while he worked in the temple. . . . He was in Nauvoo a bodyguard to the Prophet, and when asked to tell something about the days of Nauvoo he would tell it, but he was not much of a talker unless asked to do so. He

184. "Mary Elizabeth Lightner, Address at Brigham Young University, April 14, 1905," Typescript, L. Tom Perry Special Collections Library, Harold B. Lee Library, Brigham Young University, Provo, Utah, 1–3.

gave me much information about the early history of the Church because I asked him many questions. One day he said in answer to a statement I made that I thought it could not be possible for one to see a heavenly being, that I might see one without recognizing it as such—as happened once with him. I immediately became anxious to know all about it.

He told me he was once walking with the Prophet on the west side of the Mississippi River on the road to Montrose, I think. They saw a man walking along a road leading in from the south and coming towards them. The Prophet told Allen to remain where he was while he stepped over to speak with this pedestrian. Allen turned his back towards them and for a time forgot the Prophet and became engaged with his own thought, while he stood whipping a low bush with the cane he carried. The hand of the Prophet upon his shoulder aroused him. The Prophet said, "We must return immediately to Nauvoo." They walked silently and rapidly. Allen became very sorrowful over his recreancy to his duty and could not refrain from weeping. The Prophet asked him why he wept. Allen confessed, "I am an insufficient bodyguard—criminally neglectful of your welfare. I allowed that man you met to speak with you without even being ready to defend if he attacked you. He could have killed you and made his escape without my knowing who he is, which way he went or what he even looks like. You will have to dispense with my services and take a guard on which you can depend. Your life is too precious to be trusted to my care." The Prophet then said, "That man would not harm me. You saw John the Revelator."[185]

Joseph F. Smith

I was very much oppressed, once, on a mission [in Hawaii]. I was almost naked and entirely friendless, except the friendship of a poor, benighted, degraded people. I felt as if I was so debased in my condition of poverty, lack of intelligence and knowledge, just a boy, that I hardly dared look a white man in the face.

185. "Martha Cragun Cox (1852–1932) Autobiography, 1928–1930," LDS Church Archives; as cited in Mark McConkie, *Remembering Joseph: Personal Recollections of Those Who Knew the Prophet Joseph Smith* (Deseret Book, 2003), 210–11.

While in that condition I dreamed that I was on a journey, and I was impressed that I ought to hurry with all my might, for fear I might be too late. I rushed on my way as fast as I possibly could, and I was only conscious of having just a little bundle, a handkerchief with a small bundle wrapped in it. I did not realize just what it was, when I was hurrying as fast as I could; but finally I came to a wonderful mansion, if it could be called a mansion. It seemed too large, too great to have been made by hand, but I thought I knew that was my destination.

As I passed towards it, as fast as I could, I saw a notice, "Bath." I turned aside quickly and went into the bath and washed myself clean. I opened up this little bundle that I had, and there was a pair of white, clean garments, a thing I had not seen for a long time, because the people I was with did not think very much of making things exceedingly clean. But my garments were clean, and I put them on. Then I rushed to what appeared to be a great opening, or door. I knocked and the door opened, and the man who stood there was the Prophet Joseph Smith. He looked at me a little reprovingly, and the first word he said: "Joseph, you are late." Yet I took confidence and said: "Yes, but I am clean—I am clean!"

He clasped my hand and drew me in, then closed the great door. I felt his hand just as tangible as I ever felt the hand of man. I knew him, and when I entered I saw my father, and Brigham, and Heber, and Willard, and other good men that I had known, standing in a row. I looked as if it were across this valley, and it seemed to be filled with a vast multitude of people, but on the stage were all the people that I had known. My mother was there, and she sat with a child in her lap; and I could name over as many as I remember of their names, who sat there, who seemed to be among the chosen, among the exalted. The Prophet said to me, "Joseph," then pointing to my mother, he said: "Bring me that child."

I went to my mother and picked up the child, and thought it was a fine baby boy. I carried it to the Prophet, and as I handed it to him I purposely thrust my hands up against his breast. I felt the warmth; I was alone on a mat, away up in the mountains of Hawaii; no one was with me. But in this vision I pressed my hand up against the Prophet, and I saw a smile cross his countenance. I handed him the child and stepped back. President Young stepped around two steps, my father one step, and they formed a triangle.

Then Joseph blessed that baby, and when he finished blessing it they stepped back in line; that is, Brigham and father stepped back in line. Joseph handed me the baby, wanted me to come and take the baby again; and this time I was determined to test whether this was a dream or a reality. I wanted to know what it meant. So I purposely thrust myself up against the Prophet. I felt the warmth of his stomach. He smiled at me, as if he comprehended my purpose. He delivered the child to me and I returned it to my mother, laid it on her lap.

When I awoke that morning I was a man, although only a boy. There was not anything in the world that I feared. I could meet any man or woman or child and look them in the face, feeling in my soul that I was a man every whit. That vision, that manifestation and witness that I enjoyed at that time has made me what I am, if I am anything that is good, or clean, or upright before the Lord, if there is anything good in me. That has helped me out in every trial and through every difficulty.

Now, I suppose that is only a dream? To me it is a reality. There never could be anything more real to me. I felt the hand of Joseph Smith, I felt the warmth of his stomach, when I put my hand against him. I saw the smile upon his face. I did my duty as he required me to do it, and when I woke up I felt as if I had been lifted out of a slum, out of despair, out of the wretched condition that I was in.[186]

Lorenzo Snow

Related by President Snow's daughter, Lucille Snow Tracy:

The story of my birth parallels that of the Biblical Isaac and [likewise] is full of the heartbreak, joy and sorrow, which accompanied it. My father, President Lorenzo Snow, was 82 years old when he and Mama (Minnie Jane) got together to have me. Mama was 42 years old at the time, way past the menopause stage of life when women can no longer have children. Prior to their getting together for this purpose, my father had an experience in the Salt Lake Temple one night which indicated to him there was another child

186. Joseph Fielding Smith, *The Life of Joseph F. Smith* (The Deseret News Press, 1938), 445–47.

yet to be born. While he was Temple President he lived in the Salt Lake Temple, and maintained a private room there . . .

One night while in bed in this room, he was awakened by a sound. Upon opening his eyes, he beheld a young girl dressed in white (myself) saying, "Here I am Papa. Here I am Papa. It is me, your little girl." This was repeated for three nights in succession and he knew for a surety that it was from the Preexistent World of Spirits. So he conferred with mama upon the matter and told her he felt there was still another child to come. She said, "Oh no, it is impossible. Lorenzo jr. is the youngest (he being twelve at the time), and there are to be no more." However, Papa still strongly insisted, so she relented, and the Lord blessed her abundantly.[187]

Orson F. Whitney

Early on the morning of April 24, 1918 . . . while I lay on my pillow, half asleep, half awake, a pair of hands were laid upon my head. My first thought was that someone was in the house who ought not to be, and that I must lie perfectly still in order to be safe. But the touch was so soft and gentle that all fear left me, and with my own hands I took hold of those resting on my head. They were a woman's hands. Presently I saw my wife Zina, who had been dead for 18 years. She was hovering over me. I laid out my arms to her, and she came into them. It was all so real. I could not doubt that she was actually there, a guardian angel, watching over her children and me.[188]

Wilford Woodruff

The first day [March 1835] we sailed twenty-five miles, and stopped at night with a poor family who lived on the bank of the river. These kind folks gave us supper and breakfast, and, in the morning, gave us johnny-cake and a piece of pork to take with us on our journey.

---

187. Account related by Lucille Snow Tracy to Joseph Heinerman; as cited in Joseph Heinerman, *Spirit World Manifestations* (Magazine Printing and Publishing, 1978), 142–44.

188. Orson F. Whitney, *Through Memory's Halls* (Zion's Printing and Publishing Co., 1930), 413.

We traveled about fifty miles that day, and at night stopped at an old tavern, in a village called Cadron, which was deserted because it was believed to be haunted by evil spirits. We made a fire in the tavern, roasted a piece of our pork, ate our supper, said our prayers, went into a chamber, lay down on the bare floor, and were soon asleep. I dreamed I was at my father's house in a good feather bed, and I had a good night's rest. When I awoke the bed vanished, and I found myself on the bare floor and well rested, not having been troubled with evil spirits or anything else.[189]

Wilford Woodruff

On the 27th of March [1835] I arrived at Memphis, weary and hungry. I went to the best tavern in the place, kept by Mr. Josiah Jackson. I told him I was a stranger and had no money, and asked him if he would keep me over night. He inquired what my business was, and I told him I was a preacher of the gospel. He laughed and said that I did not look much like a preacher. I did not blame him, as most of the preachers he ever had been acquainted with rode on fine horses or in fine carriages, dressed in broadcloth, had large salaries, and would likely see this whole world sink to perdition before they would wade through one hundred and seventy miles of mud to save the people.

The landlord wanted a little fun, so said he would keep me if I would preach. He wanted to see if I could preach. I must confess that by this time I became a little mischievous, and pleaded with him not to set me preaching. The more I pleaded to be excused the more determined Mr. Jackson was that I should preach. He took my valise, and the landlady got me a good supper. I sat down in a large hall to eat. Before I got through, the room began to be filled by some of the rich and fashionable people of Memphis, dressed in their broadcloth and silk, while my appearance was such as you can imagine, after traveling through the mud as I had done. When I had finished eating, the table was carried out of the room over the heads of the people. I was placed in the corner of the room, with a

189. Matthias F. Cowley, *Wilford Woodruff, His Life and Labors* (Deseret News, 1909), 54.

stand having a Bible, hymn book, and candle on it, hemmed in by a dozen men, with the landlord in the center.

There were present some five hundreds persons, who had come together, not to hear a gospel sermon, but to have some fun. I read a hymn, and asked them to sing. Not a soul would sing a word. I told them I had not the gift of singing; but with the help of the Lord, I would both pray and preach. I knelt down to pray, and the men around me dropped on their knees. I prayed to the Lord to give me His spirit and to show me the hearts of the people. I promised the Lord, in my prayer, that I would deliver to that congregation whatever He would give to me. I arose and spoke one hour and a half, and it was one of the best sermons of my life. The lives of the congregation were open to the vision of my mind, and I told them of their wicked deeds and the reward they would obtain. The men who surrounded me dropped their heads. Three minutes after I closed, I was the only person in the room.

Soon I was shown to a bed, in a room adjoining a large one in which were assembled many of the men whom I had been preaching to. I could hear their conversation. One man said he would like to know how that Mormon boy knew of their past lives.[190]

Wilford Woodruff

Brigham Young also visited me [two years] after his death [in 1879]. On one occasion he and Brother Heber C. Kimball came in a splendid chariot, with fine white horses, and accompanied me to a conference that I was going to attend. When I got there I asked Brother Brigham if he would take charge of the conference. "No," said he, "I have done my work here. I have come to see what you are doing and what you are teaching the people." And he told me what Joseph Smith had taught him in Winter Quarters, to teach the people to get the Spirit of God. He said, "I want you to teach the people to get the Spirit of God. You cannot build up the Kingdom of God without that."[191]

---

190. Cowley, *Wilford Woodruff,* 55–56.

191. Brian H. Study, ed., *Collected Discourses* (B. H. S. Publishing, 1987–92), 5:237–38.

Wilford Woodruff

Joseph Smith visited me a great deal after his death, and taught me many important principles. On one occasion he and his brother Hyrum visited me while I was in a storm at sea. I was going on my last mission to preside in England. My companions were Brother Leonard W. Hardy, Milton Holmes, Dan Jones, and another brother, and my wife and two other women. We had been traveling three days and nights in a heavy gale, and were being driven backwards. Finally I asked my companions to come into the cabin with me, and I told them to pray that the Lord would change the wind. I had no fears of being lost; but I did not like the idea of being driven back to New York, as I wanted to go on my journey. We all offered the same prayer, both men and women; and when we got through we stepped on to the deck and in less than a minute it was as though a man had taken a sword and cut that gale through, and you might have thrown a muslin handkerchief out and it would not have moved it.

The night following this Joseph and Hyrum visited me, and the Prophet laid before me a great many things. Among other things he told me to get the Spirit of God; that all of us needed it. He also told me what the twelve apostles would be called to go through on the earth before the coming of the Son of Man, and what the reward of their labors would be; but all that was taken from me for some reason. Nevertheless it was most glorious, although much would be required at our hands.[192]

Wilford Woodruff

While I was at the home of my father-in-law [in October 1844] I had a peculiar dream. Much of it was unutterable and cannot be written; indeed, I do not comprehend it myself. Among other things I was called with the Twelve to hold the keys of the Kingdom in all the world. I traveled with them over much of the earth and I also traveled through many countries alone. When I finished my journey I saw many things which I cannot write, but in the end,

192. *The Discourses of Wilford Woodruff*, ed. G. Homer Durham (Bookcraft, 1946), 287.

Joseph, the Prophet, assisted me to come where he was and pointed out to me my place and work. I immediately entered into the duties of the new calling to which I was appointed. The same night I had another dream. I was in the presence of the Prophet, and was conversing with him about his death. I told him I felt bad over it, and that had I known he would have been taken so soon I should have conversed with him more while he lived. I would have asked him many questions. In reply he said that it was not his fault that I did not.[193]

Wilford Woodruff

We lost one of our Apostles a short time since. He was about the youngest man in the quorum of the Apostles. He was called suddenly away from us. There is a meaning to this. Many times things take place with us that we do not comprehend, unless it is given to us by revelation. But there is a meaning in the loss of that young Apostle. I had a manifestation of that while in San Francisco recently. One evening, as I fell asleep, I was very much troubled with evil spirits, that tried to afflict me; and while laboring to throw off these spirits and their influence, there was another spirit visited me that seemed to have power over the evil spirits, and they departed from me. Before he left me he told me not to grieve because of the departure of Abraham Hoagland Cannon [on July 19, 1896]; for the Lord had called him to fill another important mission in the spirit world, as a pure and holy Apostle from Zion in the Rocky Mountains—a labor which would not only prove a great benefit to his father's household, but to the Church and kingdom of God upon the earth. I feel to name this, because it is true.[194]

Brigham Young

While sick and asleep about noonday [on February 23, 1847] . . . I dreamed that I went to see Joseph. He looked perfectly natural, sitting with his feet on the lower round of his chair. I took hold of his right hand and kissed it many times, and said to him, "Why is

---

193. Cowley, *Wilford Woodruff*, 328

194. *Discourses of Wilford Woodruff*, 291–92.

it that we cannot be together as we used to be? You have been away from us a long time, and we want your society, and I do not like to be separated from you." Joseph, rising from his chair and looking at me with his usual earnest, expressive and pleasing countenance, said, "It is all right." I replied, "I do not like to be away from you." Joseph said, "It is all right; we cannot be together yet; we shall be, by-and-by; but you will have to do without me awhile, and then we shall be together again."

I then discovered there was a hand right between us. Joseph stood by a window, and to the southwest of him it was very light. I was in the twilight, and to the north of me it was very dark. I said, "Brother Joseph, the brethren, you know them well, better than I do, you raised them up, and brought the Priesthood to us, the brethren have a great anxiety to understand the law of adoption, or the sealing principles; and if you have a word of counsel for me, I should be glad to receive it."

Joseph stepped toward me, and, looking very earnestly, yet pleasantly, said, "Tell the people to be humble and faithful, and be sure to keep the Spirit of the Lord, and it will lead them right. Be careful and not turn away the small, still voice; it will teach what to do and where to go; it will yield the fruits of the kingdom. Tell the brethren to keep their hearts open to convictions, so that when the Holy Ghost comes to them, their hearts will be ready to receive it. They can tell the Spirit of the Lord from all other spirits; it will whisper peace and joy to their souls; it will take malice, strife and hatred, and all evil, from their hearts; and their whole desire will be to do good, bring forth righteousness, and build up the kingdom of God."[195]

Brigham Young

Related by Elder George A. Smith:

We look around today and behold our city clothed with verdure, beautiful with trees and flowers and with streams of water running in almost every direction, and the question is frequently asked, "How did you ever find this place?" I answer, "We were led to it by the inspiration of God."

---

195. *Manuscript History of Brigham Young*, Feb. 23, 1847.

After the death of Joseph Smith, when it seemed that every trouble and calamity had come upon the Saints, Brigham Young, who was President of the Twelve, then the presiding quorum of the Church, sought the Lord to know what they should do and where they should lead the people for safety. While they were fasting and praying daily on this subject, President Young had a vision of Joseph Smith, who showed him the mountain we now call Ensign Peak, immediately north of Salt Lake City, and an ensign fell upon that peak, and Joseph said, "Build under the point where the colors fall, and you will prosper and have peace."

The Pioneers had no pilot or guide, none of them had ever been in the country or knew anything about it. However, they traveled under the direction of President Young until they reached this valley. When they entered it President Young pointed to that peak, and said, "I want to go there." He went up to the point and said, "This is Ensign Peak. Now, brethren, organize your exploring parties, so as to be safe from Indians; go and explore where you will, and you will come back every time and say, 'This is the best place.'" They accordingly started out exploring parties, and visited, what we now call Cache, Malad, Tooele and Utah valleys, and other parts the country in various directions, but all came back and declared this was the best spot.[196]

Brigham Young

Now I am going to tell a dream that I had, which I think is as applicable, to the people today—the 21st day of June, 1874, as when I had it. There were so many going to California, and going this way and that way, and they did not know what they wanted, and said I—"Stay here, we can raise our food here, I know it is a good stock country, a good sheep country, and as good a country for raising silk as there is in the world, and we shall raise some of the best of wheat." . . .

After much thought and reflection, and a good deal of praying and anxiety as to whether the people would be saved after all our trouble in being driven into the wilderness, I had a dream one

196. *Journal of Discourses*, 13:86; see also Elder George Albert Smith, in Conference Report, Apr. 1927, 46–50.

night, the second year after we came in here [Salt Lake City]. . . . I thought I had started and gone past the Hot Springs, which is about four miles north of this city. I was going after my goats. When I had gone round the point of the mountain by the Hot Springs, and had got about half a mile on the rise of ground beyond the Spring, whom should I meet but brother Joseph Smith. He had a wagon with no bed on, with bottom boards, and tents and camp equipage piled on. Somebody sat on the wagon driving the team. Behind the team I saw a great flock of sheep. I heard their bleating, and saw some goats among them. I looked at them and thought—"This is curious, brother Joseph has been up to Captain Brown's and got my goats."

There were men driving the sheep, and some of the sheep I should think were three and a half feet high, with large, fine beautiful white fleeces, and they looked so lovely and pure; others were of moderate size, and pure and white; and in fact there were sheep of all sizes, with fleeces clean, pure and white. Then I saw some that were dark and spotted, of all colors and sizes and kinds, and their fleeces were dirty, and they looked inferior; some of these were a pretty good size, but not as large as some of the large fine clean sheep, and altogether there was a multitude of them of all sizes and kinds, and goats of all colors, sizes and kinds mixed among them.

Joseph stopped the wagon, and the sheep kept rushing up until there was an immense herd. I looked in Joseph's eye, and laughed, just as I had many a time when he was alive, about some trifling thing or other, and said I—"Joseph, you have got the darndest flock of sheep I ever saw in my life; what are you going to do with them, what on earth are they for?" Joseph looked cunningly out of his eyes, just as he used to at times, and said he—"They are all good in their places."

When I awoke in the morning I did not find any fault with those who wanted to go to California; I said, "If they want to go let them go, and we will do all we can to save them; I have no more fault to find, the sheep and the goats will run together," but Joseph says, "They are all good in their places."[197]

197. *Deseret News,* July 1, 1874, 341.

Brigham Young

Related by Zina Young:

> I can't remember all who were there [at Brigham's deathbed], except that Uncle Joseph Young, and several of his wives, and many of his children were there. When he was placed upon the bed in front of the window he seemed to partially revive, and opening his eyes, he gazed upward, exclaiming: "Joseph! Joseph! Joseph!" and the divine look in his face seemed to indicate that he was communicating with his beloved friend, Joseph Smith, the Prophet. This name was the last word he uttered.[198]

Notes and Commentary

We learn at least two things about departed spirits from Alonzo Hinckley and Spencer W. Kimball's accounts: (1) departed spirits visit family members for various reasons, including to comfort, and (2) departed spirits often gather around those who are moments from death to usher them into the spirit world. Elder Hinckley's father appeared to him three times to explain that he was needed on the other side of the veil. Brother Hinckley said that they spoke "face to face with one another." Shortly after these three visits, Elder Hinckley died.

Regarding family members and friends in the spirit world, President Joseph F. Smith taught, "Our fathers and mothers, brothers, sisters and friends who have passed away from this earth, having been faithful, and worthy to enjoy these rights and privileges, may have a mission given them to visit their relatives and friends upon the earth again, bring from the divine presence messages of love, of warning, or reproof and instruction, to those whom they had learned to love in the flesh."[199] Elder George Q. Cannon told the Saints not to be fearful of death. "How delightful it is," Cannon taught, "to contemplate the departure of those who have been faithful. . . . Holy angels are around their bedside to administer unto them. The Spirit of God rests down upon them, and His messengers are near them to introduce them to

---

198. Susa Young Gates, *The Life Story of Brigham Young* (The MacMillan Company, 1930), 362.

199. Joseph F. Smith, *Gospel Doctrine* (Deseret Book, 1939), 435–36.

those who are on the other side of the veil. . . . When death comes, Satan's power ceases."[200]

Another recurring theme—not only in this chapter but throughout the book—is the nature of heavenly personages. We may apply the term "angel" to different kinds of heavenly beings. Some angels are spirits who have not yet been born to earthly parents and therefore do not have physical bodies. Other angels have previously lived on the earth but have not been resurrected. A third kind of angel is one who has departed this life and has been resurrected and, therefore, has a physical body of flesh and bone.[201]

Elder Parley P. Pratt explained that men, angels, and gods are all of the same race, species, and family; however, "the great distinguishing difference between one portion of this race and another consists in the varied grades of intelligence and purity, and also in the variety of spheres occupied by each." He continued:

> An immortal man, possessing a perfect organization of spirit, flesh, and bones, and perfected in his attributes, in all the fullness of celestial glory, is called a God. An immortal man, in progress of perfection, or quickened with a lesser degree of glory, is called an angel. An immortal spirit of man, not united with a fleshly tabernacle, is called a spirit. An immortal man, clothed with a mortal tabernacle, is called a man. It may then consistently enough be said, that there are, in a subordinate sense, a plurality of Gods.[202]

Brigham Young taught that God "is not everywhere in person" but that His presence and influence are felt and seen everywhere through the Holy Spirit and angels, who are "authorized to act in His name."[203] Elder Orson Hyde similarly explained that God "makes His angels ministering spirits, and they are sent forth to minister for them who shall be heirs of salvation. The Lord is everywhere present by His ministering angels, just like any other ruler, monarch or king, who has ministers everywhere throughout His dominions; and God's ministers

---

200. George Q. Cannon, *Gospel Truth: Discourses and Writings of President George Q. Cannon*, ed. Jerreld L. Newquist (Deseret Book, 1987), 61.

201. For more on angels, see Oscar W. McConkie, *Angels* (Deseret Book, 1997).

202. Parley P. Pratt, *Key to the Science of Theology* (Deseret Book, 1965), 41.

203. *Journal of Discourses*, 12:245.

are everywhere."[204] Elder Heber C. Kimball stated that some people in the Church "think that the Almighty does not see their doings, but *if He does not*, the angels and ministering spirits do. They see you and your works, and I have no doubt but they occasionally communicate your conduct to the Father, or to the Son, or to Joseph, or to Peter, or to someone who holds the keys in connection with them."[205]

When angels reveal themselves to mortal men, they may not always appear as glorious personages but rather as ordinary men. Brigham Young taught, "When the Lord sends an angel to visit men, He gives him power and authority to appear to the people as a man, and not as an angel in his glory. . . . We may have seen the Lord and angels many times, and did not know it."[206] Paul also taught this doctrine to the early Saints: "Be not forgetful to entertain strangers: for thereby some have entertained angels unawares" (Hebrews 13:2). This is precisely what happened to the Prophet Joseph, Oliver Cowdery, and David Whitmer in 1829. They saw and talked with Moroni without immediately knowing who he was. Also, a few of David's family members saw three men working in David's field while he was away.[207]

A frequently asked question regarding angels is whether every person on earth has a guardian angel assigned to them. Concerning this doctrine, Elder Bruce R. McConkie taught, "There is an old and false sectarian tradition to the effect that all men—or if not that, at least the righteous—have guardian angels. . . . It is true that there are many specific instances in which angels, by special assignment, have performed particular works whereby faithful people have been guarded and preserved . . . but to suppose that either all men or all righteous men have heavenly beings acting as guardians for them runs counter to the basic revealed facts relative to the manner in which the Lord exercises his benevolent watchfulness over his mortal children. The fact that angels have intervened to preserve someone in a particular

---

204. *Journal of Discourses*, 2:64–65.

205. *Journal of Discourses*, 3:229.

206. *Journal of Discourses*, 11:41.

207. See Trevan G. Hatch, *Visions, Manifestations, and Miracles of the Restoration* (Granite Publishing, 2008), 189–90, 224–25.

peril does not establish the fact that all people generally have guardian angels."[208]

Elder John A. Widtsoe also explained that angels would often guard us against accidents and harm or even temptation and sin; however, "the common belief that to every person born into the world is assigned a guardian angel to be with that person constantly, is not supported by available evidence. . . . An angel may be a guardian angel though he come only as assigned to give us special help. In fact, the constant presence of the Holy Ghost would seem to make such a constant, angelic companionship unnecessary."[209] Elder George Q. Cannon—although not specifically stating that every person has a guardian angel assigned to them—taught that the Lord has assigned many angels to watch over His people: "There is not one of us that He has not given His angels charge concerning. We may be insignificant and contemptible in our own eyes and in the eyes of others, but the truth remains that we are the children of God and that He has actually given His angels—invisible beings of power and might—charge concerning us, and they watch over us and have us in their keeping."[210]

---

208. Bruce R. McConkie, *Mormon Doctrine* (Bookcraft, 1966), 341.

209. Widtsoe, *Evidences and Reconciliations*, 402–3.

210. George Q. Cannon, *Gospel Truth*, 2.

Chapter Six

Visions of the Afterlife

The scriptures tell us very little about the afterlife. There are reasons why the Lord has not revealed more. One is that He wants His children to focus on this life and not become too preoccupied with the next life. Joseph Smith supposedly taught, at least according to the diaries of one of the early Saints, that "the Lord in his wisdom had implanted the fear of death in every person that they might cling to life and thus accomplish the designs of the creator."[211]

Perhaps another reason why the Lord does not reveal more about the afterlife is that we are not ready to receive such information. Joseph Smith, referring to the vision that he and Sidney Rigdon saw of the degrees of glory in 1832, said, "I could explain a hundred fold more than I ever have of the glories of the kingdoms manifested to me in the vision, were I permitted, and were the people prepared to receive them."[212] Elder Orson Pratt stated that Joseph and Sidney were commanded to record only "some of these things" that they saw and were "strictly commanded" not to record the rest of what they beheld,

---

211. A. Karl Larson and Katharine Miles Larson, *Diary of Charles Lowell Walker*, 2 vols. (Utah State University Press, 1980), 1:595–96.

212. *History of the Church*, 5:402.

"as the world was not worthy to receive them. Neither was the Church at that time prepared to receive a full knowledge concerning these things"[213]

The Lord, however, has revealed some things pertaining to the spirit world and the degrees of glory. The following accounts, coupled with modern revelations and statements from ancient and modern prophets, provide the Latter-day Saints with more information concerning the afterlife.

Accounts of the Prophets

Melvin J. Ballard

> I lost a son six years of age, and I saw him a man in the spirit world after his death, and I saw how he had exercised his own freedom of choice and would obtain of his own will and volition a companionship, and in due time to him, and all those who are worthy of it, shall come all of the blessings and sealing privileges of the house of the Lord. Do not worry over it. They are safe; they are all right.[214]

Jedediah M. Grant

Related by Elder Heber C. Kimball:

> I went to see him [Jedediah M. Grant] one day last week, and he reached out his hand and shook hands with me; he could not speak, but he shook hands warmly with me. I felt for him, and wanted to raise him up, and to have him stay and help us whip the devils and bring to pass righteousness. Why? Because he was valiant, and I loved him. He was a great help to us, and you would be, if you were as valiant as he was, which you can be through faithfulness and obedience. I laid my hands upon him and blessed him, and asked God to strengthen his lungs that he might be easier, and in two or three minutes he raised himself up and talked for about an hour as busily as he could, telling me what he had seen and what

---

213. *Journal of Discourses*, 20:70.

214. Bryant S. Hinckley, *Sermons and Missionary Services of Melvin J. Ballard* (Deseret Book, 1949), 260.

he understood, until I was afraid he would weary himself, when I arose and left him.

He said to me, "brother Heber, I have been into the spirit world two nights in succession, and, of all the dreads that ever came across me, the worst was to have to again return to my body, though I had to do it." "But O," says he, "the order and government that were there! When in the spirit world, I saw the order of righteous men and women; beheld them organized in their several grades, and there appeared to be no obstruction to my vision; I could see every man and woman in their grade and order. I looked to see whether there was any disorder there, but there was none; neither could I see any death nor any darkness, disorder or confusion." He said that the people he there saw were organized in family capacities; and when he looked at them he saw grade after grade, and all were organized and in perfect harmony. He would mention one item after another and say, "Why, it is just as brother Brigham says it is; it is just as he has told us many a time."

That is a testimony as to the truth of what brother Brigham teaches us, and I know it is true, from what little light I have. He saw the righteous gathered together in the spirit world, and there were no wicked spirits among them. He saw his wife; she was the first person that came to him. He saw many that he knew, but did not have conversation with any except his wife Caroline. She came to him, and he said that she looked beautiful and had their little child, that died on the Plains, in her arms, and said, "Mr. Grant, here is little Margaret; you know that the wolves ate her up, but it did not hurt her; here she is all right."

"To my astonishment," he said, "when I looked at families there was a deficiency in some, there was a lack, for I saw families that would not be permitted to come and dwell together, because they had not honored their calling here." He asked his wife Caroline where Joseph and Hyrum and Father Smith and others were; she replied, "they have gone away ahead, to perform and transact business for us." The same as when brother Brigham and his brethren left Winter Quarters and came here to search out a home; they came to find a location for their brethren.

He also spoke of the buildings he saw there, remarking that the Lord gave Solomon wisdom and poured gold and silver into his hands that he might display his skill and ability, and said that the temple erected by Solomon was much inferior to the most ordinary buildings he saw in the spirit world. In regard to gardens, says brother Grant, "I have seen good gardens on this earth, but I never saw any to compare with those that were there. I saw flowers of numerous kinds, and some with from fifty to a hundred different colored flowers growing upon one stalk." We have many kinds of flowers on the earth, and I suppose those very articles came from heaven, or they would not be here.

After mentioning the things that he had seen, he spoke of how much he disliked to return and resume his body, after having seen the beauty and glory of the spirit world, where the righteous spirits are gathered together.[215]

George Albert Smith

A number of years ago I was seriously ill, in fact, I think everyone gave me up but my wife. With my family I went to St. George, Utah, to see if it would improve my health. We went as far as we could by train, and then continued the journey in a wagon, in the bottom of which a bed had been made for me. In St. George we arranged for a tent for my health and comfort, with a built-in floor raised about a foot above the ground, and we could roll up the south side of the tent to make the sunshine and fresh air available. I became so weak as to be scarcely able to move. It was a slow and exhausting effort for me even to turn over in bed.

One day, under these conditions, I lost consciousness of my surroundings and thought I had passed to the Other Side. I found myself standing with my back to a large and beautiful lake, facing a great forest of trees. There was no one in sight, and there was no boat upon the lake or any other visible means to indicate how I might have arrived there. I realized, or seemed to realize, that I had finished my work in mortality and had gone home. I began to look around, to see if I could not find someone. There was no evidence of anyone living there, just those great, beautiful trees in front of me and the wonderful lake behind me.

I began to explore, and soon I found a trail through the woods which seemed to have been used very little, and which was almost

215. *Journal of Discourses*, 4:135–36.

obscured by grass. I followed this trail, and after I had walked for some time and had traveled a considerable distance through the forest, I saw a man coming towards me. I became aware that he was a very large man, and I hurried my steps to reach him, because I recognized him as my grandfather. In mortality he weighed over three hundred pounds, so you may know he was a large man. I remember how happy I was to see him coming. I had been given his name and had always been proud of it.

When Grandfather came within a few feet of me, he stopped. His stopping was an invitation for me to stop. Then—and this I would like the boys and girls and young people never to forget—he looked at me very earnestly and said: "I would like to know what you have done with my name." Everything I had ever done passed before me as though it were a flying picture on a screen—everything I had done. Quickly this vivid retrospect came down to the very time I was standing there. My whole life had passed before me. I smiled and looked at my grandfather and said: "I have never done anything with your name of which you need be ashamed."

He stepped forward and took me in his arms, and as he did so, I became conscious again of my earthly surroundings. My pillow was as wet as though water had been poured on it—wet with tears of gratitude that I could answer unashamed.[216]

Joseph F. Smith

On the third of October, in the year nineteen hundred and eighteen, I sat in my room pondering over the scriptures; And reflecting upon the great atoning sacrifice that was made by the Son of God, for the redemption of the world; And the great and wonderful love made manifest by the Father and the Son in the coming of the Redeemer into the world; That through his atonement, and by obedience to the principles of the gospel, mankind might be saved. While I was thus engaged, my mind reverted to the writings of the apostle Peter, to the primitive saints scattered abroad throughout Pontus, Galatia, Cappadocia, and other parts of Asia, where the gospel had been preached after the crucifixion of the Lord. I

---

216. George Albert Smith, *Sharing the Gospel with Others*, comp. Preston Nibley (Deseret Book, 1949), 110–12.

opened the Bible and read the third and fourth chapters of the first epistle of Peter, and as I read I was greatly impressed, more than I had ever been before, with the following passages:

"For Christ also hath once suffered for sins, the just for the unjust, that he might bring us to God, being put to death in the flesh, but quickened by the Spirit: By which also he went and preached unto the spirits in prison; Which sometime were disobedient, when once the longsuffering of God waited in the days of Noah, while the ark was a preparing, wherein few, that is, eight souls were saved by water" (1 Peter 3:18–20). "For for this cause was the gospel preached also to them that are dead, that they might be judged according to men in the flesh, but live according to God in the spirit" (1 Peter 4:6).

As I pondered over these things which are written, the eyes of my understanding were opened, and the Spirit of the Lord rested upon me, and I saw the hosts of the dead, both small and great. And there were gathered together in one place an innumerable company of the spirits of the just, who had been faithful in the testimony of Jesus while they lived in mortality; And who had offered sacrifice in the similitude of the great sacrifice of the Son of God, and had suffered tribulation in their Redeemer's name.

All these had departed the mortal life, firm in the hope of a glorious resurrection, through the grace of God the Father and his Only Begotten Son, Jesus Christ. I beheld that they were filled with joy and gladness, and were rejoicing together because the day of their deliverance was at hand. They were assembled awaiting the advent of the Son of God into the spirit world, to declare their redemption from the bands of death. Their sleeping dust was to be restored unto its perfect frame, bone to his bone, and the sinews and the flesh upon them, the spirit and the body to be united never again to be divided, that they might receive a fullness of joy.

While this vast multitude waited and conversed, rejoicing in the hour of their deliverance from the chains of death, the Son of God appeared, declaring liberty to the captives who had been faithful; And there he preached to them the everlasting gospel, the doctrine of the resurrection and the redemption of mankind from the fall, and from individual sins on conditions of repentance. But unto the wicked he did not go, and among the ungodly and the unrepentant who had defiled themselves while in the flesh, his voice was not raised; Neither did the rebellious who rejected the testimonies and the warnings of the ancient prophets behold his presence, nor look upon his face. Where these were, darkness reigned, but among the righteous there was peace; And the saints rejoiced in their redemption, and bowed the knee and acknowledged the Son of God as their Redeemer and Deliverer from death and the chains of hell. Their countenances shone, and the radiance from the presence of the Lord rested upon them, and they sang praises unto his holy name.

I marveled, for I understood that the Savior spent about three years in his ministry among the Jews and those of the house of Israel, endeavoring to teach them the everlasting gospel and call them unto repentance; And yet, notwithstanding his mighty works, and miracles, and proclamation of the truth, in great power and authority, there were but few who hearkened to his voice, and rejoiced in his presence, and received salvation at his hands. But his ministry among those who were dead was limited to the brief time intervening between the crucifixion and his resurrection; And I wondered at the words of Peter—wherein he said that the Son of God preached unto the spirits in prison, who sometime were disobedient, when once the longsuffering of God waited in the days of Noah—and how it was possible for him to preach to those spirits and perform the necessary labor among them in so short a time.

And as I wondered, my eyes were opened, and my understanding quickened, and I perceived that the Lord went not in person among the wicked and the disobedient who had rejected the truth, to teach them; But behold, from among the righteous, he organized his forces and appointed messengers, clothed with power and authority, and commissioned them to go forth and carry the light of the gospel to them that were in darkness, even to all the spirits of men; and thus was the gospel preached to the dead.

And the chosen messengers went forth to declare the acceptable day of the Lord and proclaim liberty to the captives who were bound, even unto all who would repent of their sins and receive the gospel. Thus was the gospel preached to those who had died in their sins, without a knowledge of the truth, or in transgression, having rejected the prophets. These were taught faith in God, repentance from sin, vicarious baptism for the remission of sins, the gift of the Holy Ghost by the laying on of hands, And all other principles of the gospel that were necessary for them to know in order to qualify themselves that they might be judged according to men in the flesh, but live according to God in the spirit.

And so it was made known among the dead, both small and great, the unrighteous as well as the faithful, that redemption had been wrought through the sacrifice of the Son of God upon the cross. Thus was it made known that our Redeemer spent his time during his sojourn in the world of spirits, instructing and preparing the faithful spirits of the prophets who had testified of him in the flesh; That they might carry the message of redemption unto all the dead, unto whom he could not go personally, because of their rebellion and transgression, that they through the ministration of his servants might also hear his words.

Among the great and mighty ones who were assembled in this vast congregation of the righteous were Father Adam, the Ancient of Days and father of all, And our glorious Mother Eve, with many of her faithful daughters who had lived through the ages and worshiped the true and living God. Abel, the first martyr, was there, and his brother Seth, one of the mighty ones, who was in the express image of his father, Adam.

Noah, who gave warning of the flood; Shem, the great high priest; Abraham, the father of the faithful; Isaac, Jacob, and Moses, the great law-giver of Israel; And Isaiah, who declared by prophecy that the Redeemer was anointed to bind up the broken-hearted, to proclaim liberty to the captives, and the opening of the prison to them that were bound, were also there. Moreover, Ezekiel, who was shown in vision the great valley of dry bones, which were to be clothed upon with flesh, to come forth again in the resurrection of the dead, living souls; Daniel, who foresaw and foretold the establishment of the kingdom of God in the latter days, never again to be destroyed nor given to other people;

Elias, who was with Moses on the Mount of Transfiguration; And Malachi, the prophet who testified of the coming of Elijah—of whom also Moroni spake to the Prophet Joseph Smith, declaring that he should come before the ushering in of the great and dreadful day of the Lord—were also there. The Prophet Elijah was to plant in the hearts of the children the promises made to their fathers, Foreshadowing the great work to be done in the temples of the Lord in the dispensation of the fullness of times, for the redemption of the dead, and the sealing of the children to their parents, lest the whole earth be smitten with a curse and utterly wasted at his coming.

All these and many more, even the prophets who dwelt among the Nephites and testified of the coming of the Son of God, mingled in the vast assembly and waited for their deliverance, for the dead had looked upon the long absence of their spirits from their bodies as a bondage. These the Lord taught, and gave them power to come forth, after his resurrection from the dead, to enter into his Father's kingdom, there to be crowned with immortality and eternal life, And continue thenceforth their labor as had been promised by the Lord, and be partakers of all blessings which were held in reserve for them that love him.

The Prophet Joseph Smith, and my father, Hyrum Smith, Brigham Young, John Taylor, Wilford Woodruff, and other choice spirits who were reserved to come forth in the fullness of times to take part in laying the foundations of the great latter-day work, including the building of the temples and the performance of ordinances therein for the redemption of the dead, were also in the spirit world. I observed that they were also among the noble and great ones who were chosen in the beginning to be rulers in the Church of God. Even before they were born, they, with many others, received their first lessons in the world of spirits and were prepared to come forth in the due time of the Lord to labor in his vineyard for the salvation of the souls of men.

I beheld that the faithful elders of this dispensation, when they depart from mortal life, continue their labors in the preaching of the gospel of repentance and redemption, through the sacrifice of the Only Begotten Son of God, among those who are in darkness and under the bondage of sin in the great world of the spirits of the dead. The dead who repent will be redeemed, through obedience to the ordinances of the house of God, And after they have paid the penalty of their transgressions, and are washed clean, shall receive a reward according to their works, for they are heirs of salvation.

Thus was the vision of the redemption of the dead revealed to me, and I bear record, and I know that this record is true, through the blessing of our Lord and Savior, Jesus Christ, even so. Amen.[217]

---

217. *Improvement Era* 22 (Dec. 1918): 166–70; see also Doctrine and Covenants 138.

Joseph Smith Jr. and Sidney Rigdon

> Upon my return from Amherst Conference, I [Joseph Smith] resumed the translation of the Scriptures. From sundry revelations which had been received, it was apparent that many important points touching the salvation of men, had been taken from the Bible, or lost before it was compiled. It appeared from what truths were left, that if God rewarded every one according to the deeds done in the body the term "Heaven" as intended for the Saints' eternal home, must include more kingdoms than one. Accordingly, on the 16th of February, 1832, while translating St. John's Gospel, myself and Elder Rigdon saw the following vision [see D&C 76].[218]

Philo Dibble, who was present during the vision, recorded his experience:

> The vision which is recorded in the book of Doctrine and Covenants was given at the house of Father Johnson, in Hyrum, Ohio, and during the time that Joseph and Sidney were in the spirit and saw the heavens open, there were other men in the room, perhaps twelve, among whom I was one during a part of the time—probably two-thirds of the time—I saw the glory and felt the power, but did not see the vision. . . . Joseph would, at intervals, say: "What do I see?" as one might say while looking out the window and Beholding what all in the room could not see. Then he would relate what he had seen or what he was looking at. Then Sidney replied, "I see the same." Presently Sidney would say: "What do I see?" and would repeat what he had seen or was seeing, and Joseph would reply, "I see the same."
>
> This manner of conversation was repeated at short intervals to the end of the vision, and during the whole time not a word was spoken by any other person. Not a sound nor motion was made by anyone but Joseph and Sidney, and it seemed to me that they never moved a joint or limb during the time I was there, which I think was over an hour, and to the end of the vision. Joseph sat firmly and calmly all the time in the midst of a magnificent glory, but Sidney

218. *History of the Church*, 1:245.

sat limp and pale, apparently as limber as a rag, observing which, Joseph remarked, smilingly, "Sidney is not used to it as I am."[219]

Joseph Smith Jr.

[On January 21, 1836, at] about three o'clock, p.m., I dismissed the school, and the Presidency retired to the attic story of the printing office, where we attended the ordinance of washing our bodies in pure water. We also perfumed our bodies and our heads in the name of the Lord. At early candlelight I met with the Presidency at the west schoolroom, in the Temple, to attend to the ordinance of anointing our heads with holy oil; also the Councils of Kirtland and Zion met in the two adjoining rooms, and waited in prayer while we attended to the ordinance. I took the oil in my left hand, Father Smith being seated before me, and the remainder of the Presidency encircled him round about. We then stretched our right hands towards heaven, and blessed the oil, and consecrated it in the name of Jesus Christ.

We then laid our hands upon our aged Father Smith, and invoked the blessings of heaven. I then anointed his head with the consecrated oil, and sealed many blessings upon him. The Presidency then in turn laid their hands upon his head, beginning at the oldest, until they had all laid their hands upon him, and pronounced such blessings upon his head, as the Lord put into their hearts, all blessing him to be our Patriarch, to anoint our heads, and attend to all duties that pertain to that office. The Presidency then took the seat in their turn, according to their age, beginning at the oldest, and received their anointing and blessing under the hands of Father Smith. And in my turn, my father anointed my head, and sealed upon me the blessings of Moses, to lead Israel in the latter days, even as Moses led him in days of old; also the blessings of Abraham, Isaac and Jacob. All of the Presidency laid their hands upon me, and pronounced upon my head many prophecies and blessings, many of which I shall not notice at this time. But as Paul said, so say I, let us come to visions and revelations.

The heavens were opened upon us, and I beheld the celestial kingdom of God, and the glory thereof, whether in the body or

---

219. *Juvenile Instructor* 27 (May 15, 1892): 303–4.

out I cannot tell. I saw the transcendent beauty of the gate through which the heirs of that kingdom will enter, which was like unto circling flames of fire; also the blazing throne of God, whereon was seated the Father and the Son. I saw the beautiful streets of that kingdom, which had the appearance of being paved with gold. I saw Fathers Adam and Abraham, and my father and mother, my brother, Alvin, that has long since slept, and marvelled how it was that he had obtained an inheritance in that kingdom, seeing that he had departed this life before the Lord had set His hand to gather Israel the second time, and had not been baptized for the remission of sins.[220]

Lorenzo Snow

In my sickness [May 26, 1846] I went through in my mind the most singular scenes that any man ever did. My family generally believed that I was not in my right mind. But the scenes through which my spirit travelled are yet fresh in my memory as though they occurred but yesterday. And when my people supposed me in the greatest pain and danger I am conscious of having a great many spiritual exercises sometimes partaking of the most acute suffering that heart can conceive and others the most rapturous enjoyment that heart ever felt or imagination ever conceived.

I suppose at first I must have been left in the hands of an evil spirit, in fact I was administered to upon this supposition. I was led into the full and perfect conviction that I was entirely a hopeless case in reference to salvation, that eternities, upon eternities must pass and still I saw my case would remain the same. I saw the whole world rejoicing in all the powers and glories of salvation without the slightest beam of hope on my part, but doomed to a separation from my friends and family, all I loved most here, to eternity upon eternity. I shudder even now at the remembrance of the torments and agony of my feelings. No tongue can describe them or imagination conceive. Those who were attending me at that time describe me as being in a condition of body. I remained several hours refusing to speak. My body was cool, and my eyes and countenance

---

220. *History of the Church*, 2:379–80.

denoted extreme suffering. After this scene ended I entered another of an opposite character.

My spirit seems to have left the world and introduced into that of Kolob. I heard a voice calling me by name saying "he is worthy, he is worthy, take away his filthy garments." My clothes were then taken off piece by piece and a voice said "let him be clothed, let him be clothed." Immediately I found a celestial body gradually growing upon me until at length I found myself crowned with all its glory and power. The ecstasy of joy I now experienced no man can tell, pen cannot describe it. I conversed familiarly with Joseph, Father Smith and others, and mingled in the society of the Holy One. I saw my family all saved and observed the dispensations of God with mankind until at last a perfect redemption was effected, though great was the sufferings of the wicked, especially those that had persecuted the saints. My spirit must have remained I should judge for days enjoying the scenes of eternal happiness.[221]

Wilford Woodruff

I dreamed last night [December 30, 1882] that Captain William H. Hooper was dead. I told my family this morning that when I heard from him I should hear that he was dead. Later, Brother Jacques informed me at the Historian's office that the captain died at twenty minutes past eight. I saw Captain Hooper in the spirit world in my dream. I saw a few of the mansions in the Celestial Kingdom of God which were composed of beautiful stones and of materials that were as real as anything on earth, and that the best architects in heaven were employed in the construction of these buildings.[222]

Notes and Commentary

Numerous Saints have inquired about the conditions of the spirit world. It behooves us to examine several of those inquiries in light of

---

221. "The Iowa Journal of Lorenzo Snow," edited and with an introduction by Maureen Ursenbach Beecher, *BYU Studies* 24, no. 2 (1984): 235.

222. Matthias F. Cowley, *Wilford Woodruff, His Life and Labors* (Deseret News, 1909), 542–43.

the aforementioned accounts of the prophets, their teachings, and the scriptures. Many misconceptions about the spirit world exist among the Latter-day Saints and certainly among people of other faiths; however, the restored gospel clarifies several of these misconceptions.

Where Is the Spirit World?

When thinking about the "spirit world"—or the place where spirits reside after death until judgment—our minds usually take us to some place way out in the heavens. But is the spirit world really in heaven? Several prophets have addressed this question. Brigham Young taught that the spirit world "is not beyond the sun, but is on this earth that was organized for the people that have lived and that do and will live upon it."[223] Elder Parley P. Pratt similarly explained that the spirit world "is here on the very planet where we were born; or, in other words, the earth." Elder Pratt also stated that every planet has its "inward or spiritual spheres, as well as their outward, or temporal. The one is peopled by temporal tabernacles, and the other by spirits."[224] Throughout this book, we have seen numerous occasions when the prophets have had the veil temporarily removed from their eyes, which permitted them to see spirits. These spirits do not travel between heaven and earth, but dwell here among the living.

Are "Spirit Prison" and "Spirit Paradise" Separate Places Within the Spirit World?

According to the prophets, spirit prison and spirit paradise are the same. Joseph Smith explained that "Hades, the Greek, or Sheol, the Hebrew . . . mean a world of spirits. Hades, Sheol, paradise, spirits in prison, are all one: it is a world of spirits."[225] Brigham Young taught, "Where are the spirits of the ungodly? They are in prison. Where are the spirits of the righteous, the Prophets, and the Apostles? They are in prison, brethren; that is where they are. . . . I know it is a startling idea to say that the Prophet and the persecutor of the Prophet, all go to prison together . . . but they have not got their bodies yet, conse-

---

223. *Journal of Discourses*, 3:372.

224. Parley P. Pratt, *Key to the Science of Theology* (Deseret Book, 1965), 126–27.

225. *Teachings of the Prophet Joseph Smith* (Deseret Book, 1976), 309–10.

quently they are in prison."[226] President Young reminded the Saints of an important doctrine, which is that no man is truly happy when he is without a physical body. One reason why Satan is utterly miserable, as mentioned earlier, is that he does not have a physical body.

As shown above, when President Joseph F. Smith saw the spirit world in vision, he understood that "the dead had looked upon the long absence of their spirits from their bodies as a bondage" (Doctrine and Covenants 138:50). In Moses we read that Enoch received a vision of the spirit world, in which he saw that all the "spirits" who "were in *prison* came forth, and stood on the right hand of God; and the remainder were reserved in chains of darkness until the judgment of the great day" (Moses 7:57).

If All Spirits Are Together, Do Righteous and Wicked Spirits Associate with Each Other?

The wicked spirits do not mingle with righteous spirits unless they are being taught the gospel. President Joseph F. Smith learned from his vision that when Jesus visited the spirit world, He instructed and prepared "the faithful spirits of the prophets who had testified of him in the flesh; That they might carry the message of redemption unto all the dead, unto *whom he could not go personally, because of their rebellion and transgression*, that they through the ministration of his servants might also hear his words" (Doctrine and Covenants 138:36–37). In Elder Jedediah M. Grant's vision, he "saw the righteous gathered together in the spirit world, and there were no wicked spirits among them."[227] Elder Heber C. Kimball taught, "I ask you, brethren and sisters, if you expect to go into heaven, if you do not do his will on earth as it is done in heaven? Can those persons who pursue a course of carelessness, neglect of duty, and disobedience, when they depart from this life, expect that their spirits will associate with the spirits of the righteous in the spirit world? I do not expect it, and when you depart from this state of existence, you will find it out for yourselves."[228]

---

226. *Journal of Discourses*, 3:95.

227. *Journal of Discourses*, 4:135–36.

228. *Journal of Discourses*, 2:150.

Do Spirits Reside with God the Father in the Spirit World?

Postmortal spirits do not reside with Heavenly Father because he does not dwell in the spirit world—which is on this earth—but in "Heaven," where the Grand Council took place (see Abraham 3). One of Alma's statements concerning the spirit world confuses some people regarding this issue. Alma explained that the "spirits of all men, as soon as they are departed from this mortal body, yea, the spirits of all men, whether they be good or evil, are taken home to that God who gave them life" (Alma 40:11). Alma was speaking in general terms. He did not mean to imply that God the Father dwells among the spirits in the spirit world, as he later counseled his son: "There is a space between death and the resurrection of the body, and a state of the soul in happiness or in misery until the time which is appointed of God that the dead shall come forth, and be reunited, both soul and body, and be brought to stand before God, and be judged according to their works" (Alma 40:21).

Referring to Alma's statement that "the spirits of all men . . . are taken home to that God who gave them life," Elder George Q. Cannon explained, "He [Alma] evidently uses that phrase in a qualified sense. . . . Alma says plainly that the spirits of the righteous go into a state of happiness, etc. He says the spirits of the wicked are cast into outer darkness, etc. Now, then, how can those spirits who are cast into outer darkness be in the personal presence of God? God does not dwell where they are, and they certainly do not go where He is. And yet He is there by His Spirit and by His power."[229]

Do Pre-Born Spirits and Postmortal Spirits Reside in the Same Place and Intermingle with One Another?

Abraham explains that pre-born spirits dwell with God in Kolob, not in the spirit world that is on this earth (see Abraham 3). God "stood in the midst" of all His spirit children, many of whom were the "noble and great ones" that would eventually lead his people on earth (see verses 22–23). Joseph Smith indicated in a poem to William W.

229. George Q. Cannon, *Gospel Truth: Discourses and Writings of President George Q. Cannon*, comp. Jerreld L. Newquist (Deseret Book, 1987), 58.

Phelps that pre-born spirits come "from the council in Kolob" to their "time on the earth."[230]

The scriptures also teach that those who did not hear the gospel while in mortality must hear it in the spirit world and that they must also "be judged according to men in the flesh" (1 Peter 4:6; Doctrine and Covenants 138:32–34). According to these passages, those who reside in the spirit world—like the living—are not permitted to mingle with pre-born spirits. If they could, then their situation would not be similar to "men in the flesh," and faith would not be a factor. By conversing and mingling with pre-born spirits, they would instantly know the truth concerning several doctrines, such as premortal life, the reality of Jehovah and Satan (their brothers), the Council in Heaven, and the purposes of mortality.

Can Our Deceased Friends and Family Members See Everything We're Doing?

In speaking of the duties and capabilities of heavenly beings, President Brigham Young taught that "when an angel is appointed to perform a duty, to go to the earth to preach the Gospel, or to do anything for the advancement of his Father's kingdom in any part of the great domain of heaven, the *vision of that angel is opened to see and understand the magnitude of the work* that is expected of him to perform, and the grand results which will grow out of it."[231] Elder Charles W. Penrose more specifically stated, "As the living are not in their mortal condition, able to see and converse with the dead, so it is rational to believe, the inhabitants of the spiritual domain are, in their normal condition, shut out from intercourse with men in the flesh. By permission of the Lord, persons on either side of the veil may be manifest to those on the other, but this will certainly be by law and according to the order which God has established."[232]

The experience of Heber Q. Hale, president of the Boise Stake, is worth noting here. In 1920, President Hale recorded a vision that

---

230. *Times and Seasons* 4, no. 6 (Feb. 1, 1843): 85.

231. *Journal of Discourses*, 11:16.

232. Charles W. Penrose, *Masterpieces of Latter-day Saint Leaders* (Deseret Book, 1953), 66–67.

he saw of the spirit world. Brother Hale mentioned that immediately prior to his spirit returning to his body, "[I] beheld the whole world, as if it were but a panorama passing before my eyes. Then there came to me the unmistakable impression that *this earth and scenes and persons upon it are open to the vision of the spirits only when special permission is given, or when they are assigned to special service here.*"[233]

Do Heavenly Beings of the Spirit World Have the Same Physical and Mental Capabilities as Those in Mortality?

According to the prophets, the physical and mental capabilities are greatly enhanced upon passing from this life to the spirit world. It seems that when the mortal body and spirit are separated, the spirit is less restricted in what it can perform and accomplish. Brigham Young taught, for example, "It is not encumbered with this clog of dirt we are carrying around here so that when we advance in years we have to be stubbing along and to be careful lest we fall down. We see our youth, even, frequently stubbing their toes and falling down. But yonder, how different! They move with ease and like lightning. If we want to visit Jerusalem . . . there we are, looking at its streets. . . . Or we may visit any city we please that exists upon its surface. If we wish to understand how they are living here on these western islands, or in China, we are there."[234] Brigham similarly taught at the funeral of Brother Daniel Spencer, "As quickly as the spirit is unlocked from this house of clay, it is free to travel with lightning speed to any planet, or fixed star, or to the uttermost part of the earth, or to the depths of the sea, according to the will of Him who dictates."[235] Elder Parley P. Pratt also expounded upon the spirit traveling with ease: "They pass from one world to another with more ease, and in less time than we pass from one city to another. They have not a single attribute which

---

233. Heber Q. Hale, "A Heavenly Manifestation," unpublished manuscript, L. Tom Perry Special Collections Library, Harold B. Lee Library, Brigham Young University, Provo, Utah.

234. *Journal of Discourses*, 14:232.

235. *Journal of Discourses*, 13:77.

man has not. But their attributes are more matured, or more developed, than the attributes of men in this present sphere of existence."[236]

Not only do spirits have the ability to move about with ease, but their ability to learn greatly increases. Without the restrictions placed upon an individual clothed with a mortal body, spirits can learn more effectively without losing focus, getting bored, or falling asleep. Elder Orson Pratt taught, "I believe we shall be freed, in the next world, in a great measure, from these narrow, contracted methods of thinking. Instead of thinking in one channel, and following up one certain course of reasoning to find a certain truth, knowledge will rush in from all quarters; it will come in like the light which flows from the sun, penetrating every part, informing the spirit, and giving understanding concerning ten thousand things at the same time; and the mind will be capable of receiving and retaining all."[237] Brigham Young also stated that spirits can learn "a thousand times more in a thousand times less time."[238] Our increased ability to learn in the spirit world, however, does not eradicate the need to exercise faith. Every spirit must believe the doctrine.

Elder George Q. Cannon propounded the possibility that not all spirits will be able to learn with ease in the spirit world, but only those who are faithful and who were diligent in seeking knowledge during mortality:

> Those who have made good use of their opportunities here will have the benefit of their diligence and faithfulness there. Those who have been careless and indifferent and have not acquired knowledge and power through the exercise of faith will find themselves lacking there. We will have to work there to grow and to make progress just as we have here, though the facilities will be better there than they are here. If we can only pass into the paradise of God without Satan having any power over us, our condition will be a very happy one. But we shall find that knowledge and power will not come to us there as the rain that falls upon us, without any effort of ours to acquire them. We shall have to exercise ourselves and exert our

---

236. Parley P. Pratt, *Science of Theology*, 112–13.

237. *Journal of Discourses*, 2:247.

238. *Journal of Discourses*, 8:10.

> powers there just as we have to here. We shall be rewarded according to our diligence and faithfulness in the exercise of our agency.[239]

Spirits not only possess keen minds to help them learn with greater ease, but they possess more than five senses. Elder Orson Pratt taught that "we need not suppose our five senses connect us with all the things of heaven, and earth, and eternity, and space; we need not think that we are conversant with all the elements of nature, through the medium of the senses God has given us here. Suppose He should give us a sixth sense, a seventh, an eighth, a ninth, or a fiftieth. All these different senses would convey to us new ideas, as much so as the senses of tasting, smelling, or seeing communicate different ideas from that of hearing." "I believe," continued Elder Pratt, "there are ten thousand things with which we are surrounded, that we know nothing about by our present natural senses. When the Lord imparts to us a principle by which we can look upon the past and future, as well as the present—by which we can look upon many intricate objects of nature which are now hidden from our view, we shall find our capacity for obtaining and retaining knowledge to be greatly enlarged."[240]

Can a Person Repent in the Spirit World?

According to the prophets, a person can repent in the spirit world. The gift of repentance is always available until Judgment Day. However, the repentance process will be more difficult in the spirit world. The reason for this, President Spencer W. Kimball explained, is because in the spirit world, "one has spirit and mind but not the physical power to overcome a physical habit. He can desire to change his life, but how can he overcome the lusts of the flesh unless he has flesh to control and transform? How can he overcome the tobacco or the drink habit in the spirit world where there is no liquor nor tobacco and no flesh to crave it? Similarly with other sins involving lack of control over the body."[241]

---

239. George Q. Cannon, *Gospel Truth*, 60.

240. *Journal of Discourses*, 2:247.

241. Spencer W. Kimball, *The Miracle of Forgiveness* (Bookcraft, 1971), 163.

Elder Melvin J. Ballard spoke of repentance in the spirit world and the necessity of overcoming the flesh before death:

> Do not let any of us imagine that we can go down to the grave not having overcome the corruptions of the flesh and then lose in the grave all our sins and evil tendencies. They will be with us. They will be with the spirit when separated from the body. It is my judgment that any man or woman can do more to conform to the laws of God in one year in this life than they could in ten years when they are dead. The spirit only can repent and change, and then the battle has to go forward with the flesh afterward. It is much easier to overcome and serve the Lord when both flesh and spirit are combined as one. . . .
>
> I grant you that the righteous dead will be at peace, but I tell you that when we go out of this life, leave this body, we will desire to do many things that we cannot do at all without the body. We will be seriously handicapped, and we will long for the body; we will pray for that early reunion with our bodies. We will know then what advantage it is to have a body. . . .
>
> Some folk get the notion that the problems of life will at once clear up, and they will know that this is the gospel of Christ when they die. I have heard people say they believe when they die, they will see Peter and that he will clear it all up. I said, "You never will see Peter until you accept the gospel of the Lord Jesus Christ, at the hands of the elders of the Church, living or dead."[242]

One must remember that even though a person in the spirit world is generally happier, may move about with little effort, and have the ability to gain knowledge with greater ease, mortality is the time to prepare and overcome desires of the flesh. As Elder Ballard mentioned above, a person may accomplish more in one year during mortality while the spirit and body are united than in ten years in the spirit world while the spirit and body are separated. It appears, then, that the righteous will be blessed with increased attributes and knowledge, while the wicked and the unprepared will struggle, as they did in mortality, until long and difficult repentance has taken place.

---

242. Hinckley, *Melvin J. Ballard*, 241, 246.

Is It Easier to Accept the Gospel in the Spirit World Than It Is During Mortality?

As explained above, Peter stated that every person in the spirit world must be "judged according to men in the flesh" (1 Peter 4:6). If this is the case, it seems that accepting the gospel in the spirit world—like in mortality—will be easier *and* harder, depending on the individual. Elder Neal A. Maxwell explained this doctrine in further detail:

> We do not now know precisely how God handles things in the spirit world so that life there is an extension of walking by faith. Death does not suddenly bestow upon the disbeliever full awareness of all reality, thereby obviating the need for any faith. Instead, what follows death is a continuum of the basic structure in mortality—until the Judgment Day, when every knee shall bow and every tongue confess that Jesus is the Christ (see Romans 14:11; Philippians 2:10; Doctrine and Covenants 76:110). . . .
>
> How will God ensure this condition in the spirit world? We do not know. Yet He has certainly so handled the second estate in relation to the first estate, hasn't He? The memories of the first estate are not accessible in the second estate. . . . Furthermore, the gospel, when preached in the spirit world, will bring the same responses as here: "some believed the things which were spoken, and some believed not" (Acts 28:24).[243]

Brigham Young similarly explained that "every departed spirit is subject to the laws that govern the spirit world. . . . There are wicked men in the spirit world. Millions of them will have the privilege of receiving the Gospel in the spirit, that they may be 'judged according to men in the flesh,' and no doubt but many will reject the Gospel there."[244] Elder Bruce R. McConkie indicated that not only will many people reject the gospel in the spirit world, but some Latter-day Saints—who accepted the gospel while living—will be worthy of

243. Neal A. Maxwell, *That Ye May Believe* (Bookcraft, 1992), 94.

244. *Journal of Discourses*, 13:76–77.

the terrestrial kingdom because they did not "prove to be valiant in their testimony."[245]

A few prophets, however, maintained an opposing view—that most people, if not all, will accept the gospel in the spirit world. President Lorenzo Snow, for example, believed "that when the gospel is preached to the spirits in prison, the success attending that preaching will be far greater than that attending the preaching of our elders in this life. I believe there will be very few indeed of those spirits who will not gladly receive the gospel when it is carried to them. The circumstances there will be a thousand times more favorable."[246] President Wilford Woodruff similarly taught that "there will be very few, if any, who will not accept the Gospel."[247]

The problem with this view, as explained above, is that it contradicts the scriptures. Elder Snow's statement that "the circumstances [in the spirit world] will be a thousand times more favorable" is only partially correct. The favorable circumstances may only apply to the righteous. Therefore, it may be correctly stated that for those who were faithful and God-fearing in mortality—whether Latter-day Saint, Jew, Catholic, Protestant, Muslim, or Buddhist—the circumstances in the spirit world will be more favorable, and most of them, if not all, will accept the gospel. For the wicked, on the other hand, accepting the gospel may be far more difficult.

Considering the aforementioned accounts and statements of the prophets, it may be of interest to read the experience of Ella Jensen, who recorded in detail everything she saw and heard in the spirit world before Lorenzo Snow blessed her lifeless body and called her back to mortality (see chapter nine for the details of this account):

> I could see people from the other world and hear the most delightful music and singing that I ever heard. This singing lasted for six hours, during which time I was preparing to leave this earth, and I could hear it all through the house. At ten o'clock my spirit left

245. Conference Report, Oct. 1974, 43–47.

246. Brian H. Study, ed., *Collected Discourses* (B. H. S. Publishing, 1987–92), 3:363.

247. James R. Clark, comp., *Messages of the First Presidency of The Church of Jesus Christ of Latter-day Saints* (Bookcraft, 1965–75), 3:257.

my body. It took me some time to make up my mind to go, as I could hear and see the folks crying and mourning over me. It was very hard for me to leave them, but as soon as I had a glimpse of the other world I was anxious to go and all care and worry left me.

I entered a large hall. It was so long that I could not see the end of it. It was filled with people. As I went through the throng, the first person I recognized was my grandpa, H. P. Jensen, who was sitting in one end of the room, writing. He looked up, seemed surprised to see me and said: "Why! There is my grand-daughter, Ella." He was very much pleased, greeted me and, as he continued with his writing, I passed on through the room and met a great many of my relatives and friends. It was like going along the crowded street of a large city where you meet many people, only a very few of whom you recognize.

The next one I knew was Uncle Hans Jensen with his wife, Mary Ellen. They had two small children with them. On inquiring who they were, he told me one was his own and the other was Uncle Will's little girl. Some seemed to be in family groups. As there were only a few whom I could recognize and who knew me, I kept moving on. Some inquired about their friends and relatives on the earth. Among the number was my cousin. He asked me how the folks were getting along and said it grieved him to hear that some of the boys were using tobacco, liquor and many things that were injurious to them. This proved to me that the people in the other world know to a great extent what happens here on the earth. The people were all dressed in white or cream. . . .

Everybody appeared to be perfectly happy. I was having a very pleasant visit with each one that I knew. Finally I reached the end of that long room. I opened a door and went into another room filled with children. They were all arranged in perfect order, the smallest ones first, then larger ones, according to age and size, the largest ones in the back rows all around the room. They seemed to be convened in a sort of Primary or Sunday School presided over by Aunt Eliza R. Snow. There were hundreds of small children. It was while I was standing listening to the children sing "Gladly Meeting, Kindly Greeting" that I heard your father, President Lorenzo Snow, call me. He said: "Sister Ella, you must come back, as your mission is not yet finished here on earth." So I just spoke to Aunt Eliza R. Snow and told her I must go back.

Returning through the large room, I told the people I was going back to earth, but they seemed to want me to stay with them. I obeyed the call, though it was very much against my desire, as such perfect peace and happiness prevailed there, no suffering, no sorrow. I was so taken up with all I saw and heard, I did hate to leave that beautiful place. . . .

For more than three hours my spirit was gone from my body. As I returned I could see my body lying on the bed and the folks gathered about in the room. I hesitated for a moment, then thought, "Yes, I will go back for a little while." I told the folks I wanted to stay only a short time to comfort them.[248]

248. *Improvement Era* 32, no. 12 (Oct. 1929): 973–77.

Chapter Seven

Prophecies and Answered Prayers

Prophecy is a gift of the Spirit and therefore is available to every member of the Church. Paul taught the Saints that prophecy is given to some "by the Spirit" (1 Corinthians 12:8–10). He also told the Saints to "covet earnestly" the gifts of the Spirit, including prophecy (1 Corinthians 12:31). The prophets, however, need not "seek" after the gift of prophecy because it is given to them through their apostolic ordination.[249] I should also mention that the Lord told Joel, an Old Testament prophet, "I will pour out my spirit upon all flesh; and your sons and your daughters shall prophesy" (Joel 2:28). Scholars from all faiths, including Judaism (the Old Testament being their scripture), claim that Joel 2 refers to the last days. Furthermore, Moroni quoted Joel 2:28 to Joseph Smith when he first appeared on September 21, 1823, and stated that this prophecy would soon be fulfilled.

This chapter not only contains accounts of prophecies and answered prayers of Latter-day Saint prophets but also of manifestations

249. Jeffrey R. Holland, "Prophets, Seers, and Revelators," *Ensign* or *Liahona*, Nov. 2004, 6–9.

they received regarding future events. Some of these manifestations came by dreams or visions—many of which warned of approaching danger— and others concerned the events just prior to the Second Coming or even the Resurrection of the righteous. I included many accounts in this chapter that are less known and left out many of the more well-known accounts (Joseph Smith's prophecy of the Civil War, for example).

Accounts of the Prophets

M. Russell Ballard

Related by Glenn L. Pace:

At the close of the [sacrament] meeting [in Ethiopia on March 11, 1985], Elder Ballard offered a most sacred prayer and blessing on Ethiopia, which I recall clearly but did not make record of at the time. In his supplication to our Heavenly Father, Elder Ballard noted that we were the only Melchizedek Priesthood holders then in the country and that we were there on assignment from the First Presidency of the Church. He expressed gratitude to the members of the Church who had contributed their means during the special fast and who had offered up individual and family prayers on behalf of the people of Ethiopia. Then with as much power and boldness as I had ever witnessed, he called upon the power and authority of the holy Melchizedek Priesthood and commanded the elements to gather together to bring rain upon the land, thus to begin to relieve those who had been suffering for so many years. It hadn't rained in a year, and the prayer was offered on a clear and sunny Sunday morning. . . .

We returned to the hotel in the afternoon to rest up for the coming week, and I was sitting at a little desk writing in my journal when I heard a clap of thunder. I went to the patio just in time to see the beginning of a torrential downpour. People began to run out of their little huts and public buildings, looking up at the sky and reaching their arms toward the heavens. They were shouting and crying. The heavy downpour continued for some time. I was mesmerized as I watched the scene from the window. As the ground became saturated and began to puddle, children and adults alike began to frolic and splash on each other. They grabbed buckets and barrels to collect rain from the roofs. It was a celebration unlike any I've ever witnessed.

As I stood at the window watching the scene unfold, my emotions turned from great joy to exquisite thanksgiving. I began to weep. I knew there were only two other people in the entire country who understood what had happened. Once I had gained control of my emotions, I went down the hall and knocked on Elder Ballard's door. When he came to the door, I could tell he had been overwhelmed in a like manner. We said a prayer of thanksgiving and returned to the privacy of our own rooms and thoughts. From that day forward, wherever we traveled it rained.[250]

Heber J. Grant

Forty years ago this October conference, I met the late Elder George Teasdale of the Council of the Twelve, at the south gate, and he shook hands with me and said: "Brother Grant, I am delighted to see you. You and I are going to be"—and he stopped suddenly and his face turned red; but the Lord gave me the balance of the sentence. Four times in my life I have been permitted to read the thoughts of people. The balance of Brother Teasdale's sentence was, "sustained this afternoon as apostles of the Lord Jesus Christ to fill the vacancies in the Quorum," and that went through me like a shock of electricity.

I came to the Sunday afternoon meeting of the conference, because of this partial sentence, and the balance that was given to me, with the assurance in my heart that Brother Teasdale and myself would be sustained as apostles. Those of you who were at that conference remember that it adjourned without filling those vacancies. I do not believe that any mortal man ever more humbly supplicated God during the next few days to forgive him for his egotism than I did for thinking that I was to be chosen as an apostle.

As you are aware, within a week a revelation came to John Taylor calling Brother Teasdale and myself to those positions.[251]

250. Glenn L. Pace, *Safe Journey: An African Adventure* (Deseret Book, 2003), 28–30.

251. Conference Report, Oct. 1922, 2–3.

Orson Hyde

In the early part of March, 1840, I retired to my bed one night as usual; and while meditating and contemplating the field of my future labors, the vision of the Lord, like clouds of light, burst into my view (see Joel 2:28). The cities of London, Amsterdam, Constantinople and Jerusalem, all appeared in succession before me, and the Spirit said unto me, "Here are many of the children of Abraham whom I will gather to the land that I gave to their fathers; and here also is the field of your labors. Take, therefore, proper credentials from my people, your brethren, and also from the Governor of your state, with the seal of authority thereon, and go ye forth to the cities which have been shown you, and declare these words unto Judah, and say, 'blow ye the trumpet in the land; cry, gather together, and say, assemble yourselves, and let us go into the defensed cities. Set up the standard towards Zion-retire; stay not, for I will bring evil from the north and a great destruction. The lion is come up from his thicket, and the destroyer of the Gentiles is on his way—he is gone forth from his place to make thy land desolate, and thy cities shall be laid waste, without an inhabitant. Speak ye comfortably to Jerusalem, and cry unto her, that her warfare is accomplished—that her iniquity is pardoned, for she hath received of the Lord's hand doubly for all her sins. Let your warning voice be heard among the Gentiles as you pass; and call yet upon them in my name for aid and for assistance. With you it mattereth not whether it be little or much; but to me it belongeth to show favor unto them who show favor unto you.'" The vision continued open about six hours, that I did not close my eyes in sleep. In this time many things were shown unto me which I have never written; neither shall I write them until they are fulfilled in Jerusalem.[252]

Heber C. Kimball

Related by Elder Parley P. Pratt:

It was now April; I had retired to rest one evening at an early hour, and was pondering my future course, when there came a knock at the door. I arose and opened it, when Elder Heber C. Kimball and

---

252. *History of the Church*, 4:375–76.

others entered my house, and being filled with the spirit of prophecy, they blessed me and my wife, and prophesied as follows:

"Brother Parley, thy wife shall be healed from this hour, and shall bear a son, and his name shall be Parley; and he shall be a chosen instrument in the hands of the Lord to inherit the priesthood and to walk in the steps of his father. He shall do a great work in the earth in ministering the Word and teaching the children of men. Arise, therefore, and go forth in the ministry, nothing doubting. Take no thoughts for your debts, nor the necessaries of life, for the Lord will supply you with abundant means for all things. Thou shalt go to Upper Canada, even to the city of Toronto, the capital, and there thou shalt find a people prepared for the fulness of the gospel, and they shall receive thee, and thou shalt organize the Church among them, and it shall spread thence into the regions round about, and many shall be brought to the knowledge of the truth and shall be filled with joy; and from the things growing out of this mission, shall the fulness of the gospel spread into England, and cause a great work to be done in that land. You shall not only have means to deliver you from your present embarrassments, but you shall yet have riches, silver and gold, till you will loath the counting thereof."

This prophecy was the more marvelous, because being married near ten years we had never had any children; and for near six years my wife had been consumptive, and had been considered incurable. However, we called to mind the faith of Abraham of old, and judging Him faithful who had promised, we took courage.[253]

Spencer W. Kimball

The Lord was showing to me what great things this people [in Mexico City] would accomplish. I could see you children of Lehi with your herds and flocks on thousands of hills. In my dream I no longer saw you the servant of other people, but I saw you as the employer, the owner of banks and businesses. I saw the people of Lehi as engineers and builders building lofty bridges and great edifices. I saw you in great political positions and functioning as administrators of the land. I saw many of you as heads of

253. *Autobiography of Parley P. Pratt* (Deseret Book, 1965), 164–65.

government and of the counties, states, and cities. I saw you in legislative positions where as good legislators and good Latter-day Saints you were able to make the best laws for your brothers and sisters. I saw many of your sons become attorneys. I saw doctors, as well as lawyers, looking after the health of the people. . . . I saw you as owners of newspapers with great influence in public affairs. I saw great artists among you. Many of you I saw writing books and magazines and articles and having a powerful influence on the thoughts of the people of the country. . . . I saw the Church growing in rapid strides and I saw wards and stakes organized. I saw stakes by the hundreds: I saw a temple.[254]

Mark E. Peterson

Related by Peggy P. Barton:

At the previous April general conference, Elder Mark E. Petersen had been called to fill the vacancy caused by the excommunication of Richard R. Lyman. While the circumstances surrounding Elder Petersen's call could not mitigate the tragedy of Elder Lyman's fall, they could and did reaffirm the spiritual and revelatory powers at work in the call to service in the Twelve.

Not long before Elder Lyman's difficulties surfaced, Mark Petersen, general manager of the Deseret News, had a vivid dream. In it he saw a garbled newspaper headline, "Lyman R. Richard Dies." The same newspaper also carried a story of his call to the Twelve. The next day, he sent a reporter to the Church Administration Building to inquire about the health of the Brethren, especially Elder Lyman. Advised that everyone appeared to be well, Elder Petersen still retained the feeling that some unforeseen incident would remove Elder Lyman from the Twelve and that he would be called to replace him. When the announcement of the excommunication was put in his hand for publication, that feeling was strongly confirmed and remained with him during the months before his call in April 1944. When President Heber J. Grant extended the call to him, Elder Petersen related the dream and his spiritual

254. Spencer W. Kimball spoke to the Saints in Mexico City in 1977; *Church News*, Feb. 19, 1977, as cited in Donald Q. Cannon and Richard O. Cowan, *Unto Every Nation: Gospel Light Reaches Every Land* (Deseret Book, 2003), 275.

promptings to the Prophet, who confirmed that the Lord had taken this means to reveal the call to him in advance.[255]

George A. Smith

Related by his grandson President George Albert Smith:

I am standing on what to me is sacred ground. My grandparents and my parents and many other relatives lived here in Provo and some still live here. My father [John Henry Smith] as a young man came near losing his life in the Provo river, not far from where we are now. His father [George A. Smith], who was in Salt Lake City, felt impressed to go into a room that had been set apart for prayer. He clothed himself in Temple robes, knelt down at the altar and said: "Heavenly Father, I feel that there is something seriously wrong with my family in Provo. Thou knowest that I cannot be with them there and be here. Heavenly Father, wilt thou preserve and safeguard them, and I will be grateful to thee and honor thee."

At the time when he was praying, just as near as it was possible to indicate by checking the time, my father had fallen into the river. It was at flood time. Logs and rocks were pouring down from the canyon, and he was helpless. Those who were near saw his predicament, but they could not reach him. The turbulence of the water was such that nobody could live in it. They just stood there in horror. Father was doing everything he could to keep his head above water, but he was being thrown up and down and being dashed against the rocks and logs. All at once a wave lifted him bodily from the water and threw him upon the shore. It was a direct answer of the prayer of a servant of the Lord.[256]

Hyrum Smith

On the eighth of October, 1840, Edward Hunter was baptized by Elder Orson Hyde, then on his way to Palestine, and soon after received a visit from Elder Hyrum Smith, the Prophet's brother. He attended conference at Philadelphia, and subscribed liberally

---

255. Peggy Petersen Barton, *Mark E. Petersen* (Deseret Book, 1985), 85–86.

256. George A. Smith, *Sharing the Gospel with Others*, comp. Preston Nibley (Deseret Book, 1948), 83–84.

to the building of the Nauvoo House and the Temple. At a subsequent visit of Brother Hyrum Smith, as they were walking along the banks of the river Brandywine, the conversation turned upon the subject of the departed; and Brother Hunter was constrained to inquire about his children whom he had lost, particularly a little boy, George Washington by name, an excellent child to whom he was devotedly attached. "It is pretty strong doctrine," said Elder Smith, "but I believe I will tell it. Your son will act as an angel to you; not your guardian angel, but an auxiliary angel, to assist you in extreme trials."

The truth of this was plainly manifested to him about a year and a half later, when, in an hour of deep depression, the little boy appeared to him in a vision. Brother Hunter says: "In appearance he was more perfect than in natural life—the same blue eyes, curly hair, fair complexion, and a most beautiful appearance. I felt disposed to keep him, and offered inducements for him to remain. He then said, in his own familiar voice: 'George has many friends in heaven.'"[257]

Joseph Smith Jr.

Related by Elder B. H. Roberts:

On the 6th of August, 1842, with quite a number of his brethren, he [Joseph Smith] crossed the Mississippi river to the town of Montrose, to be present at the installation of the Masonic Lodge of the Rising Sun. A block schoolhouse had been prepared with shade in front, under which was a barrel of ice water, Judge James Adams was the highest Masonic authority in the state of Illinois, and had been sent there to organize this lodge. He and Hyrum Smith, being high Masons, went into the house to perform some ceremonies which the others were not entitled to witness. These, including Joseph Smith, remained under the bowery. Joseph, as he was tasting the cold water, warned the brethren not to be too free with it. With the tumbler still in his hand he prophesied that the saints would yet go to the Rocky Mountains; and, said he, this water tastes much like that of the crystal streams that are running from the snow-capped mountains.

257. *The Contributor* 6, no. 7 (Apr. 1885): 245.

After Joseph tasted the water, he saw a vision. Anson Call describes the event:

> I had before seen him in a vision, and now saw while he was talking his countenance change to white; not the deadly white of a bloodless face, but a living brilliant white. He seemed absorbed in gazing at something at a great distance, and said: "I am gazing upon the valleys of those mountains." This was followed by a vivid description of the scenery of these mountains, as I have since become acquainted with it. Pointing to Shadrach Roundy and others, he said: "There are some men here who shall do a great work in that land." Pointing to me, he said: "There is Anson, he shall go and shall assist in building up cities from one end of the country to the other, and you, rather extending the idea to all those he had spoken of, shall perform as great a work as has been done by man, so that the nations of the earth shall be astonished, and many of them will be gathered in that land and assist in building cities and temples, and Israel shall be made to rejoice."[258]
>
> It is impossible to represent in words this scene which is still vivid in my mind, of the grandeur of Joseph's appearance, his beautiful descriptions of this land, and his wonderful prophetic utterances as they emanated from the glorious inspirations that overshadowed him. There was a force and power in his exclamations of which the following is but a faint echo: "Oh the beauty of those snow-capped mountains! The cool refreshing streams that are running down through those mountain gorges!" Then gazing in another direction, as if there was a change of locality: "Oh the scenes that this people will pass through! The dead that will lay between here and there." Then turning in another direction as if the scene had again changed: "Oh the apostasy that will take place before my brethren reach that land!" "But," he continued, "The priesthood shall prevail over its enemies, triumph over the devil and be established upon the earth, never more to be thrown down!" He then charged us with great force and power, to be faithful to those things that had been and should be committed to our charge, with

258. B. H. Roberts, *A Comprehensive History of The Church of Jesus Christ of Latter-day Saints* (Brigham Young University Press, 1965), 2:181–82.

the promise of all the blessings that the Priesthood could bestow. "Remember these things and treasure them up."[259]

Joseph Smith Jr.

Would you think it strange if I relate what I have seen in vision in relation to this interesting theme [of the Resurrection]? Those who have died in Jesus Christ may expect to enter into all that fruition of joy, when they come forth, which they possessed or anticipated here. So plain was the vision that I actually saw men, before they had ascended from the tomb, as though they were getting up slowly. They took each other by the hand, and said to each other: "My father, my son, my mother, my daughter, my brother, my sister." And when the voice calls for the dead to arise, suppose I am laid by the side of my father, what would be the first joy of my heart? To meet my father, my mother, my brother, my sister; and when they are by my side, I will embrace them and they me. . . . All your losses will be made up to you in the resurrection, provided you continue faithful. By the vision of the Almighty I have seen it.[260]

Joseph Smith Jr.

Related by Philo Dibble:

When Joseph first came to Nauvoo, then called Commerce, a Mr. White, living there, proffered to sell him his farm for twenty-five hundred dollars, five hundred dollars of the amount to be paid down, and the balance one year from that time. Joseph and the brethren were talking about this offer when some of them said: "We can't buy it, for we lack the money." Joseph took out his purse, and, emptying out its contents, offered a half dollar to one of the brethren, which he declined accepting, but Joseph urged him to take it, and then gave each of the other brethren a similar amount, which left him without any. Addressing the brethren, he then said: "Now you all have money, and I have none; but the time will come when I will have money and you will have none!" He then said to Bishop Knight: "You go back and buy the farm!"

---

259. *History of the Church*, 5:85–86.

260. *History of the Church*, 5:361–62.

Brother Knight went to White, but learned from him that he had raised the price one hundred dollars, and returned to Joseph without closing the bargain. Joseph again sent him with positive orders to purchase, but Brother Knight, finding that White had raised the price still another hundred dollars, again returned without purchasing. For the third time then Joseph commanded him to go and buy the farm, and charged him not to come back till he had done so.

When Bishop Knight got back to White, he had raised another hundred on the place, making the whole amount twenty-eight hundred dollars. However, the bargain was closed and the obligations drawn up, but how the money was going to be raised neither Brother Knight nor the other Brethren could see. The next morning Joseph and several of the brethren went down to Mr. White's to sign the agreement and make the first payment on the land. A table was brought out with the papers upon it, and Joseph signed them, moved back from the table and sat with his head down, as if in thought for a moment. Just then a man drove up in a carriage and asked if Mr. Smith was there. Joseph hearing it, got up and went to the door. The man said, "Good morning, Mr. Smith; I am on a speculation to-day. I want to buy some land, and thought I would come and see you." Joseph then pointed around where his land lay, but the man said: "I can't go with you today to see the land. Do you want any money this morning?"

Joseph replied that he would like some, and when the stranger asked "How much?" he told him "Five hundred dollars." The man walked into the house with Joseph, emptied a small sack of gold on the table, and counted out that amount. He then handed to Joseph another hundred dollars, saying: "Mr. Smith, I make you a present of this!" After this transpired, Joseph laughed at the brethren and said: "You trusted in money; but I trusted in God. Now I have money and you have none."[261]

Joseph Smith Jr.

Related by Philo Dibble:

261. *Early Scenes in Church History* (Juvenile Instructor Office, 1882), 8:95–96.

In Nauvoo, I rented a house on the river bank. While there in business, I saw in vision my grave before me for two weeks; it mattered not whether my eyes were open or shut, it was there, and I saw no way of escape. One day Brother Joseph came and took dinner with us, and as we arose from the table I walked out upon the porch and sat down on a bench. Joseph and my wife followed me, and he came before me and said: "Philo, you must get away from here or you will die, as sure as God ever spoke by my mouth!" He then turned to my wife and said: "And you will hardly escape by the skin of your teeth!"

I immediately stepped into Joseph's carriage and rode with him to the south part of town and rented another place, after which I settled up my business as fast as I could, and made arrangements to remove. Many hearing of Joseph's prediction about me said if they had been in my place they would have remained where I was and tested the truth of it. But I assured them if they had been in my place they would have done just as I did. After I had settled my business and removed my family, we were one day at Joseph's house when he said to my wife: "You didn't believe what I told Philo the other day! Now, I will tell you what the Lord told me. He told me to go and tell Philo to come away from there, and if he obeyed he should live; if not, he should die; and I didn't want to see you a widow so soon again. If Philo had remained there fourteen days longer, he would have been a corpse."[262]

Joseph Smith Jr.

Related by John L. Smith:

When playing in the yard of the old white mansion, in Nauvoo, with Joseph and Frederick, two of his sons, a gentleman drove to the gate and asked if the Prophet Joseph Smith was at home; when he (the Prophet) sprang up from the grass plat, and, shaking the dust from his clothing, replied that he was. The gentleman then drove his one horse up to a tie post and left the lines lying loose, and got out and came into the house. When about half way to the house Joseph said, "Mr., I think you would do well to tie your horse; he might get a scare and run away and break your carriage."

262. *Early Scenes in Church History*, 8:93.

The gentleman replied, "I have driven that horse for some years and never tie him. I am a doctor and cannot afford to tie up at every place I call." Joseph repeated, "You had better tie, all the same. Your horse might get a scare and run away." The doctor replied, "No fear." Joseph seemed quite uneasy, and got up several times from his chair on the porch or stoop. Suddenly the horse started up the street and struck a wheel against a post and scattered the pieces for a block or more. The doctor sprang to his feet, and looking after the horse, cried out to Joseph, "I'll be d—d if you ain't a Prophet!"[263]

Joseph Smith Jr.

Related by Mary C. Westover:

I was very small when we lived in Nauvoo, but I must have seen Joseph Smith many times for I always attended the meetings. The most striking thing I remember of him was a prophecy he made, which I saw fulfilled immediately. I was at the funeral service of King Follett, which was held in the Nauvoo Grove. There was a heavy thunderstorm arose and as it increased the people became frightened and started to go home; but before anyone left the Prophet arose and told the multitude if they would remain still and pray in their hearts the storm would not molest them in their services. They did as they were bidden, the storm divided over the grove. I well remember how it was storming on all sides of the grove, yet it was as calm around us as if there was no sign of a storm so nearby. I thought as I sat there that the Lord was speaking through Joseph.[264]

Joseph Smith Jr.

Related by Israel A. Barlow:

My grandfather, Israel Barlow, was a very trusted bodyguard to the Prophet Joseph Smith. Shortly before the martyrdom (the exact date not being available), the Prophet called upon him and

---

263. John L. Smith, "Recollections of the Prophet Joseph Smith," *Juvenile Instructor* 27, no. 6 (Mar. 15, 1892): 172–73.

264. "Joseph Smith, the Prophet," *Young Woman's Journal* 17, no. 12 (Dec. 1906): 545.

requested that he make a journey of many miles on horseback and deliver a message from the Prophet to a certain man who lived in a neighborhood of enemies to the Prophet and to the Latter-day Saints. He was asked to make special observations of what he might see and hear while on this mission.

It was a hazardous time in the history of the Church and the Prophet was constantly in jeopardy, not only from enemies without but within the Church. The Prophet told him to leave on this errand on a certain day early in the morning and ride to a certain man's home and there deliver the message. He was instructed to accept of their hospitality, which the Prophet Joseph assured him they would extend to him. "But," said the Prophet, "let them put your horse up for you and eat supper with them, but when it becomes sundown saddle your horse and leave. They will be insistent and try to persuade you to remain overnight, but if you value your life do not stay, but leave, and listen to the direction of the Spirit."

He left promptly at sundown and rode along the country road until it became dark. Just before he came to the river bridge, a voice said to grandfather, "Ride faster." He sped up his horse and the voice repeated again, and with more emphasis, "Ride faster." And again he increased the speed of the animal when the voice said to him, "Ride for your life." He then sped for all the animal's strength. As the horse's feet clattered across the bridge he could hear the mob, which had gathered in the brush to intercept him, cursing at the top of their voices. He had crossed the bridge but a short distance when the voice said to him: "Turn to the right," and he turned his horse off the road into the brush toward the river. There he stood in silence as the mob, who had mounted their horses, came racing over the bridge at break-neck speed, and down the road they went, supposedly after him.

After they had gone by he wound his way from the river's edge to the bed of the stream, and on through the willows. In the darkness he made his way along the river in the opposite direction from which the mob had expected him to go. Finally when he thought it was safe, several miles away, he emerged from the river and made his way over the country back into Nauvoo, just as the day was breaking. There he saw the Prophet Joseph walking up and down the street in front of his home. As grandfather approached and alighted from his horse, he began to tell the Prophet of his experience. The Prophet stopped him and told him he need not tell him for he already knew. The Prophet told him that he had been up all night waiting for his return, and stated, "I saw it all; you have no need to tell me." Thereupon the Prophet laid his hand upon grandfather's shoulder and gave him a blessing and said: "Thee and thine shall never want."[265]

Joseph Smith Jr.

Related by John L. Smith:

In my early years I used to often eat at the table with Joseph the Prophet. At one time he was called to dinner. I being at play in the room with his son Joseph, he called us to him, and we stood one each side of him. After he had looked over the table he said, "Lord, we thank Thee for this Johnnycake, and ask Thee to send us something better. Amen." The corn bread was cut and I received a piece from his hand. Before the bread was all eaten, a man came to the door and asked if the Prophet Joseph was at home. Joseph replied he was, whereupon the visitor said, "I have brought you some flour and a ham." Joseph arose and took the gift, and blessed the man in the name of the Lord. Turning to his wife, Emma, he said, "I knew the Lord would answer my prayer."[266]

John Taylor

My dear child [Zina Young Williams], I have something of importance to tell you that I know will make you happy. I have been visited by your father [Brigham Young]. He came to me in the silence of the night clothed in brightness and with a face beaming with love and confidence told me things of great importance and among others that the school [now Brigham Young University] being taught by Brother [Karl. G.] Maeser was accepted in the heavens and was a part of the great plan of life and salvation; that Church schools should be fostered for the good of Zion's children; that we

265. Ora Haven Barlow, *The Israel Barlow Story and Mormon Mores* (Publishers Press, 1968), 194–95.

266. "Recollections of the Prophet Joseph Smith," *Juvenile Instructor* 27, no. 6 (Mar. 1892): 172–73.

rejoice to see the awakening among the teachers and the children of our people; for they would need the support of this knowledge and testimony of the Gospel, and there was a bright future in store for the preparation for the children of the covenant for future usefulness in the Kingdom of God, and that Christ himself was directing, and had a care over this school.[267]

Wilford Woodruff

During the night [in February 1835] I had the following dream: I thought an angel came to us, and told us we were commanded of the Lord to follow a certain straight path, which was pointed out to us, let it lead us wherever it might. After we had walked in it awhile we came to the door of a house, which was in the line of a high wall running north and south, so that we could not go around. I opened the door and saw the room was filled with large serpents, and I shuddered at the sight. . . . As I stepped into the room the serpents coiled themselves up, and raised their heads some two feet from the floor, to spring at me. There was one much larger than the rest, in the center of the room, which raised his head nearly as high as mine and made a spring at me. . . . Just before the serpent reached me he dropped dead at my feet; all the rest dropped dead, swelled up, turned black, bust open, took fire and were consumed before my eyes, and we went through the room unharmed, thanking God for our deliverance.

I awoke in the morning and pondered upon the dream. . . . I related to my companion my dream, and told him we should see something strange. We had great anticipations of meeting Mr. Akeman, supposing him to be a member of the Church. When we arrived at his house, he received us very coldly, and we soon found that he had apostatized. . . . Word was sent through all the settlements on the river for twenty miles that two Mormon preachers were in the place. A mob was soon raised, and warning sent to us to leave immediately or we would be tarred and feathered, ridden on a rail, and hanged. I soon saw who the serpents were. My companion

267. Leonard Arrington, *The Presidents of the Church* (Deseret Book, 1986), 108–9.

wanted to leave; I told him, no. I would stay and see my dream fulfilled.

There was an old gentleman and lady named Hubbel, who had read the Book of Mormon and believed. Father Hubbel came to see us, and invited us to make our home with him while we stayed in the place. We did so, and labored for him some three weeks with our axes, clearing land, while we were waiting to see the salvation of God.

February 14th, 1835, was an important day to me. In company with Brother Brown, I took my axe and went into the woods to help Brother Hubbel clear some land. We chopped till 3 o'clock in the afternoon. The spirit of the Lord came upon me like a rushing of mighty wind. The voice of the spirit said, "Go up again and visit Mr. Akeman and again bear testimony to him of the truth of the Book of Mormon and of the work of God." . . .

I carried my ax to the house and walked up to Mr. Akeman's about one and a half mile through a pleasant grove. . . . As I approached the house I saw the door open and Mr. Akeman walking the floor. I felt particularly impressed to ask if he was well. He said he never felt better in health. I told him I had come to bear testimony again to him of the truth of the Book of Mormon and of the work of God and of the danger of opposing that work. He was soon filled with wrath and indignation and he opposed me in the strongest terms and raged against the leaders of the Church. My mouth was more closed up than ever before. I felt that the house was filled with devils and with an awful darkness. . . . My tongue seemed glued to my mouth. I could not speak. I arose to my feet to leave the house. I felt as though the floor moved under my feet and when I stepped upon the ground I felt as though I was surrounded by evil spirits. . . .

Mr. Akeman followed me out of the door and kept within about four rods of me. Neither of us spoke a word. I knew he was following, but when he was about four rods from the house, the strange feeling left me. When Mr. Akeman reached the place where my feelings so instantly changed, he fell dead at my feet as though he had been struck with a thunderbolt from heaven. I heard him fall to the earth, but I did not look behind me. . . . I continued to walk down to Mr. Hubbel's as fast as I could, meditating all the while upon the strange dealings of God with me. I still did not know that Mr. Akeman was dead.

I arrived at Mr. Hubbel's just at dark . . . when I heard a horse coming up on the full ran. . . . A man rode up to our door and cried out: "Mr. Akeman is dead. I want you to go there immediately." In a moment my eyes were opened, so that I understood the whole matter. I felt satisfied with the dealings of God with me in calling me to go and warn him. . . . His family, as well as ourselves, felt it was the judgment of God upon him. I preached his funeral sermon. Many of the mob died suddenly. We stayed about two weeks after Akeman's death and preached, baptized Mr. Hubbel and his wife, and then continued on our journey.[268]

Wilford Woodruff

I have had some revelations of late, and very important ones to me, and I will tell you what the Lord has said to me. Let me bring your minds to what is termed the manifesto. . . . The Lord has told me to ask the Latter-day Saints a question, and He also told me that if they would listen to what I said to them and answer the question put to them, by the Spirit and power of God, they would all answer alike, and they would all believe alike with regard to this matter.

The question is this: Which is the wisest course for the Latter-day Saints to pursue—to continue to attempt to practice plural marriage, with the laws of the nation against it and the opposition of sixty millions of people, and at the cost of the confiscation and loss of all the Temples, and the stopping of all the ordinances therein, both for the living and the dead, and the imprisonment of the First Presidency and Twelve and the heads of families in the Church, and the confiscation of personal property of the people (all of which of themselves would stop the practice); or, after doing and suffering what we have through our adherence to this principle to cease the practice and submit to the law, and through doing so leave the Prophets, Apostles and fathers at home, so that they can instruct the people and attend to the duties of the Church, and also

268. Matthias F. Cowley, *Wilford Woodruff, His Life and Labors* (Deseret News, 1909), 51–54.

leave the Temples in the hands of the Saints, so that they can attend to the ordinances of the Gospel, both for the living and the dead?

The Lord showed me by vision and revelation exactly what would take place if we did not stop this practice. If we had not stopped it, you would have had no use for . . . any of the men in this temple at Logan; for all ordinances would be stopped throughout the land of Zion. Confusion would reign throughout Israel, and many men would be made prisoners. This trouble would have come upon the whole Church, and we should have been compelled to stop the practice. Now, the question is, whether it should be stopped in this manner, or in the way the Lord has manifested to us, and leave our Prophets and Apostles and fathers free men, and the temples in the hands of the people, so that the dead may be redeemed. A large number has already been delivered from the prison house in the spirit world by this people, and shall the work go on or stop? This is the question I lay before the Latter-day Saints. You have to judge for yourselves. I want you to answer it for yourselves. I shall not answer it; but I say to you that that is exactly the condition we as a people would have been in had we not taken the course we have. . . .

I saw exactly what would come to pass if there was not something done. I have had this spirit upon me for a long time. But I want to say this: I should have let all the temples go out of our hands; I should have gone to prison myself, and let every other man go there, had not the God of heaven commanded me to do what I did do; and when the hour came that I was commanded to do that, it was all clear to me. I went before the Lord, and I wrote what the Lord told me to write. . . . I leave this with you, for you to contemplate and consider. The Lord is at work with us.[269]

Wilford Woodruff

Now, I will refer to a thing that took place with me in Tennessee. I was in Tennessee in the year 1835, and while at the house of Abraham O. Smoot, I received a letter from Brothers Joseph Smith and Oliver Cowdery, requesting me to stay there, and stating that

269. Cache Stake Conference, Logan, Utah, Sunday, November 1, 1891; reported in *Deseret Weekly*, Nov. 14, 1891; also printed in Official Declaration 1.

> I would lose no blessing by doing so. Of course, I was satisfied. I went into a little room and sat down upon a small sofa. I was all by myself and the room was dark; and while I rejoiced in this letter and the promise made to me, I became wrapped in vision. I was like Paul; I did not know whether I was in the body or out of the body. A personage appeared to me and showed me the great scenes that should take place in the last days. One scene after another passed before me. I saw the sun darkened; I saw the moon become as blood; I saw the stars fall from heaven; I saw seven golden lamps set in the heavens, representing the various dispensations of God to man—a sign that would appear before the coming of Christ. I saw the resurrection of the dead. In the first resurrection those that came forth from their graves seemed to be all dressed alike, but in the second resurrection they were as diverse in their dress as this congregation is before me today, and if I had been an artist I could have painted the whole scene as it was impressed upon my mind, more indelibly fixed than anything I had ever seen with the natural eye.[270]

In another account of this vision, President Woodruff wrote the following:

> I knelt down and prayed. I arose from my knees and sat down. The room was filled with light. A messenger came to me. We had a long conversation. He laid before me as if in a panorama, the signs of the last days, and told me what was coming to pass. I saw the sun turned to darkness, the moon to blood, the stars fall from heaven. I saw the resurrection day. I saw armies of men in the first resurrection, clothed with the robes of the Holy Priesthood. I saw the second resurrection. I saw a great many signs that were presented before me, by this personage; and among the rest, there were seven lions, as of burning brass, set in the heavens. He says, "That is one of the signs that will appear in the heavens before the coming of the Son of Man. It is a sign of the various dispensations."[271]

---

270. *Journal of Discourses*, 22:333–34.

271. Brian Stuy, ed., *Collected Discourses* (B.H.S. Publishing, 1992), 1:217.

Brigham Young

Related by President Wilford Woodruff:

> On the twenty-fourth [of July 1847], I drove my carriage, with President [Brigham] Young lying on a bed in it, into the open valley, the rest of the company following. When we came out of the canyon, into full view of the [Salt Lake] valley, I turned the side of my carriage around, open to the west, and President Young arose from his bed and took a survey of the country. While gazing on the scene before us, he was enwrapped in vision for several minutes. He had seen the valley before in vision, and upon the occasion he saw the future glory of Zion and Israel, as they would be, planted in the valleys of the mountains. When the vision had passed, he said, "It is enough. This is the right place. Drive on." So I drove to the encampment already formed by those who had come along in advance of us.[272]

Brigham Young later mentioned his vision of the Salt Lake Valley:

> We have built cities in this mountainous region, because there was no other place where we could do so. We have not got through with our work here yet. The people have hardly commenced to realize the beauty, excellence, and glory that will yet crown this city. I do not know that I will live in the flesh to see what I saw in vision when I came here. I see some things, but a great deal more has yet to be accomplished.[273]

Notes and Commentary

Many people in the Church have had experiences when the Spirit reveals certain things to them regarding the immediate future. This is precisely what happened to several men in Latter-day Saint history prior to receiving a call to serve in the Quorum of the Twelve. Heber J. Grant learned by discerning the thoughts of George Teasdale that he would soon be called to the Twelve. Franklin D. Richards also learned of his call to the Twelve before the call was extended. Brother

---

272. Preston Nibley, *Brigham Young: The Man and His Work* (Deseret Book, 1936), 98–99.

273. *Journal of Discourses* 12:94.

Richards talked with Brigham Young in a dream, who asked, "Would you accept it if I should appoint you one of the quorum?" Brother Richards said that he would. Two years later, he was called.[274]

At least two individuals were told by family members or priesthood leaders that they would be called to the Twelve. When Hugh B. Brown was a boy, his mother saw his image appear in the face of Elder Francis Lyman while speaking at a Church conference. Elder Brown recalled:

> Mother and I went to conference . . . in the horse and buggy. As we were coming home she told me of an experience she had had while Francis M. Lyman was addressing the conference. She said: "As I looked upon him, he ceased to be Francis M. Lyman and became Hugh B. Brown, and I saw you as occupying the position he then held. I know as I know I live that that's what is going to happen to you. If you will just behave yourself and do what is right, the time will come when you will be called into the Council of the Twelve."[275]

On May 29, 1899, James L. McMurrin, president of the European Mission, approached the pulpit near the conclusion of a priesthood meeting and said, "The Lord has accepted our labors, and at this time we stand pure before him. . . . Yes, brethren, there are angels in this room. . . . Let me say to you, Brother David [McKay], Satan has desired you that he may sift you as wheat, but God is mindful of you, and if you will keep the faith, you will yet sit in the leading councils of the Church."[276] Six years later, on April 9, 1906, thirty-two-year-old David O. McKay was called into the Quorum of the Twelve.

Many accounts in this book describe heavenly beings appearing to accept a dedication of a temple or to show approval of a certain course of action of the Church. One related account I wish to highlight is the aforementioned experience of President John Taylor. Shortly after Brigham Young died in 1877, he appeared to President Taylor and

---

274. West, *Franklin D. Richards*, 81–82.

275. Campbell and Poll, *Hugh B. Brown*, 220.

276. David O. Mckay, in Conference Report, Oct. 1968, 86; Jeanette McKay Morrell, *Highlights in the Life of President David O. McKay* (Deseret Book, 1966), 35–38.

told him that the Brigham Young Academy, established on October 16, 1875, "was accepted in the heavens and was a part of the great plan of life and salvation." Brigham also said that "there was a bright future in store for the preparation for the children of the covenant for future usefulness in the Kingdom of God, and that Christ himself was directing, and had a care over this school."[277]

Over the next sixty years, at least three individuals recorded experiences that are fascinating supplements to President Taylor's manifestation and which add prophetic validity to his experience. The first of these individuals was Karl G. Maeser, who was appointed to be the first president of Brigham Young Academy.[278] Before Brigham Young died, he counseled Brother Maeser, saying, "Whatever you teach, even the multiplication tables, do it with the spirit of the Lord."[279]

Twelve years after Brigham Young founded the school, Brother Maeser received a manifestation about its future. In the 1880s, Brigham Young Academy struggled financially and the future of the institution looked bleak. The financial situation grew increasingly worse until the professors agreed to teach an entire year without pay in hopes of saving the academy.

In a letter to L. John Nuttall, Brother Maeser wrote, "The affairs of this institution are in such an unsettled condition financially and executively, that I cannot see my way clear at any point. . . . I am worn out and sick in spirit, dear Brother, about this dragging and planless condition of things, and with all my love for this Academy, I feel that I owe it to my very life, which is needlessly wearing out here in an apparently hopeless task, to accept any change that will promise to me opportunities for permanent usefulness."[280]

Brother Maeser decided to leave the academy and accept a teaching position at the University of Deseret. However, just before he and his family packed up their belongings to relocate, he had a dream.

---

277. Arrington, *Presidents of the Church*, 108–9.

278. Warren N. Dusenberry was technically the first president of Brigham Young Academy, but he only held that position for a few months until a permanent president was appointed, which was Karl G. Maeser.

279. Susa Young Gates, *Life Story of Brigham Young* (Macmillan, 1930), 292.

280. Ernest L. Wilkinson ed., *Brigham Young University: The First One Hundred Years* (Brigham Young University Press, 1976), 4:399–400.

The following morning, he related to his daughter, who had inquired about the move, "I have changed my mind. I have had a dream—I have seen Temple Hill filled with buildings—great temples of learning, and I have decided to remain and do my part in contributing to the fulfillment of that dream."[281] The school soon recovered, and by 1903—two years after Karl G. Maeser died—the name was changed to Brigham Young University. In 1909, the university commenced constructing the Maeser Memorial Building.

A few years later, in 1912, Brigham Young University experienced additional financial setbacks. The Maeser Building was only partially complete, and the university administrators were selling some of the property to keep the school from going bankrupt. During this time, eighteen students were preparing to receive their diplomas at the approaching graduation. These students would be the first four-year graduates of Brigham Young University. On the day of commencement, Alfred Kelly, a student at the university, arose to speak. After standing for several minutes in silence, Kelly related a vision he had seen a few days prior. President Jeffrey R. Holland, while president of Brigham Young University, related Kelly's experience as follows:

> Early one morning . . . with a feeling of desperation regarding his approaching assignment, he walked north from his downtown apartment to where the partially completed Maeser Building stood (as Horace Cummings would later describe it) as an "air castle" come to earth on Temple Hill. He wanted to gain inspiration from this hope of a new campus, but he felt only grim disappointment. The sky was starting to glow from the morning light, but the darkly silhouetted Maeser Building seemed only a symbol of gloom.
>
> Kelly then turned his eyes to view the valley below that was also still in shadow. The light from the rising sun was just beginning to illuminate the western hills back of Utah Lake with an unusual golden glow. As morning came, the light gradually worked down from the hilltops, moved across the valley floor, and slowly advanced to the spot where Kelly stood. He said he partially closed his eyes as the light approached and was startled by what he could still see. He stood as if transfixed. In the advancing sunlight everything he saw took on the appearance of people, young people about

281. Wilkinson, *Brigham Young University*, 4:400.

> his age moving toward Temple Hill. He saw hundreds of them, thousands of young people coming into view. He knew they were students, he said, because they carried books in their arms as they came.
>
> Then Temple Hill was bathed in sunlight, and the whole of the present campus was illuminated not with one partially completed building, nor with homes in a modern subdivision, but rather what Kelly described to that graduating class as "temples of learning," large buildings, beautiful buildings, hundreds of buildings covering the top of that hill and stretching clear to the mouth of Rock Canyon. The students then entered these temples of learning with their books in hand. As they came out of them, Kelly said their countenances bore smiles of hope and of faith. He observed that they seemed cheerful and very confident. Their walk was light but firm as they again became a part of the sunlight as it moved to the top of Y Mountain, and then they gradually disappeared from view.
>
> Kelly sat down to what was absolutely stone-deaf silence. Not a word was spoken. What about the sales pitch? No one moved or whispered. Then longtime BYU benefactor Jesse Knight jumped to his feet and shouted, "We won't sell an acre. We won't sell a single lot." And he turned to President George Brimhall and pledged several thousand dollars to the future of the university. Soon others stood up and joined in, some offering only a widow's mite, but all believing in the dream of a Provo schoolboy, all believing the destiny of a great university which that day had scarcely begun.[282]

The third individual, Sidney B. Sperry, also saw the future of Brigham Young University in vision. Brother Sperry is known for being one of the first Latter-day Saints to receive a PhD in religious studies at a prestigious institution—the University of Chicago. Brother Sperry's vision was prophetic, not just concerning the future of Brigham Young University but also of the Provo Temple. In the 1930s, the university struggled financially as it had in the past. Closing the university appeared to be the only solution. Professor Sperry, a member of the

282. Jeffery R. Holland, "Who We Are and What God Expects Us to Do" (Brigham Young University devotional, Sept. 15, 1987), speeches.byu.edu; taken from B. F. Larsen, "Fifty Years Ago" (Brigham Young University alumni meeting, May 25, 1962), B. F. Larsen biographical file, BYU Archives, 45; see also Wilkinson, *Brigham Young University*, 4:404–7.

religion faculty, was "profoundly disturbed" over the financial situation. One night during this difficult time, as Sperry lay sleepless, a vision was opened to him. He saw "Brigham Young University in the future." He beheld "beautiful modern buildings extending along the entire East Bench and great crowds of people going to and from the University." Along with these buildings, he saw a "temple." The next morning he told some of his colleagues about his vision and then said, "I know that BYU is destined to be one of the great universities in the world, and that some day we will have a Temple here."[283]

283. Memorandum of conference between W. Cleon Skousen and Sidney B. Sperry, 1951; as cited in Wilkinson, *Brigham Young University*, 4:410.

Chapter Eight

The Gift of Tongues

The gift of tongues is a gift of the Spirit that accompanied Christ's first-century followers as well as Christ's latter-day followers. This gift is intriguing to many people but is also misunderstood. The gift of tongues refers to two specific gifts of the Spirit: "speaking with tongues" and the "interpretation of tongues" (see Doctrine and Covenants 46:24–25). These two gifts, according to Elder Bruce R. McConkie, serve at least two purposes: (1) they are given to some of the Saints to help them learn to "speak foreign tongues, to understand the words spoken by aliens, and to translate" languages, and (2) they are given to some for "speaking or understanding alien and unknown languages without premeditation."[284]

Paul taught that the gift of tongues is a sign, not only for those who believe but also for those who do not believe (1 Corinthians 14:22). The most well-known scriptural account of the Saints speaking in tongues was recorded in Acts 2. Shortly after Jesus's forty-day ministry, thousands of people—both believers and nonbelievers—gathered on the day of Pentecost to hear the Apostles speak. At this gathering,

---

284. Bruce R. McConkie, *A New Witness for the Articles of Faith* (Deseret Book, 1985), 374.

many people heard "a sound from heaven as of a rushing mighty wind" (verse 2), and "all were filled with the Holy Ghost" (verse 4). The Apostles quickly discovered that they did not need translators, for everyone heard the sermons in their own tongue (see verse 8). The nonbelievers were amazed, and three thousand of them were baptized that same day (see verse 41).

Some Christian groups have misunderstood this gift, and many have claimed that the incoherent gibberish that is blurted out in their meetings is of God. However, it is only of God—as explained above, as well as displayed in the accounts below—if it enlightens, edifies, teaches, and ultimately advances God's work. Joseph Smith once stated that some brothers and sisters have "had the gift of tongues falsely; they would speak in a muttering, unnatural voice, and their bodies be distorted . . . whereas, there is nothing unnatural in the Spirit of God."[285] The following accounts provide examples of how the gift of tongues assists the prophets in the latter days.

Accounts of the Prophets

Hugh B. Brown

Related by President Thomas S. Monson:

> Arrived Apia, Western Samoa, in the late morning [October 17, 1965] and met with 1322 members of the Apia Stake and surrounding missionaries. . . . At the session, each speaker was supplied a translator, so that the remarks made in English could be translated for the members who spoke only Samoan. As President Hugh B. Brown commenced speaking, a translator was provided. As President Brown concluded his introductory remarks, a counselor in the mission presidency leaned forward and spoke to the stake president, these men being native Samoans. They had observed that the congregation was receiving the message of President Brown without the aid of interpreter. The interpreter was, therefore, excused from his assignment, and President Hugh B. Brown spoke for a full 40 minutes, with his remarks being understood by

285. *History of the Church*, 4:580.

English and Samoan-speaking members alike. All assembled felt the inspiration of this divine gift of the interpretation of tongues.[286]

Alonzo A. Hinckley

One day, when I was alone, visiting among the people at Rotterdam, it was my duty to go back to the homes in which I had left tracts and repossess the literature. As I went I gathered the booklets, [and] some power that I cannot understand possessed me until I quaked and trembled. I stood and looked at the house at which I was to call and felt as if I could not go to the door. But I knew my duty and so, with fortitude and determination, I went to the house, raised the knocker and dropped it. Almost instantly, the door opened and an irate woman stepped out and closed it behind her. She talked in a very loud shrill voice, berating me most severely.

I did not realize for a moment, that I was understanding Dutch as clearly as though she had spoken English. I felt no supernatural power, or influence, or feeling. I just knew every word she was saying. She spoke so loud that a carpenter, who was working across the street, building a porch on a little store, heard her and, I supposed, thought I was abusing the woman, for he came over to where we stood and brought his son with him and, greatly to my alarm, he carried a broadax. The man took his position near me and listened to the woman, who continued her tirade against me in a shouting voice.

I did not grow angry at the woman's abuse, but my soul was filled with a burning desire to speak her language and testify of the divinity of the gospel of the Lord Jesus Christ. I thought if I could only explain to her the importance of my message and the good it would do her, she would not berate me as she does now. In a few moments she ceased her abuse, and I began speaking. I spoke in the Dutch language. I defended the truth and bore testimony of the restoration of the Gospel. I had forgotten the big man who stood near me with his ax, and I looked at the woman and delivered my message of truth; he put his arm across my shoulders and, looking

286. Eugene E. Campbell and Richard D. Poll, *Hugh B. Brown: His Life and Thought* (Bookcraft, 1975), 268.

the woman in the face, said, "The Mormon Church may have its black sheep, but this is a man of God."

The woman answered, "I know it." After our conversation, I went back home, hardly touching the ground. It dawned upon me that the prayers I had offered, and perhaps as a result, in part, of the hard study I had made, and the prayers of those at home, had been answered in a moment, for I had spoken the Dutch language intelligently for the first time in my life. In ecstasy, I rushed home to tell Brother Thatcher in the office, and to tell the president of the mission; but when I attempted to speak, to my great dismay I was the same as before, I could not understand nor speak the language.

President Farrell asked me if I would go to meeting that night. "Yes, President Farrell," I answered, "after a man has been blessed of the Lord as I have been, I will gladly go, but I beg of you not to call upon me to speak even if someone translates what I say." "Very well," he said, "I promise you, Brother Hinckley, that if you go you will not be asked to speak." I went to meeting, and everything progressed nicely, as I thought, until Brother DeBry, the branch president, arose and, contrary to Brother Farrell's promise, said, "We will now hear from Elder Hinckley." President Farrell stepped forward, greatly embarrassed, and asked, "Brother Hinckley, shall I interpret for you?" I felt a power I cannot describe. "Wait, President Farrell," I said as I stood upon my feet; and then I began to speak, not in my native tongue, but in the Dutch language. And then and there, I delivered the first discourse in my life in the tongue of the mission. The following morning I was sent to preside over the Amsterdam District.[287]

David O. McKay

Related by Jeanette McKay Morrell:

On Friday, June 13, there was a mission-wide conference of missionaries and members in Rotterdam, attended by 1,024, which represented one-third of the membership of the mission. At this meeting there was a presentation of a Delft blue china plate to

287. Bryant S. Hinckley, *Faith of Our Pioneer Fathers* (Deseret Book, 1956), 231–33.

President and Mrs. McKay, and one also to Elder and Mrs. David Lawrence McKay. During his remarks, the President said:

"Today, Sister McKay and I stood on the ruins of the place where thirty years ago a very remarkable experience occurred to me. I was speaking to an audience here in Rotterdam, and President Zappey was interpreting, when it happened that the gift of interpreting tongues was given to me. There may be some here today who were present at that time. President Zappey was making a statement following my remarks, and even though I could not understand the language, I knew that he had given the wrong interpretation, and I told him so and corrected him. He turned to me and said that I really had no need for an interpreter since I understood the language so well. This is an illustration of the spirit directing the minds of each."[288]

David O. McKay

One of the most important events on my world tour of the missions of the Church was the gift of interpretation of the English tongue to the Saints of New Zealand, at a session of their conference, held on the 23rd day of April, 1921, at Puke Tapu Branch, Waikato District, Huntly, New Zealand. The service was held in a large tent, beneath the shade of which hundreds of earnest men and women gathered in anxious anticipation of seeing and hearing an Apostle of the Church, the first one to visit that land.

When I looked over that vast assemblage and contemplated the great expectations that filled the hearts of all who had met together, I realized how inadequately I might satisfy the ardent desires of their souls, and I yearned, most earnestly, for the gift of tongues that I might be able to speak to them in their native language. Until that moment I had not given much serious thought to the gift of tongues, but on that occasion, I wished with all my heart, that I might be worthy of that divine power. In other missions I had spoken through an interpreter but, able as all interpreters are, I nevertheless felt hampered, in fact, somewhat inhibited, in presenting my message. Now, I faced an audience that had assembled with

---

288. Jeanette McKay Morrell, *Highlights in the Life of President David O. McKay* (Deseret Book, 1966), 110–11.

unusual expectations, and I then realized, as never before, the great responsibility of my office. From the depth of my soul, I prayed for divine assistance. When I arose to give my address, I said to Brother Stuart Meha, our interpreter, that I would speak without his translating, sentence by sentence and then to the audience I continued:

"I wish, oh, how I wish I had the power to speak to you in your own tongue, that I might tell you what is in my heart; but since I have not the gift, I pray, and I ask you to pray, that you might have the spirit of interpretation, of discernment, that you may understand at least the spirit while I am speaking, and then you will get the words and the thought when Brother Meha interprets."

My sermon lasted forty minutes, and I have never addressed a more attentive, more respectful audience. My listeners were in perfect rapport—this I knew when I saw tears in their eyes. Some of them at least, perhaps most of them, who did not understand English, had the gift of interpretation. Brother Sidney Christy, a native New Zealander, who had been a student at Brigham Young University, at the close of my address, whispered to me, "Brother McKay, they got your message!" "Yes," I replied, "I think so, but for the benefit of some who may not have understood, we shall have Brother Meha give a synopsis of it in Maori." During the translation, some of the Maoris corrected him on some points, showing that they had a clear conception of what had been said in English.[289]

Franklin D. Richards

Related by President Heber J. Grant:

Karl G. Maeser read a vicious attack upon the "Mormons"—about the "Danites" and the "Destroying Angels," and so on, and so forth. Then he found in the same article that the "Mormons" were industrious, that they were frugal, that there was not a poorhouse in all the territory of Utah, that the fifteen percent of Gentile population, among them then furnished eighty-five per cent of the criminals, according to United States statistics, compiled by the Gentiles themselves. He found that there was not one saloon in the entire territory of Utah, and that the only place where whiskey was

289. Clare Middlemiss, *Cherished Experiences from the Writings of President David O. McKay* (Deseret Book, 1955), 73–74.

sold was in Salt Lake City; and, to the disgrace of the city government, they were selling it. That is what he found on the temperance question. He found that there was not a single house of ill fame in the whole of Utah. He found that the people went to bed at night with their front and back doors open. After reading all this he said to himself: "The man who wrote this illustrated article for the magazine is a liar. The fruits of honesty, industry sobriety, and brotherly love do not grow among immoral and wicked people," so he sent for some tracts, investigated the gospel and embraced it. On the night of his baptism, which occurred at midnight, he looked up to heaven and said, in substance: "O, God, if what I have done tonight meets with your approval, and you will give to me the witness of the Spirit that this gospel, that I believe, is in very deed the truth, that I may know it, I pledge my life, if need be, to its promulgation and its advancement." . . .

God heard and answered that prayer. Walking from the river in which he was baptized, Karl G. Maeser was conversing upon the principles of the gospel with the late Apostle Franklin D. Richards, and Brother William Budge was acting as interpreter, Brother Richards talking in English and Brother Maeser in German. They began their walk of several miles to return home. After walking a short distance Brother Maeser announced to Brother Budge that he need not interpret the answers, that he understood them. Immediately thereafter, Brother Franklin said, "You need not interpret those questions; I understand them." They walked for miles, Franklin D. Richards answering questions in English, Karl G. Maeser asking them in German, neither knowing the other's language, yet by the inspiration of the Spirit of God, both understanding each other. . . .

When these two men reached the bridge that spans the river Elbe, on their way into the city of Dresden, they were separated, and when they reached the other side of the bridge Brother Maeser again began asking questions, but Brother Richards could not then understand him, nor could Brother Maeser understand anything further that was said in reply; and they were obliged to revert to Brother Budge's interpretation. Then Brother Maeser turned to Brother Richards and said, "What does this mean, we could understand each other for miles, and now we can't understand?" "Brother Maeser," said Apostle Richards, "the Lord has given to you a portion of the fruit of the gospel of Jesus Christ, as restored in our day. For some wise reason he has allowed you to enjoy one of the manifestations of the Spirit accompanying the true gospel of Christ." Brother Maeser told me, with tears rolling down his cheeks, although it had been nearly 50 years since he had that manifestation, that he realized that God had heard and answered his prayers.[290]

Joseph Smith Jr.

On the 22nd day of January [1833], I spoke to the conference in another tongue, and was followed in the same gift by Brother Zebedee Coltrin, and he by Brother William Smith, after which the Lord poured out His Spirit in a miraculous manner, until all the Elders spake in tongues, and several members, both male and female, exercised the same gift. Great and glorious were the divine manifestations of the Holy Spirit. Praises were sung to God and the Lamb; speaking and praying, all in tongues, occupied the conference until a late hour at night, so rejoiced were we at the return of these long absent blessings.[291]

Joseph Smith Jr.

Related by E. Cecil McGavin:

The Prophet once received an invitation to visit a tribe of Indians across the river and tell them of the Book the Great Spirit had given him. The Indian agent promised to interpret his speech to the assembled redmen. The Prophet gladly accepted the invitation, journeyed to the appointed place, and addressed the Indians. When the agent arose to interpret the speech of the unpopular leader, he failed to tell what his visitor had said, for he was anxious to stir up the Indians against the Mormons. Instead of a faithful translation of the speech, he told them that the chief of the Mormons intended to muster his armies of pale face warriors, arm them with rifles and swords, march them into the region where Indian tepees

290. George C. Lambert, *Gems of Reminiscence: Faith-Promoting Series*, no. 17 (George C. Lambert, 1915), 104–7.

291. *History of the Church*, 1:322–23.

now covered the ground, and drive the redmen and their families toward the setting sun, watering the thirsty soil with their blood as they fled. Paleface plows would uncover the graves of the redmen, and houses of logs would replace the leather lodges of the Indians.

The Indians listened but a moment to this false interpretation until they began to grunt and move about nervously. Soon they were picking up stones or pieces of wood to be used as cudgels with which to kill the pale face leader who dared to come into their strongholds with such a message of doom. Their rugged features were wrinkled in scorn and anger as they stared ominously at their visitor who had come as a preacher, but would be made a prisoner. In a miraculous manner akin to the universal spirit of discernment that permeated the place of meeting on the day of Pentecost, Joseph Smith understood every word his deceitful interpreter was saying. This knowledge came to him before the angry warriors had taken up their arms to silence him.

He stepped forward with as much bravery as any warrior in the audience ever manifested, pushed aside the falsifying interpreter, and began to speak as if to men of his own speech. The moment his voice was heard, a calm spirit of understanding settled upon the warriors. They unloosed their hold on stones or other weapons, for they understood every word the stranger said as if he spoke to them in their own tongue. His discourse was long and eloquent, every word of which fell upon the ears of his hearers as if he had spent his life in their wigwams, learning their speech as well as they themselves knew it. This was such a miracle to the natives that they saw in it the invisible hand of the Great Spirit. A spirit seemed to whisper to their troubled thoughts that the pale face chief was a true son of the Great Spirit. When the results of this meeting were told to other tribes, other delegations of redmen began to visit Nauvoo, seeking advice from the pale face chief.[292]

Brigham Young

A few weeks after my baptism [April 14, 1832] I was at Brother Kimball's house one morning, and while family prayer was being offered up, Brother Alpheus Gifford commenced speaking in

292. E. Cecil McGavin, *Nauvoo the Beautiful* (Bookcraft, 1972), 81–82.

tongues. Soon the Spirit came on me, and I spoke in tongues, and we thought only of the day of Pentecost, when the Apostles were clothed upon with cloven tongues of fire. In September 1832, Brother Heber C. Kimball took his horse and wagon, Brother Joseph Young and myself accompanying him and started for Kirtland to see the Prophet Joseph. We visited many friends on the way, and some branches of the Church. We exhorted them and prayed with them, and I spoke in tongues. Some pronounced it genuine and from the Lord, and others pronounced it of the devil.

We proceeded to Kirtland and stopped at John P. Greene's, who had just arrived there with his family. We rested a few minutes, took some refreshment, and started to see the Prophet. We went to his father's house and learned that he was in the woods, chopping. We immediately repaired to the woods, where we found the Prophet, and two or three of his brothers chopping and hauling wood. Here my joy was full at the privilege of shaking the hand of the Prophet of God, and received the sure testimony, by the spirit of prophecy, that he was all that any man could believe him to be, as a true Prophet. He was happy to see us, and bid us welcome. We soon returned to his house, he accompanying us.

In the evening a few of the brethren came in, and we conversed together upon the things of the kingdom. He called upon me to pray; in my prayer I spoke in tongues. As soon as we arose from our knees the brethren flocked around him, and asked his opinion concerning the gift of tongues that was upon me. He told them it was the pure Adamic language. Some said to him they expected he would condemn the gift Brother Brigham had, but he said, "No, it is of God, and the time will come when Brother Brigham Young will preside over this Church."[293]

Brigham Young

The Twelve continued their journey [in August 1844] through the day and night by stage. While upon their journey they overtook a company of Norwegians who were traveling with ox teams, and heavily loaded wagons, one of which was stuck fast in the mud, blocking up the road, while several of them were whipping the oxen

293. *Millennial Star* 25 (Jan. 3, 1863): 439–40.

and bawling to them in the Norwegian language, which seemed to frighten the oxen, but they were unable to move the wagons on. After sitting and looking at them a moment, President Young got out of the coach and stepped up, and took the whip out of the hands of one of the Norwegians, telling them all to stand out of the way. He then talked to the oxen in a tongue which was not understood by Norwegians or English, and touching them lightly with the whip, they instantly pulled the wagon out of the mud and continued the journey, much to the astonishment of the Norwegians and the surprise and amusement of the passengers on the stage.[294]

Notes and Commentary

As on the day of Pentecost when many heard the sermons in their own tongue, the people of Western Samoa understood Hugh B. Brown of the First Presidency in their own tongue. A similar experience was recorded when David O. McKay spoke to the Saints in New Zealand in 1921. This is a perfect example of how the "interpretation of tongues" is bestowed by the Holy Ghost. Joseph Smith taught that the gift of tongues, whether interpreting or speaking, "was particularly instituted for the preaching of the Gospel to other nations and languages."[295] The Prophet Joseph also taught that the gift of tongues is among the most dangerous of the gifts of the Spirit because it is one that Satan can imitate the easiest. "The devil," Joseph explained, "can speak in tongues; the adversary will come with his work; he can tempt all classes; [he] can speak in English or Dutch."[296] On another occasion, Joseph taught that any gift, including the gift of tongues, if used improperly, will "prove an injury, a snare and a curse instead of a blessing."[297]

President Joseph F. Smith, like the Prophet Joseph, taught that the gift of tongues is given primarily to spread the gospel and will only be given when necessary. "I believe in the gifts of the Holy Spirit unto men," explained President Smith, "but I do not want the gift

294. *History of the Church,* 7:224.

295. *History of the Church,* 2:162.

296. *History of the Church,* 3:392.

297. *History of the Church,* 5:32.

of tongues, except when I need it. I needed the gift of tongues once and the Lord gave it to me. I was in a foreign land, sent to preach the Gospel to a people whose language I could not understand. Then I sought earnestly for the gift of tongues, and by this gift and by study, in a hundred days after landing upon those islands I could talk to the people in their language as I now talk to you in my native tongue. . . . If you have need of this gift of tongues, seek for it and God will help you in it. But I do not ask you to be very hungry for the gift of tongues, for if you are not careful the devil will deceive you in it."[298]

President Harold B. Lee recorded another account that is worth noting here. Although the recipient of the gift was not a prophet, President Lee recounted the following experience to illustrate the importance of the Spirit and the gift of tongues:

> Something happened at a recent general conference that will give you a key to how the Lord can open the mind of a man and give him spiritual understanding beyond his natural self. There were eleven translators or interpreters down in the basement of the Tabernacle translating in eleven different languages. For most of the talks they had scripts, so they could study them and, as the speakers spoke in English, they would repeat the words in the various languages for the benefit of those who were listening on earphones. One of these brethren was translating for the Swedish Saints. At the priesthood meeting I spoke extemporaneously, so he had no script to follow. But he reported that something miraculous happened. This is what he told me:
>
> The whole conference was a spiritual experience, but at the general priesthood meeting I had an experience that I have never had before. I knew that there were some Swedish brethren attending the conference who had never been here before and perhaps would never come again. Therefore, I had a great desire that they receive everything that our prophet had to deliver. Not having a script, I commended myself into the hands of the Lord, and as you began to speak, I was startled by the fact that I knew one or two words and even three ahead of the time when you would say them. At first, I was so startled that I did not dare to pronounce them as they were given.

298. Conference Report, Apr. 1900, 41.

Usually I close my eyes and listen and then interpret as I hear the speakers deliver, but this time I was prompted to look at your face on the television screen. In this very unusual situation, I looked at you and began to translate the words as they came. However, to my amazement I did not receive just the words in my mind; with my inner eyes, I saw them emanating from the vicinity of the temple of your head and coming toward me. I did not see them actually as written on something, and yet, I saw them and how they were spelled, and I experienced the power of the Spirit as I received them.

One of the things that made it even more dramatic was that when a complex sentence was about to be delivered, I received more words so that I could reconstruct the grammar into good Swedish and deliver it at the very moment you pronounced the words. Never before had I experienced the great force with which the interpreted message was flowing as I did at that time.[299]

---

299. Harold B. Lee, *Ye Are the Light of the World: Selected Sermons and Writings of Harold B. Lee* (Deseret Book, 1974), 351–53.

Chapter Nine

Healing the Sick and Raising the Dead

When Jesus began His ministry in Galilee, it immediately became clear to all who encountered Him that not only was He a messianic candidate, but He had the power to heal "all manner of sickness and all manner of disease among the people" (Matthew 4:23). After Jesus "called unto him" twelve men, who would learn from him and eventually lead the other disciples, he gave them power to "heal the sick, cleanse the lepers, [and] raise the dead" (Matthew 10:1, 8). Luke recorded that after Jesus was resurrected and ascended to heaven, the Apostles continued to perform many miracles. Multitudes of people "brought forth the sick into the streets, and laid them on beds and couches, that at the least the shadow of Peter passing by might overshadow some of them. There came also a multitude out of the cities round about unto Jerusalem, bringing sick folks, and them which were vexed with unclean spirits: and they were healed every one" (Acts 5:15–16).

James, the brother of Jesus, explained that if any are sick, they should "call for the elders of the church; and let them pray over him, anointing him with oil in the name of the Lord: And the prayer of faith shall save the sick, and the Lord shall raise him up" (James 5:14–15). Jesus also revealed to Joseph Smith that "the elders of the church, two or more, shall be called, and shall pray for and lay their hands upon them in my name" (Doctrine and Covenants 42:44). Joseph Smith taught that because healing is a gift of the Spirit (see 1 Corinthians 12:10; Moroni 10:11), one must receive the gift in the "way marked out by the Lord," which is to be baptized and receive the gift of the Holy Ghost before receiving the gift to heal.[300]

Latter-day Saints are extremely familiar with the gift of healing. Accounts of healings and raisings of the dead in our history could fill countless volumes. It is no wonder that the people who claim to be true followers of Jesus are also those who claim to possess the gift of healing. Healing in The Church of Jesus Christ of Latter-day Saints is performed not by mesmerizing chants, superstitious formulas, medicines, or charismatic prayers but by the laying on of hands and humbly blessing the sick in the name of Jesus Christ. The experiences related below, concerning healings and the raising of the dead, are but a small percentage of what the prophets have experienced in Latter-day Saint history.

Accounts of the Prophets

Ezra T. Benson and Others

Concerning Lorenzo Snow, related by W. W. Cluff:

> We arrived at Honolulu, the capital of the islands, about the 27th of March, 1864. On the 29th we sailed for Lahaina, on the schooner Nettie Merrill, Captain Fisher, for the island of Maui, a distance of about ninety miles from Honolulu. On the morning of the 31st of March, we came to anchor about one mile from the mouth of the little harbor of Lahaina.
>
> Apostles Ezra T. Benson, Lorenzo Snow, Brother Alma L. Smith, and myself got into the small boat to go on shore. Brother Joseph F. Smith, as he afterwards stated, had some misgivings about going in that boat, but the manifestation was not sufficiently strong to indicate any general accident. He preferred to remain on board

300. *History of the Church*, 4:555.

the vessel until the boat returned. The boat started for the shore. It contained some barrels and boxes, the captain, a white man, two or three native passengers, and the boat's crew, who were also natives. The entrance to the harbor is a very narrow passage between coral reefs, and when the sea is rough, it is very dangerous, on account of the breakers. Where the vessel lay, the sea was not rough, but only presented the appearance of heavy swells rolling to the shore.

As we approached the reef it was evident to me that the surf was running higher than we anticipated. I called the captain's attention to the fact. We were running quartering across the waves, and I suggested that we change our course so as to run at right angles with them. He replied that he did not think there was any danger, and our course was not changed. We went but little farther, when a heavy swell struck the boat and carried us before it about fifty yards. When the swell passed it left us in a trough between two huge waves. It was too late to retrieve our error, and we must run our chances. When the second swell struck the boat, it raised the stern so high that the steersman's oar was out of the water, and he lost control of the boat. It rode on the swell a short distance and swung around just as the wave began to break up. We were almost instantly capsized into the dashing, foaming sea.

I felt no concern for myself about drowning, for while on my former mission I had learned to swim and sport in the surf of those shores. The last I remember of Brother Snow, as the boat was going over, I saw him seize the upper edge of it with both hands. Fearing that the upper edge of the boat, or the barrels, might hit and injure me as the boat was going over, I plunged head foremost into the water. After swimming a short distance, I came to the surface without being strangled or injured. The boat was bottom upwards, and barrels, hats and umbrellas were floating in every direction. I swam to the boat and as there was nothing to cling to on the bottom, I reached under and seized the edge of it.

About the same time Brother Benson came up near me and readily got hold of the boat. Brother Alma L. Smith came up on the opposite side of the boat from Brother Benson and myself. He was considerably strangled, but succeeded in securing a hold on the boat.

A short time afterwards the captain was discovered, about fifty yards from ups. Two sailors, one on each side, succeeded in keeping him on the surface, although life was apparently extinct.

Nothing yet had been seen of Brother Snow, although the natives had been swimming and diving in every direction in search of him. We were only about one-fourth of a mile from shore. The people, as soon as they discovered our circumstances, manned a life boat and hurried to the rescue. We were taken into the boat, when the crew wanted to row for the shore, and pick up the captain by the way. We told them that one of our friends was yet missing, and we did not want to leave. We discovered that a second boat had left the shore and could reach the captain as soon as the one we were in. Seeing this, the crew of our boat consented to remain and assist us.

The captain was taken ashore, and by working over him sometime was brought to life. Probably his life would not have been much endangered but for a sack of four or five hundred silver dollars which he held in his hand, the weight of which took him at once to the bottom. The natives dove and brought him up, still clinging to the sack. When his vitality was restored, the first thing he inquired about was the money; intimating to the natives, with peculiar emphasis, that it would not have been healthy for them to have lost it.

Brother Snow had not yet been discovered, and the anxiety was intense. The natives were, evidently, doing all in their power. Finally, one of them, in edging himself around the capsized boat, must have felt Brother Snow with his feet and pulled him, at least, partly from under it, as the first I saw of Brother Snow was his hair floating upon the water around one end of the capsized boat. As soon as we got him into our boat, we told the boatmen to pull for the shore with all possible speed. His body was stiff, and life apparently extinct.

Brother A. L. Smith and I were sitting side by side. We laid Brother Snow across our laps, and, on the way to shore, we quietly administered to him and asked the Lord to spare his life, that he might return to his family and home. On reaching the shore, we carried him a little way to some large empty barrels that were lying on the sandy beach. We laid him face downwards on one of them, and rolled him back and forth until we succeeded in getting the water he had swallowed out of him.

During this time a number of persons came down from the town; among them was Mr. E. P. Adams, a merchant. All were willing to do what they could. We washed Brother Snow's face with camphor, furnished by Mr. Adams. We did not only what was customary in such cases, but also what the Spirit seemed to whisper to us. After working over him for some time, without any indications of returning life, the bystanders said that nothing more could be done for him. But we did not feel like giving him up, and still prayed and worked over him, with an assurance that the Lord would hear and answer our prayers.

Finally we were impressed to place our mouth over his and make an effort to inflate his lungs, alternately blowing in and drawing out the air, imitating, as far as possible, the natural process of breathing. This we persevered in until we succeeded in inflating his lungs. After a little, we perceived very faint indications of returning life. A slight wink of the eye, which, until then, had been open and death-like, and a very faint rattle in the throat, were the first symptoms of returning vitality. These grew more and more distinct, until consciousness was fully restored.

When this result was reached, it must have been fully one hour after the upsetting of the boat. A Portuguese man, living in Lahaina, who, from the first, rendered us much assistance, invited us to take Brother Snow to his house. There being no Saints in the place, we gladly accepted his kind offer. Every possible attention was given for Brother Snow's comfort. We will here append my brother's [Lorenzo Snow] account of the upsetting of the boat, and what he can recollect of the sensations of a man drowning and afterwards coming to life:

"As we were moving along, probably more than a quarter of a mile from where we expected to land, my attention was suddenly arrested by Captain Fisher calling to the oarsmen in a voice which denoted some alarm, 'Hurry up, hurry up!' I immediately discovered the cause of alarm. A short distance behind us, I saw an immense surf, thirty or forty feet high, rushing towards us swifter than a race horse. We had scarcely a moment for reflection before the huge mass was upon us. In an instant our boat, with its contents, as though it were a feather, was hurled into a gulf of briny waters, and all was under this rolling, seething mountain wave. It took me by surprise. I think, however, that I comprehended the situation—in the midst of turbulent waves—a quarter of a mile from the shore, without much probability of human aid.

"I felt confident, however, there would be some way of escape; that the Lord would provide the means, for it was not possible that my life and mission were thus to terminate. This reliance on the Lord banished fear, and inspired me up to the last moment of consciousness. In such extreme cases of excitement, we seem to live hours in a minute, and a volume of thoughts crowd themselves into one single moment. It was so with me in that perilous scene.

"Having been somewhat subject to faint, I think that after a few moments in the water I must have fainted, as I did not suffer the pain common in the experience of drowning persons. I had been in the water only a few moments, until I lost consciousness. The first I knew afterwards, I was on shore, receiving the kind and tender attentions of my brethren. The first recollection I have of returning consciousness, was that of a very small light—the smallest imaginable. This soon disappeared, and I was again in total darkness. Again it appeared much larger than before, then sank away and left me, as before, in forgetfulness. Thus it continued to come and go, until, finally, I recognized, as I thought, persons whispering, and soon after, I asked in a feeble whisper, 'What is the matter?' I immediately recognized the voice of Elder Cluff, as he replied, 'You have been drowned; the boat upset in the surf.' Quick as lightning the scene of our disaster flashed upon my mind. I immediately asked, 'Are you brethren all safe?' The emotion that was awakened in my bosom by the answer of Elder Cluff will remain with me as long as life continues: 'Brother Snow, we are all safe.' I rapidly recovered, and very soon was able to walk and accompany the brethren to our lodgings."[301]

George Q. Cannon

We had a meeting at a place called Waiehu [Hawaii]. After the meeting was over, three persons requested to be administered to, one of whom was a blind man. He had been blind for upwards of thirty years, but his sight was restored to him. He began to amend

301. Eliza R. Snow, *Biography and Family Record of Lorenzo Snow* (Deseret News, 1884), 276–81.

from the time hands were laid upon him, and the next morning he was able to see. He was afterwards able to go about without any guide; and I have frequently seen him come into meeting, winding this way among the people, without any aid, to a seat which he was accustomed to occupy near the speaker. His restoration caused a great stir in the neighborhood, for his blindness was well known. He had a son, a mature man, who could barely recollect when his father was able to see and go about without aid.[302]

Matthew Cowley

A little over a year ago a couple came into my office carrying a little boy. The father said to me, "My wife and I have been fasting for two days, and we've brought our little boy up for a blessing. You are the one we've been sent to." I said, "What's the matter with him?" They said he was born blind, deaf, and dumb, had no co-ordination of his muscles, and couldn't even crawl at the age of five years. . . . I had implicit faith in the fasting and the prayers of those parents. I blessed that child, and a few weeks later I received a letter: "Brother Cowley, we wish you could see our little boy now. He's crawling. When we throw a ball across the floor, he races after it on his hands and knees. He can see. When we clap our hands over his head, he jumps. He can hear." Medical science had laid the burden down. God had taken over. The little boy was rapidly recovering or really getting what he'd never had.[303]

Matthew Cowley

I've told the story about the little baby nine months old who was born blind. The father came up with him one Sunday and said, "Brother Cowley, our baby hasn't been blessed yet; we'd like you to bless him." I said, "Why have you waited so long?" "Oh, we just didn't get around to it. . ." I said, "All right, what's the name?" So he told me the name, and I was just going to start when he said, "By the way, give him his vision when you give him a name. He was born blind." Well, it shocked me, but then I said to myself, why not?

302. George Q Cannon, *My First Mission* (Juvenile Instructor Office, 1879), 64.

303. Matthew Cowley, *Matthew Cowley Speaks* (Deseret Book, 1954), 245–48.

Christ told his disciples when he left them they could work miracles. And I had faith in that father's faith. After I gave that child its name, I finally got around to giving it its vision. That boy's about twelve years old now. The last time I was back there I was afraid to inquire about him. I was sure he had gone blind again. That's the way my faith works sometimes. So I asked the branch president about him. And he said, "Brother Cowley, the worst thing you ever did was to bless that child to receive his vision. He's the meanest kid in the neighborhood, always getting into mischief." Boy, I was thrilled about that kid getting into mischief![304]

Gordon B. Hinckley

I recall once when I arrived in Hong Kong I was asked if I would visit a woman in the hospital whose doctors had told her she was going blind and would lose her sight within a week. She asked if we would administer to her and we did so, and she states that she was miraculously healed. I have a painting in my home that she gave me which says on the back of it, "To Gordon B. Hinckley in grateful appreciation for the miracle of saving my sight." I said to her, "I didn't save your sight. Of course, the Lord saved your sight. Thank Him and be grateful to Him."[305]

Harold B. Lee

There is a power beyond the sight of man that heals not only sick bodies but sick souls. . . . I met a young man in Japan where we were holding a servicemen's conference. . . . He had his right arm in a sling and . . . said, "I am not a member of the Church but I understand you are going to be down in Manila in another few weeks. We will be there with the Seventh Fleet and I hope to be able to tell you when you get there that I am now a member of the Church."

The weeks went by and I had almost forgotten the incident until, as we held a conference at Clark Field in Manila, . . . I spotted the same man whom I had met in Japan. . . . He said, "You noticed I had my arm in a sling and it was paining me terribly all through

304. Cowley, *Matthew Cowley Speaks*, 247–48.

305. Dallin H. Oaks, "Miracles," *Ensign*, June 2001, 12.

that service, but after we had shaken hands on the stand suddenly the throbbing pain seemed to stop and I took my arm out of the sling and began to flex it and there was no pain. I went back to the ship, never needed any treatment, the infection seemed to have been gone, and I sensed the fact that I had been in the presence of a power that had taken away the pain of my body. I am going back home now to prove that I am worthy of the love of my sweet wife."

A few years later I was with a companion in Norfolk, Virginia, where we were organizing a new stake and right down in the front seat there sat this same man with a beautiful woman by his side, his wife, and we sustained him as a member of the elder's presidency of that stake. Yes, the Lord can heal sick bodies but the greatest miracle we see is the healing of sick souls.[306]

Harold B. Lee

In Brazil . . . two of the elders came to me and said, "We have a family here that is investigating. They have a little boy who is six years old who has never walked. When we told him that there was going to be an apostle here tonight for the conference, the little boy said, 'When the apostle comes, he will bless me and I will walk. . .'" The elder said, "Would you be kind enough to join with us in blessing this little boy?" I replied that I would.

The president was busy with some other things at the conference, so I went with the two elders and the father carried this little boy in his arms and carried him in and sat him on a chair. The mother and two smaller children sat there, and the only impression I had as the elders and I put our hands on his head was that the little fellow sat there and cried all the time we were blessing him. He was overcome by something.

On my way home I got a letter from President Moyle who said, "We are anxious to have you come home and tell us about the healing that came to that little boy down in Brazil." I hadn't heard anything about the outcome of the blessing, but when I arrived home I was shown a picture showing this little boy standing on his feet for the first time. That miracle didn't come because of me; it didn't come because of the elders; this was because the Lord himself, by

306. Baccalaureate Address, Ricks College, May 6, 1970; *Ensign*, Feb. 1974, 16.

my hand and the hands of the elders, put his hands upon the head of that little boy by our hands and he received the strength . . . to stand on his feet for the first time since his birth.[307]

David O. McKay

On Sunday, June 29, 1952, Sister McKay and I were in Berlin, Germany, near the Iron Curtain. Arrangements had been made for a meeting of the Saints, investigators, and friends in the "Mercedes Palast" theater, the largest hall in North Berlin. Prior to the meeting I had received word through the presidency of the East German Mission that one of the members of the Church in that mission—a sister—had lost her husband and eldest son under communist rule. She had been driven from her home, and was subsequently exposed to the rigors of the weather and lack of nutrition until she finally became paralyzed and had been confined to her bed for five years. She had heard of my coming to Berlin, and being unable to travel herself, she expressed the desire that her two little children—a boy and a girl about ten and twelve years of age—be sent over to meet the President of the Church. This good sister said: "I know if I send my children to shake hands with President McKay, and then they come home and take my hand—if I can hold their little hands in mine—I know that I shall get better."

Arrangements were made for them to take the trip. Some of the Saints contributed to the clothing of the little children, and the missionaries contributed to pay their expenses. I asked the mission president to point out these little children as they came to the meeting. Two little children among thousands who were assembled! Anticipating meeting them, I took a new handkerchief, and when that little girl and boy came along, I went to them and shook their hands, and said, "Will you take this handkerchief to your mother with my blessing?" I later learned that after I had shaken hands with them, they would not shake hands with anyone else, for they did not want to touch anyone with their hands until they got back to their mother. We heard no more about it; however, the incident was well-known throughout the crowd. I saw the children

307. Joint Nottingham and Leicester Conference, Nottingham Stake, England, Sept. 2, 1973; *Ensign*, Feb. 1974, 18.

again in the conference house that night. They were sleeping on the top floor of the mission home—sweet little darlings!

When Sister McKay returned to Salt Lake City, she wrote to the mission president's wife and asked her to find out how the mother of the two little children was getting along. In her reply, the mission president's wife said, "This sister thanks the Lord every day for the blessing and the handkerchief which President McKay sent through her two children, and she has the faith that she will fully recover, and I believe so, too. Immediately after the children came home, her feet and toes began to get feeling in them, and this feeling slowly moved up into her legs, and now she gets out of bed alone and seats herself on a chair, and then, with her feet and the chair, works all the way around to the kitchen sink, where she has the children bring her the dishes to wash, and other things, and is very thankful that she is able to help now." That is the faith of a mother in the Russian zone. God bless her, and bless all who are over there![308]

David O. McKay

Related by Melvin Mickelson:

If I were to labor in the service of our Master all the days of my life, I could only repay in part the blessings he has so freely given to me, by the faith and humility of our great leader, President David O. McKay. He, through the power of the priesthood, made it possible for me to enjoy the blessing of sight.

In the month of March 1939, while trucking grain to Salt Lake City from Gem Valley, Idaho, and returning loaded with coal, I was aware of quite a severe headache, but kept on going even though I realized the trouble was in my eyes, particularly my right eye. As this pain increased, I became sick and was getting ready to go to a doctor when I received word that my uncle, Theodore Mickelson, living in Tetonia, Idaho, had passed away and that the family desired that I speak at his funeral. This seemed an opportunity to speak for one whom I loved very much.

308. Clare Middlemiss, *Cherished Experiences from the Writings of President David O. McKay* (Deseret Book, 1955), 149–51.

I thought perhaps I could see a doctor in Idaho Falls, Idaho. I went to a doctor there, and, when he looked at my eyes, he said that my trouble was more than he would like to take care of. He then recommended another doctor in another town whom I went to see. This doctor seemed quite excited about my condition, and he, being a specialist, treated my eyes. At this time I was unable to see anything out of my right eye, and the pain was increasing by the hour. However, I stayed and spoke at the funeral of my uncle.

As soon as I finished speaking, I was brought home by my brother-in-law, Vernon H. Mendenhall. I went immediately to see a doctor at Soda Springs, Idaho, who exclaimed that I was blind the minute he examined my eyes. He suggested that I go at once to Salt Lake City, Utah. We arrived there about five o'clock the next morning. My wife, Mary, called an eye physician, who came to his office about six a.m. After she told him what was wrong he examined my eyes, and then he exclaimed, "Mary, you are a week or ten days too late in coming for aid to save your husband's eye. We may have to remove both of them." I was suffering with iritis. After talking with Mary and me, he decided to fight the infection with medicine.

The doctor worked hard and was very kind as the treatments were severe and painful. I realized that if I had gone to the doctor as my wife had suggested when I first took sick, most of the trouble could have been stopped. The doctor advised me to keep on my feet and walk around if it were possible. This was accomplished only by my wife leading me, for the sight in one eye was completely gone, and the other had sympathized to a point I could not see to get around. For one week the doctor treated my eyes, only to say each day that they were getting worse.

Then one morning the doctor told me he would have to remove my right eye. By so doing the other eye might be saved. About two hours after we had left the doctor's office, President McKay came to our door and told us he had heard of my sickness and wondered if I would like a blessing. No one could deny the feeling of peace which came with him. As he blessed me, the pain eased and then left me. As President McKay left the room, my wife's words of faith were, "You will be all right." I had felt bad because I could not attend the meeting in the temple with the bishops that day, for at that time I was bishop of Lago Ward, Bannock Stake; but I had received a blessing which shall never be forgotten. The next morning I returned to the doctor's office. After examining my eyes, he said, "Some miracle has happened. We won't have to remove that eye. Why, you will receive fifteen to twenty percent of your eyesight." The next day he told me seventy-five percent of my vision would come back, and on the third day, perhaps all of my vision.[309]

Marriner W. Merrill

Related by his son:

Indians were never very troublesome in Cache Valley and the country north, yet at times threatening situations arose. It was during one of these occasions that Father and a number of other men from northern Cache Valley were called to go to the protection of the settlers further north. A heavy rain fell just before their departure which made the roads and the country side extremely muddy and slippery. As Father took a detour, he had gone out a short distance from the company when his horse slipped and fell with Father under him. When the other men of the party reached the scene Father was motionless and from all appearance, dead.

Father relates that his spirit left his body and stood, as it were, in the air above it. He could see his body and the men standing around and he heard their conversation. At this option he could re-enter its body or remain in spirit. His reflection upon his responsibility to his family and his great desire to live caused him to choose to enter his body again and live. As he did so he regained consciousness and experienced severe pains incident to the injuries which he had suffered from the accident.[310]

David W. Patten

Related by Abraham O. Smoot:

I have witnessed the power of God displayed in the healing of persons who were sick in hundreds of instances, in some cases that would probably be considered by the world as very wonderful, but to which the Saints, whose experience has been similar to my own,

---

309. Middlemiss, *Writings of President David O. McKay*, 161–63.

310. Bryant S. Hinckley, *The Faith of Our Pioneer Fathers* (Deseret Book, 1959), 183.

had become accustomed. I think Elder David W. Patten possessed the gift of healing to a greater degree than any man I ever associated with. I remember on one occasion when I was laboring with him as a missionary in Tennessee, he was sent for to administer to a woman who had been sick for five years and bed-ridden for one year and not able to help herself. Brother Patten stepped to her bedside and asked her if she believed in the Lord Jesus Christ. She replied that she did. He then took her by the hand and said, "In the name of Jesus Christ, arise!"

She immediately sat up in bed, when he placed his hands upon her head and rebuked her disease, pronounced blessings upon her head and promised that she should bear children. She had been married for seven years and had never had any children, and this promise seemed very unlikely ever to be fulfilled. But she arose from her bed immediately, walked half a mile to be baptized and back again in her wet clothes. She was healed from that time, and within one year became a mother, and afterwards bore several children.[311]

Parley P. Pratt

After conversing with these interesting persons [in Toronto, Canada] till a late hour, we retired to rest. Next day Mrs. Walton requested me to call on a friend of hers, who was also a widow in deep affliction, being totally blind with inflammation in the eyes; she had suffered extreme pain for several months, and had also been reduced to want, having four little children to support. She had lost her husband, of cholera, two years before, and had sustained herself and family by teaching school until deprived of sight, since which she had been dependent on the Methodist society; herself and children being then a public charge. Mrs. Walton sent her little daughter of twelve years old to show me the way. I called on the poor blind widow and helpless orphans, and found them in a dark and gloomy apartment, rendered more so by having every ray of light obscured to prevent its painful effects on her eyes. I related to her the circumstances of my mission, and she believed the same. I laid my hands upon her in the name of Jesus Christ, and said unto her, "your eyes shall be well from this very hour." She threw

311. *Early Scenes in Church History* (Juvenile Instructor Office, 1882), 8:29.

off her bandages; opened her house to the light; dressed herself, and walking with open eyes, came to the meeting that same evening at sister Walton's, with eyes as well and as bright as any other person's.

The Methodist society were now relieved of their burden in the person of this widow and four orphans. This remarkable miracle was soon noised abroad, and the poor woman's house was thronged from all parts of the city and country with visitors; all curious to witness for themselves, and to inquire of her how her eyes were healed. "How did the man heal your eyes?" What did he do?—tell us," were questions so oft repeated that the woman, wearied of replying, came to me for advice to know what she should do. I advised her to tell them that the Lord had healed her, and to give Him the glory, and let that suffice. But still they teased her for particulars. "What did this man do?" "How were your eyes opened and made well?"

"He laid his hands upon my head in the name of Jesus Christ, and rebuked the inflammation, and commanded them to be made whole and restored to sight; and it was instantly done." "Well, give God the glory; for, as to this man, it is well known that he is an impostor, a follower of Joseph Smith, the false prophet." "Whether he be an impostor or not, I know not; but this much I know, whereas I was blind, now I see! Can an impostor open the eyes of the blind?" "Perhaps, then, you intend to be his disciple, to join the Mormons?" "He said nothing to me about joining the Mormons, but taught me the gospel, and bore testimony that God had restored its power to the earth. Would you like to be partakers thereof? Or why do you inquire so earnestly about my eyes being healed?"

"Oh, we are John Wesley's disciples. We are the Christian Church. We know John Wesley, but as to this man, we know not whence he is." "How is this that you know not whence he is, and yet he hath opened my eyes? Did John Wesley open the eyes of the blind? Can an impostor do it?" "Ah, we see how it is. You are determined to forsake the Christian Church, the good old way, for the sake of these fools, these weak impostors—the Mormons. Well, farewell. But remember, you will have no more support from our society, no more encouragement of any kind; you shall not even teach a school for us. How then will you live?"

Such contentions and discouragement as these, poured into the ears of a poor mother from day to day, together with railings, lyings, and various sophistry and slander, soon caused her to waver, and like thousands of other poor, weak mortals, she shrank back into the net of sectarian delusion, and was seen by the Saints no more. In the meantime our meetings commenced at Mrs. Walton's. At first very few attended, but they gradually increased till her rooms, and sometimes her yard, were well filled with attentive hearers.[312]

Parley P. Pratt

I then journeyed in connection with a young Elder, named H. Brown, as far as Henderson County, in northern New York, where lived Elder Brown's father, and where there was quite a branch of the Church. I visited with them for a few days, resting from my toils and ministering among them. Taking leave of these friends, I went to Sackett's Harbor, where all were yet strangers to the fullness of the gospel. Leaving an appointment at a hotel that I would return in a few days thence, and address the people wherever they saw fit to assemble, I crossed over the bay to a country neighborhood, called Pillar Point. In this neighborhood there had been some preaching by our Elders; but no branch of the Church organized, though there had been one or two instances of healing, and some few were believing. Here I appointed a meeting for evening in a school house; it was crowded full of people; indeed, all could not get in.

As the meeting closed a man named William Cory stepped forward, and earnestly begged of me to go home with him and minister to his wife, as she was lying at the point of death in consequence of a lingering sickness, not having risen up in her bed for six days without swooning or going into fits. He further said that he was worn out by being up with her every night, and that his neighbors were weary with watching, and it was doubted whether she could survive through the night without relief. The Spirit would not suffer me to go with him that night, but I promised to call in the morning. At this many voices were heard, saying: "Yes, yes, there's a case in hand; let him heal her and we'll all believe." Others exclaimed: "I wonder if she'll be at his meeting tomorrow! We shall

312. *Autobiography of Parley P. Pratt*, ed. Facer Proctor and Maurine Jensen (Deseret Book, 2000), 175–77.

see, and if so, we'll all believe." Expressions like these, joined with my own weakness, only tended to dampen my courage and confidence in the case.

I went home with a friend who invited me to partake of his hospitality for the night. As we entered his house, we found one of his children very sick with a violent pain in the head, to which it had been subject from its birth, and which came at regular periods, and was never relieved till it gathered and broke at his ear—so said his parents. The little fellow was rolling from side to side in his bed, and screeching and screaming with pain. I stepped to the bedside, and laid my hands upon his head in the name of Jesus Christ; he was instantly made whole and went to sleep. Next morning he got up well, and continued so; he said that the pain all left him as soon as my hands touched his head.

In the morning, before I arose, I had a vision, as follows: I saw a log house, and entered it through a door at the northwest corner; in the northeast corner lay a woman sick in bed; in the southeast corner was a small door opening into an adjoining room, and near it a stairway, where stood a ladder; the fireplace being in the south end. As I entered the house and laid my hands on the woman, she rose up and was made whole; the house being crowded, she took her seat near the fire and under the ladder, or near by it, and she praised God with a shout of glory, clapping her hands for joy, and exclaimed: "Thank God, I'm every whit whole." I awoke from my vision and related the same to the family where I stayed. The man harnessed his horses, and with seven or eight persons in the wagon, including myself, we started for meeting, intending to call and see Mrs. Cory on our way, as I had appointed the previous evening. On alighting at her house I saw it was the same that I had seen in the vision; there were the doors, the stairway, ladder, fireplace, bed, and sick woman, just as I had seen and described.

I laid my hands upon the woman, and said: "In the name of Jesus Christ, be thou made whole this instant." I then commanded her to arise and walk. Her husband burst into tears; the people looked surprised; but the woman arose and walked to the fire, and happened to take her seat near the ladder, as I had related in the vision before I saw her. She then clapped her hands for joy, gave a shout of "Glory to God in the highest," and testified that she was every whit whole. We invited her to accompany us to the meeting;

she immediately made ready, walked out, helped herself into the wagon, and rode some two miles over a very rough road. She then got out of the wagon, and walked with a strong and quick step into the meeting, where she sat till the discourse was over; when she arose and testified what the Lord had done for her. She then rode home, and was baptized in connection with several others, who came forward and obeyed the fullness of the gospel. We afterwards laid our hands on them for the gift of the Holy Ghost, when it fell upon them in great power, insomuch that all in the room felt its power and influence and glorified God; some spake in tongues, others prophesied and bore testimony to the truth.

The next evening I went over to Sackett's Harbor in order to preach; many of the people from Pillar Point, who had witnessed these things, went with me, and, among others, Mr. Cory with his wife, who had been so miraculously healed. A great rabble came out to hear, or rather to disturb the meeting; and among others, some half dozen clergymen of different orders, who were loud in their challenges and calls for miracles; "give us a miracle—we want a miracle—heal the sick—raise the dead, and then we'll believe." The lying, rage, and confusion excited by these wicked spirits, broke up the meeting, and I had much ado to get out of the crowd without being stoned or torn to pieces.[313]

Hyrum Smith

Related by James A. Little:

When the temple was enclosed, in a meeting of the brethren called to consult about its completion, the Prophet Joseph Smith desired that a hard finish be put on its outside walls. None of the masons who had worked on the building knew how to do it. Looking around on those present his eyes rested on Lorenzo and he said, "Brother Lorenzo, I want you to take hold and put this hard finish on the walls. Will you do it?" Lorenzo replied, "Yes, I will try."

The following day with horse and buggy he went to Cleveland, twenty-two miles, determined if possible to find a man who understood the business. He had been there but a short time inquiring after such a man, when he met a young man, Artemus Millet, who

313. *Autobiography of Parley P. Pratt*, 135–38.

said he understood the business, had just completed a job and wanted another. Lorenzo at once engaged him, put him and his tools into the buggy and returned to Kirtland. The materials and fixtures were soon on hand to make the mortar, and work was commenced on the 2nd of November, 1835. Before the mortar was dry, Lorenzo, with a suitable tool made by himself, marked off the walls into blocks in imitation of regular stone work, and at the proper time commenced penciling. It was the last of November and the weather daily grew colder. A Brother Stillman assisted him a day or two, but said he could not stand the cold and quit the work. Lorenzo persevered day after day, determined if possible to complete the task. When badly chilled he went into his house to get warm and again returned to the work.

The task was completed on the 8th of January, 1836, but Lorenzo was sick the last two days. He had caught a bad cold accompanied with a very severe cough, and in a few days was confined to his bed. His disease was pronounced "quick consumption," and he sank rapidly. When for two weeks he had been unable to walk, [Frederick G.] Williams, one of the brethren, came to see him. Considering his case a bad one he returned the next day and brought with him Dr. Seely, an old practicing physician, and another doctor whose name is forgotten. They examined the patient and Dr. Seely asserted that he had not as much lungs as would fill a tea saucer. He appeared a somewhat rough, irreligious man. With what he probably considered a good natured fling at the belief of the Saints in miracles, he said to Father Young, "Unless the Lord makes your son a pair of lungs there is no hope for him." Again we will let the subject of our narrative tell his experience, when his life seemed to hang only by a thread:

"I was so low and nervous that I could scarcely bear any noise in the room. The next morning after the visit of the doctors, my father came to the door of the room to see how I was, and I recall his gazing earnestly at me with tears in his eyes. As I afterwards learned he went from there to the Prophet Joseph and said to him: 'My son, Lorenzo, is dying; can there not be something done for him?' The Prophet studied a few moments and replied, 'Yes; of necessity I must go away to fill an appointment which I cannot put off. But you go and get my brother Hyrum, and with him get together twelve or fifteen good faithful brethren; go to the house of Brother Lorenzo and all join in prayer; one by mouth and the others repeat after him in unison. After prayer divide into quorums of three. Let the first quorum who administer anoint Brother Young with oil, then lay hands on him, one being mouth, and the other two repeating in unison with him. When all the quorums have, in succession, laid their hands on Brother Young and prayed for him, begin again with the first quorum by anointing, continuing the administration in this way until you receive a testimony that he will be restored.'

"My father came with fifteen of the brethren and these instructions were strictly followed. The administrations were continued until it came the turn of the first quorum the third time. Brother Hyrum Smith led. The spirit rested mightily upon him and he was full of blessing and prophecy. He said that I should regain my health, live to go with the Saints into the bosom of the Rocky Mountains to build up a place there, and that my cellar should overflow with wine and fatness. At that time I had not heard about the Saints going to the Rocky Mountains; possibly Brother Smith had. After he was through the administration he seemed surprised at some things he had said, and wondered at the manifestations of the spirit. I coughed no more and rapidly recovered. I had been pronounced by the best physicians in the country past all human aid. I am now a living witness of the power of God through the administrations of the Elders."[314]

Joseph Smith Jr.

Related by the author:

In 1831, an incident occurred in the Smith home that led to the baptism of at least three individuals. Ezra Booth, a Methodist preacher of Mantua, Ohio accompanied his wife, Elsa Johnson, her husband, and others to the Smith home in Hiram, Ohio. They went to visit with the Prophet Joseph about his newly established church. During the discussion, the topic turned to spiritual gifts that were demonstrated in the days of the New Testament apostles. Someone in the group commented on the condition of Elsa Johnson, who had

314. James A. Little, "Biography of Lorenzo Dow Young," *Utah Historical Quarterly* 14, no. 1 (1946): 44–46 (pages 26–132 for bibliography).

been afflicted for many years with rheumatism and was unable to lift her arm, saying, "Here is Mrs. Johnson with a lame arm; has God given any power to man now on the earth to cure her?"

Soon after, when the conversation had turned to another topic, the Prophet Joseph stood and walked across the room to where Elsa was seated and taking her by the hand said in the most "impressive manner," "Woman, in the name of the Lord Jesus Christ I command thee to be whole." He immediately exited the room leaving the company to marvel at what they had just witnessed. Elsa suddenly lifted her arm and the company rejoiced at the miracle they had witnessed. Elsa returned home and was able to perform the tasks that she had not been able to do for a long time. Because of this miracle, Ezra Booth, as well as Mr. and Mrs. Johnson, requested that the Prophet Joseph baptize them.[315]

Joseph Smith Jr.

Related by Philo Dibble:

> When Joseph came to Kirtland his fame spread far and wide. There was a woman living in the town of Hiram, forty miles from Kirtland, who had a crooked arm, which she had not been able to use for a long period. She persuaded her husband, whose name was Johnson, to take her to Kirtland to get her arm healed. I saw them as they passed my house on their way. She went to Joseph and requested him to heal her. Joseph asked her if she believed the Lord was able to make him an instrument in healing her arm. She said she believed the Lord was able to heal her arm.
>
> Joseph put her off till the next morning, when he met her at Brother Whitney's house. There were eight persons present, one a Methodist preacher, and one a doctor. Joseph took her by the hand, prayed in silence a moment, pronounced her arm whole, in the name of Jesus Christ, and turned and left the room. The preacher asked her if her arm was whole, and she straightened it out and replied: "It is as good as the other." The question was then asked if it would remain whole. Joseph hearing this, answered and said: "It is as good as the other, and as liable to accident as the other."

---

315. B. H. Roberts, *A Comprehensive History of The Church of Jesus Christ of Latter-day Saints* (Brigham Young University Press, 1965), 1:278.

The doctor who witnessed this miracle came to my house the next morning and related the circumstance to me. He attempted to account for it by his false philosophy, saying that Joseph took her by the hand, and seemed to be in prayer, and pronounced her arm whole in the name of Jesus Christ, which excited her and started perspiration, and that relaxed the cords of her arm.[316]

Joseph Smith Jr.

Related by Elder Parley P. Pratt:

After the gush of feelings consequent on our happy meeting had subsided, I accompanied Joseph Smith over the Mississippi in a skiff to visit some friends in Montrose [on July 22, 1839]. Here many were lying sick and at the point of death. Among these was my old friend and fellow servant, Elijah Fordham, who had been with me in that extraordinary work in New York City in 1837. He was now in the last stage of a deadly fever. He lay prostrate and nearly speechless, with his feet poulticed; his eyes were sunk in their sockets; his flesh was gone; the paleness of death was upon him; and he was hardly to be distinguished from a corpse. His wife was weeping over him, and preparing clothes for his burial.

Brother Joseph took him by the hand, and in a voice and energy which would seemingly have raised the dead, he cried: "BROTHER FORDHAM, IN THE NAME OF JESUS CHRIST, ARISE AND WALK." It was a voice which could be heard from house to house and nearly through the neighborhood. It was like the roaring of a lion, or the heavy thunderbolt. Brother Fordham leaped from his dying bed in an instant, shook the poultices and bandages from his feet, put on his clothes so quick that none got a chance to assist him, and taking a cup of tea and a little refreshment, he walked with us from house to house visiting other sick beds, and joining in prayer and ministrations for them, while the people followed us, and with joy and amazement gave glory to God. Several more were called up in a similar manner and were healed.[317]

---

316. *Early Scenes in Church History,* 8:79.

317. *Autobiography of Parley P. Pratt,* 355.

Joseph Smith Jr.

Related by Joseph Curtis:

About the month of August, 1856, William D. Huntington and I went into Hobble Creek Canyon to get a tree or log suitable for making drums. After we had finished our labor and started for home, both of us riding on the log, our conversation naturally turned upon the doctrines of the Church and experiences of the past, when the life and labors of the Prophet Joseph were touched upon. This subject aroused into more than usual earnestness the mind and conversation of my associate.

He said that in Nauvoo he lived in the family of and worked for Joseph Smith at the time the Prophet had such a wonderful time with the sick, when nearly everybody was stricken down and he himself was among the afflicted, and was one of those who were healed by Joseph. He said he had been sick some weeks and kept getting weaker, until he became so helpless that he could not move. Finally he got so low he could not speak, but had perfect consciousness of all that was passing in the room. He saw friends come to the bedside, look at him a moment and commence weeping, then turn away. He further stated that he presently felt easy, and observing his situation found that he was in the upper part of the room near the ceiling, and could see the body he had occupied lying on the bed, with weeping friends, standing around as he had witnessed in many cases where people had died under his own observation.

About this time he saw Joseph Smith and two other brethren come into the room. Joseph turned to his wife Emma and asked her to get him a dish of clean water. This she did; and the Prophet with the two brethren accompanying him washed their hands and carefully wiped them. Then they stepped to the bed and laid their hands upon the head of his body, which at that time looked loathsome to him, and as the three stretched out their hands to place them upon the head, he by some means became aware that he must go back into that body, and started to do so. The process of getting in he could not remember; but when Joseph said "amen," he heard and could see and feel with his body. The feeling for a moment was most excruciating, as though his body was pierced in every part with some sharp instruments.

As soon as the brethren had taken their hands from his head he raised up in bed, sitting erect, and in another moment turned his legs off the bed. At this juncture Joseph asked him if he had not better be careful, for he was very weak. He replied, "I never felt better in my life," almost immediately adding, "I want my pants." His pants were found and given him, which he drew on, Joseph assisting him, although he thought he needed no help. Then he signified his intention to sit in a chair at or near the fireplace. Joseph took hold of his arm to help him along safely, but William declared his ability to walk alone, notwithstanding which, the help continued.

Astonishment had taken the place of weeping throughout the room. Every looker-on was ready to weep for joy; but none were able or felt inclined to talk. Presently William said he wanted something to eat. Joseph asked him what he would like, and he replied that he wanted a dish of bread and milk. Emma immediately brought what he called for, as one may easily comprehend, every hand was anxious to supply the wants of a man who, a few moments before was dead, really and truly dead! Brother Huntington ate the bowl of bread and milk with as good a relish as any he ever ate. In a short time all felt more familiar, and conversation upon the scene that transpired followed. William related his experiences, and the friends theirs. Joseph listened to the conversation and in his turn remarked that they had just witnessed as great a miracle as Jesus did while on the earth. They had seen the dead brought to life. At the close of his narrative to me William Huntington remarked: "Now I have told you the truth, and here I am a live man, sitting by the side of you on this log, and I testify that Joseph Smith was a Prophet of God."[318]

Joseph Smith Jr. and Parley P. Pratt

About this time a young lady, by the name of Chloe Smith, being a member of the Church, was lying very low with a lingering fever, with a family who occupied one of the houses on the farm of Isaac Morley, in Kirtland. Many of the Church had visited and prayed

---

318. Levi Curtis, "Recollections of the Prophet Joseph Smith," *Juvenile Instructor* 27, no. 12 (June 15, 1892): 385–86.

with her, but all to no effect; she seemed at the point of death, but would not consent to have a physician. This greatly enraged her relatives, who had cast her out because she belonged to the Church, and who, together with many of the people of the neighborhood, were greatly stirred up to anger, saying, "these wicked deceivers will let her lie and die without a physician, because of their superstitions; and if they do, we will prosecute them for so doing." Now these were daily watching for her last breath, with many threats.

Under these circumstances, President Smith and myself, with several other Elders called to see her. She was so low that no one had been allowed for some days previous to speak above a whisper, and even the door of the log dwelling was muffled with cloths to prevent a noise. We kneeled down and prayed vocally all around, each in turn; after which President Smith arose, went to the bedside, took her by the hand, and said unto her with a loud voice, "in the name of Jesus Christ arise and walk!" She immediately arose, was dressed by a woman in attendance, when she walked to a chair before the fire, and was seated and joined in singing a hymn. The house was thronged with people in a few moments, and the young lady arose and shook hands with each as they came in; and from that minute she was perfectly restored to health.[319]

Joseph Smith Jr.

Related by Elder Orson F. Whitney and Elder Heber C. Kimball:

Twelve months had elapsed since the word of the Lord came for the Apostles to depart and "go over the great waters" to promulgate the Gospel. They had fulfilled the revelation in so far as to take leave of the Saints in Far West, at the time and place appointed, but the toils and trials incident to settling their new home had unavoidably delayed their departure from America.

One of these trials was an epidemic which swept over Nauvoo and the neighboring towns, prostrating many of the inhabitants with sickness; partly due, no doubt, to the swamps in and around the lower portions of the new settlement, but greatly enhanced by the physical weakness of the Saints, resulting from their recent privations and sufferings in Missouri. So general and widespread was

319. *Autobiography of Parley P. Pratt*, 79–80.

the sickness that scarcely a family in Nauvoo or the vicinity entirely escaped the scourge. But this unhappy condition of affairs—rendered doubly disheartening from following so closely upon the Missouri troubles—was not without its recompense. It was the occasion of a marvelous and miraculous display of divine power in behalf of the Lord's afflicted people. Heber thus describes the event:

"July 22nd, the Prophet Joseph arose from his bed of sickness, when the power of God rested upon him, and he went forth administering to the sick. He commenced with the sick in his own house, then visited those who were camping in tents in his own dooryard, commanding the sick in the name of the Lord Jesus Christ to arise from their beds and be whole; when they were healed according to his words. He then went from house to house, and from tent to tent, upon the bank of the river, healing the sick by the power of Israel's God, as he went among them. He did not miss a single house, wagon or tent, and continued this work up to the upper stone house, where he crossed the river in a boat, accompanied by Parley P. Pratt, Orson Pratt, John E. Page, John Taylor and myself, and landed at Montrose. He then walked into the cabin of Brother Brigham Young, who was lying very sick, and commanded him in the name of the Lord Jesus Christ to arise and be made whole. He arose, healed of his sickness, and then accompanied Joseph and his brethren of the Twelve, and went into the house of Brother Elijah Fordham, who was insensible, and considered by his family and friends to be in the hands of death. Joseph stepped to his bedside, looked him in the eye for a minute without speaking, then took him by the hand and commanded him in the name of Jesus Christ to arise from his bed and walk. Brother Fordham immediately leaped out of his bed, threw off all his poultices and bandages, dressed himself, called for a bowl of bread and milk, which he ate, and then followed us into the street. We then went into the house of Joseph B. Noble, who was also very sick, and he was healed in the same manner.

"Joseph spoke with the voice and power of God. When he had healed all the sick by the power given unto him he went down to the ferry boat, when a stranger rode up almost breathless, and said that he had heard that Joseph Smith was raising the dead, and healing all of the sick, and his wife begged him to ride up and get Mr.

Smith to go down and heal her twin children, about three months old. Joseph replied, 'I cannot go, but will send someone.' In a few minutes he said to Elder Woodruff, 'You go and heal those children, and take this pocket handkerchief, and when you administer to them, wipe their faces with it, and they shall recover.' Brother Woodruff did as he was commanded, and the children were healed.

"The mob spirits, when they saw men whom they thought were dying, arise from their beds, and pray for others, stood paralyzed with fear; yet those same men would have killed Joseph and his brethren if they had had an opportunity. Joseph recrossed the river to his own home and I returned to mine, rejoicing in the mercies and goodness of God. This was a day never to be forgotten by the Saints; nor by the wicked; for they saw the power of God manifest in the flesh."[320]

Wilford Woodruff expounded on Joseph's healing handkerchief as follows:

While waiting for the ferry-boat, a man of the world, knowing of the miracles which had been performed, came to him and asked him if he would not go and heal two twin children of his, about five months old, who were both lying sick nigh unto death. They were some two miles from Montrose. The Prophet said he could not go; but, after pausing some time, he said he would send someone to heal them; and he turned to me and said: "You go with the man and heal his children." He took a red silk handkerchief out of his pocket and gave it to me, and told me to wipe their faces with the handkerchief when I administered to them, and they should be healed. He also said unto me: "As long as you will keep that handkerchief, it shall remain a league between you and me." I went with the man, and did as the Prophet commanded me, and the children were healed. I have possession of the handkerchief unto this day.[321]

Joseph F. Smith

Related by President Joseph Fielding Smith:

---

320. Orson F. Whitney, *Life of Heber C. Kimball*, Collector's Edition (Bookcraft, 1992), 262–64.

321. Wilford Woodruff, *Leaves From My Journal* (Covenant Communications, 2005), 84.

> It was on the seventh day of August, 1906, that President [Joseph F.] Smith and party arrived in Rotterdam, having come from the boat at Antwerp two days before. There was living in that city a boy of eleven years of age, John Roothoff by name, who had suffered greatly for a number of years with his eyes. His mother was a faithful member of the Church, as also was the boy, who was slowly losing his sight and was unable to attend school. The boy said to his mother: "The Prophet has the most power of any missionary on earth. If you will take me with you to the meeting and he will look into my eyes, I believe they will be healed."
>
> According to his desire he was permitted to accompany his mother to the meeting. At the close of the meeting, as was the custom, President Smith moved towards the door and began to shake hands and speak encouragingly to the people as they passed from the hall. As John Roothoff approached him, led by his mother and his eyes bandaged, President Smith took him by the hand and spoke to him kindly. He then raised the bandage slightly and looked sympathetically into the inflamed eyes, at the same time saying something in English which the boy did not understand. However he was satisfied. President Smith had acted according to the boy's faith; and according to his faith it came to pass. When he arrived home, he cried out with great joy: "Mama, my eyes are well; I cannot feel any more pain. I can see fine now, and far too."[322]

Lorenzo Snow

On Monday, January 16, 1843, the first British emigrant company of the year sailed from Liverpool to New Orleans under the direction of Lorenzo Snow. The following was related by Eliza R. Snow:

> The commander of the ship Swanton, Captain Davenport and officers of the crew, were kind and courteous which contributed much to ameliorate the discomfort incident to life on the ocean. The steward, a German by birth, was a young man, very affable in manner, and gentlemanly in deportment—a general favorite and highly respected by all. During the latter part of the voyage he took sick, and continued growing worse and worse until death seemed inevitable. All means proved unavailing, and the captain,

322. Joseph Fielding Smith, *The Life of Joseph F. Smith* (Deseret Book, 1938), 397.

by whom he was much beloved, gave up all hope of his recovery, and requested the officers and crew to go on one by one and take a farewell look of their dying friend, which they did silently and solemnly as he lay unconscious and almost breathless on his dying couch.

Immediately after this sad ceremony closed, one of our sisters by the name of Martin, without my brother's knowledge, went to the captain and requested him to allow my brother to lay hands on the steward, according to our faith and practice under such circumstances, saying that she believed that the steward would be restored. The captain shook his head, and told her that the steward was now breathing his last, and it would be useless to trouble Mr. Snow. But Sister Martin was not to be defeated; she not only importuned, but earnestly declared her faith in the result of the proposed ministration, and he finally yielded and gave consent.

As soon the forgoing circumstance was communicated to my brother, he started toward the cabin where the steward lay, and in passing through the door met the captain who was in tears. He said: "Mr. Snow, it is too late; he is expiring; he a breathing his last! My brother made no reply, but took a seat beside the dying man. After devoting a few moments to secret prayer, he laid his hands on the head of the young man, prayed, and in the name of Jesus Christ rebuked the disease and commanded him to be made whole. Very soon after, to the joy and astonishment of all, he was seen waking the deck, praising and glorifying God for his restoration. The officers and sailors acknowledged the miraculous power of God, and on landing at New Orleans, several of them were baptized, also the first mate, February 26th, 1843.[323]

Lorenzo Snow and Rudger Clawson

Related by Leroi C. Snow, Lorenzo Snow's son:

At that time he [Lorenzo Snow] received a patriarchal blessing, under the hands of the Prophet's father, Joseph Smith Sr. This blessing was given in the Kirtland Temple. Among other things were these promises: "The dead shall rise and come forth at thy bidding."

323. *The Contributor* 12, no. 12 (Oct. 1891), 446–48.

For several long weeks Ella Jensen had lingered, almost between life and death, with scarlet fever. In order to relieve the tired parents from their weary hours of loving care, kind neighbors took turns in staying at the Jensen home over night to help look after the sick girl. Among these thoughtful friends was Leah Rees (now Mrs. Wilford Reeder of Brigham City). She occasionally played the little, old-fashioned harmonium and sang for Ella's entertainment. This particular evening the sick girl became very much worse. Leah had come about eight o'clock to remain until about eight the next morning. Ella was so weak that she could hardly speak above a whisper.

"Ella asked me to sing and play for her," Leah says, "but, goodness, I was so worried about her condition, I felt more like crying. I sat down at the organ and began to play and sing but broke down and had to quit." After Ella had gone to sleep, Leah lay down on a couch in the room, and also dropped off to sleep. Leah continues with her own story:

"About three or four o'clock in the morning I was suddenly awakened by Ella calling me. I hurried to her bed. She was all excited and asked me to get the comb, brush and scissors, explaining that she wanted to brush her hair and trim her finger nails and get all ready, 'for,' she said, 'they are coming to get me at ten o'clock in the morning.' I asked who was coming to get her. 'Uncle Hans Jensen,' she replied, 'and the messengers. I am going to die and they are coming at ten o'clock to get me and take me away. . .' As I was brushing her hair, she asked me to call her parents. I explained that they were tired and asleep and that it would be better not to disturb them. 'Yes,' Ella replied, 'you must call them. I want to tell them now.' The parents were called and as they entered the room the daughter told them that her Uncle Hans, who was dead, had suddenly appeared in the room, while she was awake, with her eyes open, and told her that messengers would be there at ten o'clock to conduct her into the spirit world." . . .

At about eight o'clock Leah left the house, realizing that the sick girl was gradually sinking. The father and mother remained at the bedside. Relatives and friends who had heard of Ella's sudden relapse came to see her. Towards ten o'clock, Uncle Jake, the father, who was holding his daughter's hand, felt the pulse become very weak. A few moments later he turned to his wife saying: "Althea, she is dead, her pulse has stopped." The heart-broken parents wept and grieved at the loss of their beautiful daughter. Jacob Jensen, Ella's father, and uncle of the writer of this article, was familiarly known to the people of Brigham City as "Uncle Jake." Here are his own words to me:

"Ella had been sick for several weeks. She awoke one morning with the idea that she was about to die, and told us that her Uncle Hans had appeared in her room and said he was coming for her that morning. . . . She wanted to see all the folks and bid them good-bye. All who were near came in, all but Grandma Jensen. She was in town and I sent for her. She arrived just when the others of us had said good-bye. Ella put her arms around her grandmother's neck and kissed her good-bye. It was not more than a minute after that when her pulse stopped and she passed away. I was holding her hand and felt her pulse stop. . . .

"I went out to the barn, hitched up, and drove to the tabernacle where your father, President Lorenzo Snow, whom we all loved so much, was in meeting. I went into the vestry, behind the main hall, wrote a note and had it sent to your father, who was speaking to the congregation. When the note was placed upon the pulpit, President Snow stopped his talking, read the note and then explained to the Saints that it was a call to visit some people who were in deep sorrow and asked to be excused.

"President Snow came into the vestry and after I told him what had happened he meditated a moment or two and then said: 'I will go down with you.' Just as we were about to leave, President Snow stopped me, saying: 'Wait a moment, I wish you would go into the meeting and get Brother Clawson, I want him to go also.' President Clawson was then president of the Box Elder stake. (President Rudger Clawson is now president of the Council of Twelve and lives in Salt Lake City.)

"I went in and got him and took them both down to my home, about a mile and a half south of Brigham City. We went into the house. My wife and children were there. After standing at Ella's bedside for a minute or two, President Snow asked if we had any consecrated oil in the house. I was greatly surprised, but told him yes and got it for him. He handed the bottle of oil to Brother Clawson and asked him to anoint Ella. Your father was then mouth in confirming the anointing. During the administration I was particularly impressed with some of the words which he used and can well remember them now. He said: 'Dear Ella, I command you, in the name of the Lord, Jesus Christ, to come back and live, your mission is not ended. You shall yet live to perform a great mission.' He said she should yet live to rear a large family and be a comfort to her parents and friends. I well remember these words."

President Rudger Clawson relates his experiences and after telling of Brother Jensen's coming to the meeting house toward the close of the morning session and being invited by President Snow to go along, says:

"As we entered the home we met Sister Jensen, who was very much agitated and alarmed. We came to Ella's bedside and were impressed by the thought that her spirit had passed out of the body and gone beyond. Turning to me President Snow said: 'Brother Clawson, will you anoint her,' which I did. We then laid our hands upon her head and the anointing was confirmed by President Snow, who blessed her and among other things, used this very extraordinary expression, in a commanding tone of voice, 'Come back, Ella, come back. Your work upon the earth is not yet completed, come back.' Shortly afterward we left the home."

Uncle Jake, Ella's father, continues his account: "After President Snow had finished the blessing, he turned to my wife and me and said; 'Now do not mourn or grieve any more. It will be all right. Brother Clawson and I are busy and must go, we cannot stay, but you just be patient and wait, and do not mourn, because it will be all right.'"

As already stated, it was ten o'clock in the morning when Ella died. It was towards noon when Jacob Jensen reported to President Snow at the tabernacle service, and not long after twelve o'clock, noon, when President Snow and President Clawson left the home after the administration. Uncle Jake says that he and his wife remained at the bedside. The news of the death spread about the city. Friends continued to call at the home, express their sympathy to the sorrowing parents and leave. Continuing in Uncle Jake's words:

"Ella remained in this condition for more than an hour after President Snow administered to her, or more than three hours in all after she died. We were sitting there watching by the bedside, her mother and myself, when all at once she opened her eyes. She looked about the room, saw us sitting there, but still looked for someone else, and the first thing she said was: 'Where is he? Where is he?' We asked, 'Who? Where is who?' 'Why, Brother Snow,' she replied. 'He called me back.' We explained that Brother Snow and Brother Clawson were very busy and could not remain, that they had gone. Ella dropped her head back on the pillow, saying: 'Why did he call me back? I was so happy and did not want to come back.'"

Then Ella Jensen began to relate her marvelous experiences, marvelous both as to the incidents themselves, and as to the great number of them that occurred in the short space of between three and four hours.[324]

Lorenzo Snow

Related by Eliza R. Snow:

One of the precious gifts of the everlasting Gospel conferred on Brother Lorenzo, that of healing the sick by the power of faith and the instrumentality of the sacred ordinances which God has revealed, is a prominent one. Early in his experience in the Church, when he received his patriarchal blessing under the hands of the Patriarch, Joseph Smith, father of the Prophet, had received a promise of this gift, and he was told that the sick should even send handkerchiefs to him for his blessing, by which they should be made whole.

A very striking instance in fulfillment of this prediction occurred in the winter of 1866. Brother William Smith, of Kaysville, Davis County, Utah, was taken very sick; his faith centered in God and in the ordinances of His house, instead of human medical skill; and he and his wife had, from experience, great faith in Brother Snow as an administrator, but he was forty miles away. It was winter, the weather very cold and stormy, and the roads almost impassable, and they thought it preposterous to send for him, and tried to content themselves with the services of those present.

But with all the faith that was exercised, with all that patient, skillful and careful nursing—all that love and affection could do for him—he continued to grow worse, and gradually sank until

324. "Raised From the Dead," *Improvement Era* 32, no. 11 (1929): 881–86.

his life was despaired of and his case considered hopeless by all but his heart-stricken, loving wife. She was hoping and praying with all the fervor affection inspires, when, by the promptings of the Spirit, which brings "all things to remembrance," she recollected that when Brother Snow was at her home in Wiberson, England, in reading a copy of his patriarchal blessing, she was struck with the prediction that the sick should send handkerchiefs to him, etc. Like a lamp suddenly lighted, and like the sunbeams streaking forth from under a heavy cloud, her heart took courage and the light of eternity seemed to spread a halo around; and the thought was immediately suggested to her that, as her husband, now almost unconscious, was too far gone to act for himself, she might act for him, and forthwith she started to carry the suggestion into effect.

No time was lost in commissioning a messenger to go with all possible dispatch and take to Brother Snow a new silk handkerchief, with a note from Sister Smith containing her request, also instructions relative to, and descriptive of her husband's condition. The messenger accomplished the trip, to and from, as expeditiously as the state of the roads would possibly admit. When Brother Snow was made acquainted with the situation, his sympathies were much aroused. From long acquaintance, he had full confidence in their faithfulness and integrity. They had befriended him when on a mission in a foreign land, and from first acquaintance, with him and them, confidence was mutual.

We now copy from Brother Snow's journal: "I took the handkerchief and a bottle of perfumery, and on retiring to my closet, I prayed, and then I consecrated the perfumery and sprinkled it on the handkerchief. I then again bowed before the Lord, and in earnest supplication besought Him to remember the promises He made through His servant, the Patriarch, whom He had now taken to Himself, and let the healing and life-inspiring virtues of His Holy Spirit be imparted to this handkerchief, and from thence to Brother Smith when it shall be placed upon him, speedily restoring him to life, health and vigor."

As soon as the messenger returned, with the handkerchief neatly folded in an envelope, it was unfolded and spread over the head and face of Brother Smith, the apparently dying man, with almost instantaneous effect. His immediate recovery was observed with surprise and astonishment by all around, and well might they exclaim: "It is the Lord's doings, and it is marvelous in our eyes."[325]

Bud Jensen recorded the time when he was healed by Lorenzo Snow's handkerchief:

> I left Salt Lake City on the 10th of May, 1899, and went to St. Johns, Kansas, headquarters of the Southwestern States Mission, with Elder Walter E. Hamblin, son of Jacob Hamblin. We were sent to the South Texas Conference. There I labored as a missionary with different companions in the low, swampy country where nearly all the people had chills and fever. My health was fairly good for the first fourteen months. After that I was taken with chills and fever. They had a number of different kinds of chills and I had about all of them, including intestinal malaria, which often is fatal, and finally became so sick I was not able to travel at all so I was called to conference headquarters to take charge of the books and lived with a family named Findley.
>
> I wrote home and told my folks that I had been transferred to conference headquarters because I was not able to travel any longer in the field on account of chills and fever. They talked the matter over with President Lorenzo Snow, and wanted to have me transferred to another mission. He had father get a white silk handkerchief of which President Snow blessed and sent to me. After receiving the handkerchief and reading the letter, promising that the fever would leave me if I would remain faithful in my missionary work, I went out into the woods by myself hardly able to walk. I had prayer there and applied this handkerchief to my head and the parts that were aching and hurt most and I received almost immediate relief.
>
> I walked back toward the house and met Sister Findley. She looked at me in surprise and said: "My goodness, Elder Jensen, you look like a changed man. What has happened? What have you been doing?" I replied, "I feel like a changed man. I am ever so much better." We went into the house and I told her about receiving the handkerchief and receiving the blessing through it. She said it was one of the greatest testimonies she had ever heard of. From that

325. Eliza R. Snow, *Lorenzo Snow*, 263–65.

time on I was able to travel and to attend to my work in the mission field until I was released.

I was released from the office work because I was so much better. I was conference president at that time and traveled in the various counties visiting among the Saints. In the spring of 1901 I was transferred from Texas to Missouri and labored there until July when I came home. All the Saints in that neighborhood and the elders knew of my condition and they all felt that it was a very great testimony. I told of it wherever I went and everyone seemed pleased to hear about it.[326]

Orson F. Whitney

It was April 8, 1877, when I left Columbia for Elyria, Ohio. Arriving at my destination, I walked three miles into the country, to the farm where dwelt the Frinks. They were not aware of my coming, but had been praying that an Elder of the Church might be led that way, several of their neighbors, with whom Sister Frink had conversed, having expressed a desire to hear more of the Gospel, and hear it from the lips of a "Mormon" missionary. I was the only one in that part of the country.

On the other side of the country road passing the farm house where I was staying, stood the residence of Truman Frink's brother, a bitter anti-Mormon, who had been heard to say that if one of our Elders crossed his threshold he would kick him into the street. . . . His wife, Margaret Frink, was an excellent woman, childless by him but by a former husband the mother of several daughters, all married. The eldest, a widow with one child, shared her mother's home.

Mrs. Frink had been confined to her room with an attack of neuralgia, which for many weeks had caused her intense pain. Her daughter had learned . . . that . . . healing was practiced by the Latter-day Saints. . . . She therefore invited me to come and bless her mother, that she might be healed. Sister Angie seconded the suggestion—if, indeed, she did not originate it—and again I was all but paralyzed at the prospect.

326. LeRoi C. Snow, "Spiritual Gifts Through Signs and Tokens," *Deseret News* (Church Section), Aug. 8, 1942.

Never did I feel so helpless—or so humble. I besought the Lord with all my soul to stand by me in this critical hour, to perfect my faith, and use me, if He could consistently, as an instrument for showing forth His merciful power upon the afflicted one. I then consecrated, as best I could, some olive oil provided by Sister Frink, and went with her and her husband to Mrs. Frink's abode. It was evening and the family were all at home. The daughter met us at the door, and ushered us into her mother's apartment, on the right of a hallway leading through the house, with rooms on either side. We had heard, as we entered, men's gruff voices and loud laughter in a room to the left; and presently Eli Frink thrust his head through a rear doorway, glanced around suspiciously, and then retired without uttering a word.

Mrs. Frink, with her head bandaged, was sitting up, but still suffering much pain. Laying my hands upon her head, which I previously had anointed, I proceeded to bless her. Scarcely had I begun, when a power fell upon me that I had never felt before. . . . It was a warm glow in my throat and breast—not painful, but powerful, almost preventing utterance, and it ran like liquid flame to the very tips of my fingers. The effect was instant. "Thank God!" said the sufferer, "the pain has gone . . ." I was so overcome by a sense of gratitude for this signal manifestation of divine favor, that I sank into a chair and burst into tears.[327]

Wilford Woodruff

December 3 [1838] found my wife very low. I spent the day in taking care of her, and the day following I returned to Eaton to get some things for her. She seemed to be sinking gradually, and in the evening the spirit apparently left her body, and she was dead. The sisters gathered around, weeping, while I stood looking at her in sorrow. The spirit and power of God began to rest upon me until, for the first time during her sickness, faith filled my soul, although she lay before me as one dead.

I had some oil that was consecrated for my anointing while in Kirtland. I took it and consecrated it again before the Lord, for

327. Orson F. Whitney, *Through Memory's Halls* (Zion's Printing and Publishing Co., 1930), 85–87.

anointing the sick. I then bowed down before the Lord, prayed for the life of my companion, and in the name of the Lord anointed her body with the oil. I then laid my hands upon her, and in the name of Jesus Christ I rebuked the power of death and of the destroyer, and commanded the same to depart from her and the spirit of life to enter her body. Her spirit returned to her body, and from that hour she was made whole; and we all felt to praise the name of God, and to trust in Him and keep His commandments.

While I was undergoing this ordeal (as my wife related afterwards) her spirit left her body, and she saw it lying upon the bed and the sisters there weeping. She looked at them and at me, and upon her babe; while gazing upon this scene, two persons came into the room, carrying a coffin, and told her they had come for her body. One of these messengers said to her that she might have her choice—she might go to rest in the spirit world, or, upon one condition, she could have the privilege of returning to her tabernacle and of continuing her labors upon the earth. The condition was that if she felt she could stand by her husband, and with him pass through all the cares, trials, tribulations, and afflictions of life which he would be called upon to pass through for the gospel's sake unto the end, she might return. When she looked at the situation of her husband and child she said, "Yes, I will do it." At the moment that decision was made the power of faith rested upon me, and when I administered to her, her spirit reentered her tabernacle, and she saw the messengers carry the coffin out of the door.[328]

Brigham Young, Wilford Woodruff, and Willard Richards

Related by President Wilford Woodruff:

The first meeting I held in Elder Kington's house brother Pitt was present. I will say first, however, that Mary Pitt, brother Pitt's sister, was something like the lame man who lay at the gate of the Temple called "Beautiful" at Jerusalem—she had not been able to walk a step for fourteen years, and confined to her bed nearly half that time. She had no strength in her feet and ankles and could only move about a little with a crutch or holding on to a chair. She wished to be baptized. Brother Pitt and myself took her in our

328. Matthias F. Cowley, *Wilford Woodruff, His Life and Labors*, 97–98.

arms, and carried her into the water and I baptized her. When she came out of the water I confirmed her. She said she wanted to be healed and she believed she had faith enough to be healed. I had had experience enough in this Church to know that it required a good deal of faith to heal a person who had not walked a step for fourteen years. I told her that according to her faith it should be unto her.

It so happened that on the day after she was baptized, Brother Richards and President Brigham Young came down to see me. We met at Brother Kington's. Sister Mary Pitt was there also. I told President Young what Sister Pitt wished, and that she believed she had faith enough to be healed. We prayed for her and laid hands upon her. Brother Young was mouth, and commanded her to be made whole. She laid down her crutch and never used it after, and the next day she walked three miles.[329]

J. Rueben Clark, Harold B. Lee, and Henry D. Moyle

Concerning Spencer W. Kimball, related by Edward L. Kimball:

In the spring of 1950 he [Spencer W. Kimball] began to worry more about an annoying hoarseness that had hung on since before Christmas. Nothing seemed to explain it. There was no congestion, no cough. He made an appointment with Leland Cowan, a cancer specialist. Dr. Cowan examined the throat carefully, noted a spot of white on one vocal cord, and arranged a second appointment. Spencer walked from Dr. Cowan's office in fear. That night he wrote in his journal: "Cancer! Cancer of the throat would render me useless from now on for the Church. I have done so very little in these six short years—there is so much to do—it is a black outlook indeed."

At the Thursday report meeting in the Temple Elder Kimball looked so glum that President Clark asked the cause. When told, he sympathized, "Surely you don't need anything else to worry you." But just that attitude by the Brethren plagued Spencer more. The only Church work he could get now was what he dug up on his own. The Brethren's rest policy sent him into depression.

329. *Journal of Discourses*, 15:344.

For the next month Spencer pinned his hope to every hint of improvement. If he awoke in the morning less hoarse he brightened. But by April Dr. Cowan had sent him to Dr. Smith and Dr. Rigby, who proposed a biopsy to obtain a specimen for laboratory examination. Just that cutting of the vocal cord alone could leave Spencer with a harsh, raspy voice which could hinder his work for the rest of his life. "I am so useless anyway—I have done so little—my efforts have been so puny—my service so small—how can I face inactivity because of physical handicap?"

But on the other hand, if he refused the test, there might be cancer which would spread up from his throat into his head, ending his usefulness that way, too. He agonized over the image of his sister Helen's distorted, cancer-eaten face and wished for death by heart attack before that ever happened to him. He agreed to let the doctor cut. "My children do not yet know the possibilities—practically no one else does. I shall keep it to ourselves until it is more surely diagnosed. I hope to go on forward to the last ounce and inch. I hope to repay in a small measure My Father."

At St. Mark's Hospital in Salt Lake City he was put under total anesthesia and operated on, then wheeled on a table back toward his room. Still drugged, Spencer sensed his table stop by an elevator and heard the orderly, angry at something, profaning the Lord's name. Half-conscious, he pleaded with labored sounds: "Please don't say that. I love Him more than anything in this world. Please." An absolute silence. Then the orderly answered softly: "I shouldn't have said that. I'm sorry."

In two days the doctor phoned Spencer at home. What he had was an infection which would need to be cauterized. But no cancer. For that happy news, though, Spencer had paid with his good voice. He spoke into his dictaphone and played the belt back. The sounds from his scraped throat were like the grating of harsh materials. Even in a quiet place he could not be heard beyond a few feet. One day he talked in a meeting for five minutes with his raw throat and then finished, perspiring from the exertion. He prayed for relief, but he ended each prayer, "Thy will be done." He had a foreboding he would lose his voice.

But a week later he recorded a miraculous recovery. Elders J. Reuben Clark, Harold B. Lee and Henry D. Moyle had met with him, first to console him and build his faith, then to give him a priesthood blessing. As they left a calmness lighted his mind, and when he awoke next morning he could talk with strength. Jubilant, he refused to listen to his doctors, who still insisted he have his throat infection cauterized. In two days they agreed with him that there was no hurry. By two weeks they concluded there was no need at all.[330]

Heber C. Kimball, Joseph Smith, and Willard Richards

Related by Elder Heber C. Kimball:

The rough oak boxes in which the bodies of Joseph and Hyrum were brought from Carthage, were made into canes and other articles. I have a cane made from the plank of one of those boxes, so has brother Brigham and a great many others, and we prize them highly, and esteem them a great blessing. I want to carefully preserve my cane, and when I am done with it here, I shall hand it down to my heir, with instructions to him to do the same. And the day will come when there will be multitudes who will be healed and blessed through the instrumentality of those canes, and the devil cannot overcome those who have them, in consequence of their faith and confidence in the virtues connected with them. . . .

In England, when not in a situation to go, I have blessed my handkerchief, and asked God to sanctify it and fill it with life and power, and sent it to the sick, and hundreds have been healed by it; in like manner I have sent my cane. Dr. [Willard] Richards used to lay his old black cane on a person's head, and that person has been healed through its instrumentality, by the power of God. I have known Joseph, hundreds of times, send his handkerchief to the sick, and they have been healed. There are persons in this congregation who have been healed by throwing my old cloak on their beds.[331]

---

330. Edward L. Kimball and Andrew E. Kimball Jr., *Spencer W. Kimball: Twelfth President of The Church of Jesus Christ of Latter-day Saints* (Bookcraft, 1977), 263–64.

331. *Journal of Discourses*, 4:294.

Notes and Commentary

Notice that several of the accounts relate that people who were blind, bedridden, or with disease were healed after several years of remaining in that condition. Elder George Q. Cannon, for example, healed a man who had been blind for over thirty years. Also notice—like the woman who knew she would be healed if she could touch the hem of Jesus's robe (see Matthew 9:20)—that many people had faith sufficient to be healed if they could shake hands with, or be in the presence of, a prophet of God.

For instance, when a six-year-old boy from a nonmember family—who had never walked—heard that an Apostle (Harold B. Lee) was coming to speak in his city, he requested that his parents take him to the Apostle so that he could heal him. A woman in Germany, who was confined to her bed for five years, believed that if her children could get near enough to David O. McKay to shake his hand, then she would be healed if they subsequently returned home and grasped her hand.

Another intriguing theme in this chapter is healing through inanimate objects. Many people have heard of the time when the Prophet Joseph blessed a handkerchief, gave it to Wilford Woodruff, and told him to take and bless two children with it. However, most people are unaware that Lorenzo Snow, Heber C. Kimball, Willard Richards, and others also blessed objects and used them to heal. Elder Kimball—as shown above—stated, "I have blessed my handkerchief, and asked God to sanctify it and fill it with life and power, and sent it to the sick, and hundreds have been healed by it; in like manner . . . there are persons in this congregation who have been healed by throwing my old cloak on their beds."[332] Joseph Smith Sr. told Lorenzo Snow in his patriarchal blessing that "the diseased shall send to thee their handkerchiefs and aprons and by thy touch their owners shall be healed."[333] A similar statement is found in Acts 19:11–12: "And God

---

332. *Journal of Discourses*, 4:294.

333. Lorenzo Snow was blessed by Joseph Smith Sr. on December 15, 1836, in Kirtland, Ohio, LDS Church Archives; as cited in Irene M. Bates and E. Gary Smith, *Lost Legacy: The Mormon Office of Presiding Patriarch* (University of Illinois Press, 2003), 48.

wrought special miracles by the hands of Paul: So that from his body were brought unto the sick *handkerchiefs or aprons*, and the diseases departed from them, and the evil spirits went out of them" (emphasis added).

It seems strange that objects could be used to bless the sick, for on one hand, this smacks of Catholic influence (Catholics being notorious for claiming that certain inanimate objects possess "holy" power—a crucifix, an ancient artifact, or an object from the Holy Land, for example). On the other hand, exercising the priesthood need not always be limited to one specific set of requirements. While it is true that, if at all possible, two elders should be present and anoint with oil, this does not prohibit any priesthood holder from blessing the sick if the situation cannot accommodate the traditional, ideal procedure.[334]

334. See Joseph Fielding Smith, *Answers to Gospel Questions* (Deseret Book, 1957), 1:144–50.

About the Author

Glenn T. H. Kimball is a lifelong member of the Church and has studied religion and Latter-day Saint history for decades. He studied religion in graduate school and has extensively researched his Kimball family history alongside Latter-day Saint history.